"*Writing is the art of applying the seat of the pants to the seat of the chair*".

Mary Heaton Vorse.

"*The most valuable talent is that of never using two words when one will do*".

Thomas Jefferson

CHAPTER 1

When I left Secondary School in 1946 at the age of fourteen, I was acutely aware that life held few opportunities for me if I were to stay in the little Yorkshire village where I was born. That villages name was Swinefleet which was in the West Riding of the County and situated on the banks of the river Ouse.

I came from a large family which had originated in the village. My Father was a bed-ridden invalid who had worked rarely throughout the whole of his life. My Mother was a sickly person who, through no fault of her own, spent most of her time looking after my Father and picked up any casual jobs such as cleaning for the better off villagers whenever such opportunities arose. My three sisters and four brothers had, upon coming of school leaving age, left home as quickly as they were able and were scattered far and wide. I, being the youngest, seemed destined to remain with my parents and bring in a wage packet every week to add support to the family home.

When I was only thirteen years of age I already had ambitions to flee the family nest when my time came just as my siblings had done before me. It was at this early age that I had the good fortune to pass an examination for entry into the Trinity House Nautical School in Hull at the mouth of the river Humber. Alas, I had no choice but to disclose to my parents just what I was about and tell them of my ambitions to become a sailor just as soon as I possibly could. Along with my success in the examination I had been called for interview with the head of the Nautical School who I was informed was called Captain Beer. I was briefed at great length by my Mother as to what questions I should put to the good Captain. Such things as my uniform, which would be paying for that?

5

My day to day living costs while undergoing training at the Nautical School, who would pay? The nearest Rail Station being at Goole, from where I would travel to Hull. Who would provide the wherewithal for the fares? My parents were in no position to provide for such expenses. She went on for some considerable time always aided and abetted by my Father who seemed equally keen to avoid seeing their weekly income rapidly disappearing out of the door.

The day arrived for the interview and my train fare was met from School funds as well as a prized sum of sixpence which would ensure that at least I would eat at lunchtime which was a rare treat for me.

Being the good son that I was I carefully said what my parents had told me to say to the Captain. He listened most carefully and at the end of it all he informed me that I was now being taken for a Standard Ministry of Transport eyesight test which was apparently a requirement before I was allocated a place at the Nautical School. Needless to say I was refused a place at the school. The excuse was put forward that my eyesight was not up to Ministry of Transport standards.

Even now when I am in my mid seventies, I have never had to wear spectacles and I can to this very day read the small print in a newspaper without the aid of any enhancement.

I left school on a Friday afternoon and started work as a farm laborer the very next day which was a Saturday morning at half past seven and went on until five o'clock at night. I was not impressed. My Mother had taken steps to ensure that the household income would benefit from my labors just as soon as it became humanly possible. She had secured a job for me and it was also her way to collect my wages from the Farmer every Friday night which happened to be pay day. I received the princely sum of Half a Crown from my parents which they gave to me as a reward for my week's work which involved in excess of forty five hours each week in all kinds of weather. This kindness I might add was very grudgingly given.

Remember this was 1946 and World War Two had just ended. There was little wonder that I thought my own war was only just beginning.

By the spring of 1947 I had secretly and without my parent's knowledge, applied for and secured a position with a Jobbing Printer in Goole, which was just three miles from the village of Swinefleet. I was very excited at the prospect of escaping from the farm. It was a fact that even in this very early stage of my working life I knew that if one wanted something badly enough you jolly well had to fight for it. I had to put up with an awful lot of aggravation when I did at last inform my parents of my intentions. I had made a change to the pattern of my working life and I was now much more independent. I was now in a position where I would draw my own wages each week. In fact I retained a whole Pound for myself and still received the usual two shillings and sixpence from the amount I passed over every Friday night to my parents.

It was now early spring when, during my usual lunchtime stroll around the shops in Goole's Boothferry Road, I saw a display in the shop window of Marks and Spencer's. Young men were being offered, providing they were aged at least fifteen, the opportunity to become an Army Apprentice where they would learn an Engineering trade and then go on and serve as a Soldier in the British Army. I registered there and then and took the forms away with me. It seemed that as my fifteenth birthday fell on the first of September I would be of age by the middle of September and thus qualify to enlist in mid September which seemed to be the plan.

It also became painfully obvious that my enrolment forms required the signature of both my parents to indicate that they gave their full approval to my joining the British Army. There was no way that this would be forthcoming so I did the only thing I could do, I forged their signatures and signed the forms myself.

I handed the forms back to the recruiting Sergeant the very next day. He accepted them with a smile and assured me that I would not regret my action.

I was sworn in at Jermyn Street Recruiting Office in Hull on the 3rd of September 1947 (just three days after I was 15 years old). I received the Kings shilling which I promptly spent on fish and chips to celebrate pulling off my coup and escaping what would only have been a life tied to my Mothers apron strings.

Life as an Army Apprentice was just great and I enjoyed every minute of it. It seems hard to believe all these years later, but believe it or not, I had never tasted a boiled egg, or worn a pair of underpants, or possessed a pair of Pajamas or even a vest before I joined up. Life was indeed a little grim for the youngest of eight children living in a small Yorkshire village on the banks of the river Ouse in the 1930's and 1940's and it didn't have a lot to do with the country being at war with Hitler.

It had taken a bit of scrimshanking but I had made it. Charles Hebden, Soldier of the King had arrived.

At the age of 18 I was ready to enter the Army proper. By this time I was a fully qualified Fitter and Turner and I found myself posted to the Royal Engineers where I was destined to spend the next twelve years of my life that being the time I would have to serve in return for being trained as a Tradesman. At least that was the plot at that time. What actually happened was quite different as you will see.

This point was not the only significant turning point in my life. During the time I had spent at the Arborfield Army Apprentices School I had become terribly smitten by a most delightful young lady who at the time was a telephonist on the School's switchboard. She was called Jean Lois Marshal and although I didn't realize it at the time, she was to become Mrs. Charles Hebden, bear me four children and accompany me round a number of countries worldwide. The children of course went with us, well most of the time anyway. Jean left her post in Arborfield at the same time as I moved of to Malvern in Worcestershire to complete my initiation into the Royal Engineers.

It was called Sapper training and was something else believe me. At Merebrook Camp, this lay alongside the river Avon in Worcestershire and was designed to thoroughly piss off the new recruits to the Royal Engineers. We were subjected to a form of torture at a place known as the Spars Ground. Now there are Spars and there are Spars, but these particular Spars were enormous wooden affairs the size of a decent telephone pole. I couldn't hazard a guess as to what they weighed but we, strapping 18 year olds, fit as Butchers Dogs, were paired off and the two of us were required to shoulder the "Spar" and then at the double relocate the thing some 100 yards further down stream. Engage in such

8

exercise from eight in the morning to twelve thirty, for lunch you invariably opted for a hurried kip and then continued from thirteen hundred round to sixteen thirty before you called it a day. Our development was nothing less than miraculous. Muscles appeared as knots on cotton.

When we had proven to our Instructors that we could shift Spars in large quantities and not drop them, well not very often anyway, we were then treated to a more sophisticated form of misery. We were now working in groups of four soldiers who assembled and then disassembled all those mysterious bits that go together to form a Bailey bridge. These bits are made of steel or iron and are even heavier, in the main than those bloody Spars. I was more than happy when our Sapper training session (six weeks) came to an end and I was posted on to the Royal Engineers Depot at Chatham in Kent.

Life in the Depot was the complete opposite to the life I had endured since leaving Boy's Service. It was boring in the extreme. Muster parade at 0800hrs. March to the Workshops, ten minutes away, sit around all day with nothing to do, and I mean nothing. 16.30 march back to the Barracks and dismiss. The routine was exactly the same five days each week. I stuck it for six ball aching weeks then made a decision. I jacked in my trade and the extra money that went with the Technical Qualifications. That was a bit of a sin really after completing a three year Apprenticeship to get there in the first place.

I then volunteered myself as a Regimental Policeman. The post had been advertised on the Daily Part 1 Orders for the whole time I had been at the Depot but no one seemed to want the job. I now think it was the promise of a stripe to the person who would take it on which swayed me towards it, but I did so want to get on and this seemed to be an opportunity for me to get my foot on the first rung of the promotion ladder. It proved that the promotion to Lance Corporal didn't mean a great deal anyway as I was now an Acting, Unpaid Lance Corporal but I was one step up from being a Sapper anyway.

It was almost time for the Regimental Runner to deliver copies of the Daily Part 1 Orders to the Guardroom. This was a regular thing which took place around 1600 hrs each day Monday to Friday. On Saturday there was an exception in that they arrived about mid-day. Sunday, being the Sabbath, no Part 1 Orders were published.

There was a good sound reason why the Orders were delivered to the Guardroom; it enriched the duties of the Provost Sergeant who would then detail one of his Regimental Policemen to make a tour of the whole Depot and post a copy of the Orders at strategic points throughout in order that all could read and inwardly digest. Ignorance of the contents would not be accepted in any way from anyone. To be selected by the Sergeant to fulfill this duty was something that was always welcomed by his staff. It meant escape from the constant attention of their lord and master, if only for a short period anyway.

It was here within the confines of the Guardroom that I was to experience my first taste of power over my fellow man. I maximized the opportunity to not only verbally abuse the inmates of the Detention Cells but also to vent untold wrath upon the goods and chattels belonging to these men. In fact I gave them one hell of a life. I felt safe in the knowledge that they were in no position to retaliate in any way, shape or form for fear of an increase to the period of detention they had been sentenced to in the first place. I adopted this attitude as a means of displaying to the Provost Sergeant what an excellent disciplinarian I was. I knew that it would impress him and eventually he would judge me to be far better material than the other Acting, Unpaid Lance Corporals who, I saw as my competition to becoming a fully paid Lance Corporal over and above them.

It sounds quite pathetic on reflection but in fact such was my desire to not only getting on the first rung of the ladder but to make my way up it at the very earliest opportunity. My ambitions knew no bounds.

The method worked and my Acting, Unpaid status was soon a thing of the past. I received my sixpence per day increase as a Lance Corporal and within a period of six months I was sewing on my second stripe.

This of course was all due to the patronage of the Provost Sergeant, Jacob Silver. He ruled "His" Guardroom with a veritable rod of iron. Jacob Silver was not a very nice person. He was not liked and was certainly not respected by his peers in the Regimental Sergeants Mess.

10

However, this seemed not to bother him to any great extent. He was known by all and sundry as"The Animal" and thought of one person only that being himself. He was a five foot six inch underdeveloped male person who sported a closely shaven head and the barest pencil line of a moustache. A pair of red-rimmed piggy eyes peered out from his hatchet like face which in itself was invariably bright red. This was undoubtedly due to the constant rising of his blood pressure by frequent bouts of tantrum that he was prone to. He had bad teeth and the breath to match. This scenario was coupled with a vocabulary, which in many quarters was described as "imaginative". The few basic phrases he was capable of stringing together were invariably linked by the foulest expletives imaginable. The detainees hated him with ferocity even greater than that they reserved for me. The soldiers passing through the Guardroom, as was the way things were done in those days, either on their way to town or perhaps just returning to Barracks, were very wary of him and clearly hated the sight of him. His superiors hated him though being Officers; they preferred to describe their hatred as "not too keen on the chap". In fact everybody hated him and not a good word was ever spoken about him.

By far and away the one person with the most pent-up hatred for "The Animal" was me. These feelings were not so much inspired by the man himself but rather the fact that he was a bloody Sergeant and I was yet only a Corporal who had to pander to his every whim.

I must do something about it.

It was most unfortunate but I openly applauded even the most moronic of his actions. I also showed myself willing to perform extra duties. I never bitched about the job of being a Regimental Policeman, which the others did frequently. In fact I arse-hole crept to the repulsive bastard on every possible occasion. It seemed to have worked so far and I now had hopes that I would soon become a member of the Regimental Sergeants Mess. When that day arrived, as surely it would, I would displace Sergeant Jacob Silver from his prized position and I would laugh in his face.

The Regimental Runner arrived and threw some ten or fifteen sets of

11

Orders onto the Guardroom table. The three Regimental Policemen present watched with a hint of a smirk on their faces. The Runner stared Silver straight in the eye but said not a word. The Sergeant, in return, eyed the Runner, obviously boiling inside; his eyes could not hide the fact that to take a knife and slit the Runners throat would have given him great pleasure. Sergeant Silver somehow expected all persons below the rank of Sergeant to be afraid of the power he thought he held. It was fairly obvious that the Runner did not subscribe to this theory. He couldn't give a shit what Silver thought. He was simply not afraid of the Sergeants dubious antics and from his vantage point in the Regimental Headquarters where he spent the majority of his time, he felt safe in the knowledge that Silver wouldn't have the stomach to pick on him.

Still seething inwardly the Sergeant picked up a copy of the Orders but his stare remained fixed on the Runner. Not a word passed between them as the Runner turned and left the Guard room slamming the door behind him.

I sat at the much scrubbed table which sat in the middle of the floor in the Guardroom. Spread out before me was a copy of the "Sun" newspaper. It was not the current days copy but that didn't matter as I was interested in what appeared on page three at the time. I was only whiling away the time waiting for 1600hrs when the Sergeant would grandly announce the names of two of us Policemen, one of us which would select two prisoners. These he would pilot down to the Cookhouse where a half bucket of hot sweet tea would be collected. The tea would be taken back to the Guardroom, at the double of course, where the Guardroom staff would consume it. If there was ever any left in the bucket, an infrequent occurrence I might add, the prisoners were then permitted to share this amongst themselves.

The second person selected by the Sergeant would take up the delivery of the daily Part 1 Orders. This he would do by using the Guardroom bicycle, an honor indeed. The bicycle, which lay idle most of the day, was generally reserved for the exclusive use of the Provost Sergeant when he would tour the Depot on it. The purpose of his tour was to ensure that there was no felony being committed by any of the unfortunate bodies that were passing through the Depot en-route to some far off place either at Home or Abroad.

I considered myself to be the favorite for the task of distribution. I had been particularly smarmy to Silver that morning and I think he rather looked on e as his ally within the confines of the Guardroom. I was not to be disappointed as the rat faced turd pointed directly at me then to the pile of Orders on the table and finally with his thumb at the door. Not a word was spoken nor any sound heard with the exception of a low rumbling belch emanating from somewhere about the person of the Sergeant.

It was woe betide any of us Policemen who became the subject of a complaint of anything to do with the delivery of Orders. Such complaints were in all cases dealt with by the Sergeant himself. His wrath knew no bounds whatever the felony. Complaints could comprise such things as the sheets were wet as a result of a sudden downpour while they were being delivered. Another reason, and this was quite a frequent one, Orders were scattered all over the floor and not displayed properly on the Notice Board. Perhaps someone had pinched all the Drawing Pins from the board and the unfortunate Policeman making the delivery had no option but to deposit them nearby prior to beating a hasty retreat.

It was invariably the case that when I was making the deliveries I was permitted to have use of the Regimental Bicycle. I whistled as I pedaled along the familiar route. Barrack Blocks first, then each of the four Company Offices. The NAAFI, WRVS Room, Padre, Sergeants Mess where I always lingered a little dreaming of the day I would become a fully fledged member and not just a poxy Corporal who pedaled around on a bike posting bits of paper around the place. Finally, I headed for the Officers Mess. This would be my final port of call before returning to the Guardroom. I mounted the broad steps which fronted the building and led up to the main entrance. Stiffening my back just that tad further to give myself the appearance of being "as Regimental as a Button Stick" as the saying goes. I had glanced at the Orders a few times during my travels but had taken little notice of their content as I concentrated on the route I was taking, however, as I was about to close the Notice board door there in the Officers Mess, something caught my eye in the section headed Regimental Notices.

AIRBORNE FORCES...PARACHUTING...EXTRA PAY.

I muttered to myself as I tried to read all that was written in the notice but there I was, reading Daily Part 1 Orders in the Officers Mess. I quickly left the building having first made sure that the Orders in the Notice board were lined up and sitting square to each other.

Hurrying back to the Guardroom I decided that I must collar a spare copy of the Orders and check out this notice thing very closely indeed. It might prove to be just what I had been waiting for. A chance for adventure and do some real soldiering. I'd show 'em, I bet I would be a Sergeant before you could say "Jack Robinson" given a chance to shine.

My mind was so taken up with fantasy thoughts that I almost missed a Second Lieutenant who hove into view some hundred or so yards away across the other side of the Barrack Square. I acknowledged him by treating him to a very smart salute in spite of my being mounted on a bicycle. I gave him the full treatment. Longest way up and shortest way down whilst remaining in full control of my transport. The lieutenant failed to respond. It was highly likely that he hadn't been expecting such a display from such a distance let alone from a bicycle mounted soldier. In fact, he most probably hadn't even seen me for from the direction he seemed to be heading, his mind was probably concentrating on other matters. He seemed to be heading for the Adjutants Office in Regimental Headquarters where he would no doubt receive a good strong telling off for some wrong doing, either real or imaginary, plus a couple of extra Orderly Officers duties to keep him out of mischief over the weekend to come.

Entering the Guardroom as casually as I could, didn't want to give the game away, I looked round for any sign of the now highly important copy of the days Orders. I took extra care not to reveal my keen interest to Silver as that would undoubtedly make him hog any spare copy there was, just to be awkward. I slumped into my usual chair at the Trestle Table. Silver had the copy alright. He had them in his hand but was

14

making little effort to read them. Bide your time I thought, don't even look at the old sod or he might take umbrage and ask what the hell I was looking at. He would put them down at some stage or other and then I would bag them.

The telephone rank breaking the tension. This tension always existed in the Guardroom when Jacob Silver and his staff all sat around and waited for something to happen. No one except the great man himself was ever allowed to answer the telephone, when he was there anyway. I was going to say he jumped up from his seat, but that's not true. He more slowly rose like a Slug and slowly made his way to the instrument which was fastened on the wall at ear level just as one would have expected it to be in a Military Establishment. Damn it I thought, the old sod still had the Orders clutched in his claw like hand.

The phone call, which lasted all of 15 seconds, was being given his undivided attention. At the end of it he crashed the handset back into it's cradle and headed for the door slinging the copy of Orders back on the table and grunted out the simple statement "Orderly Room", "Important". This was for the benefit of all present including him presumably, just to prove what an important part he was of the British Army in general and the Royal Engineers Depot in particular.

He was hardly out of the door before I was reading the "Notice" which had created such a stir in me.

Addressing no one in particular I announced "Bog" and headed for the Ablutions clutching the copy of Orders which now had become the number one priority in my life. Behind the privacy of the Bog door I sat and re-read the Notice at my leisure. It promised all that I craved and above all it seemed to be a heaven sent opportunity for me to get away from that blasted Guardroom and all that went with it. Knowing that the copy I now held was a spare copy; it was highly unlikely that it would be missed. I folded it neatly and slipped it into my Battledress pocket. Finishing time was 1800hrs and it couldn't come quickly enough for me. That was the time I would be able to retire to my own bunk and once again read it through, just in case I had missed something.

Sure enough, I had grasped all the basics that were required when I had read it earlier in the day but nevertheless I read it over and over again to make sure that I had missed nothing.

Searching my locker I came up with a pad of lined writing paper and a Biro. Armed thus, I composed my application for service with the Malayan Scouts who were at present serving in the Malayan Emergency. After reading through it several times, I placed it in an envelope and firmly made up my mind that I would hand it in to the Company Office the very next morning just as the Orders had instructed.

I waited for two whole days. There was no sign of being called in by the Company Commander in response to my application. In fact, I took to hanging around near the Company Office at the least opportunity just in case they had forgotten to send for me and I thought this just might jog someone's memory if they should happen to catch sight of me.

Almost a full week had gone by when I finally received the call. This filled me with a sense of great excitement about the whole thing, making me believe that I would be on my way to Malaya by the coming weekend or perhaps at the worst, early the following week.

The Company Commander questioned me about my reasons for applying and this he followed up with a thinly veiled attempt to put me off by describing some of the pitfalls such a venture held for a young man such as me. I paid little or no attention to what the fatherly figure had to say on the subject. My mind was elsewhere. Parachuting and chasing Bandits in the Jungle. "...we will forward your application, but you must expect to wait some time as is usually the case with this sort of thing." This was the end bit of what the Major had to say on the subject and it was just about all that I had taken in. I did assure the Major however, that I was fully determined to go and do my bit for King and Country. He offered a smile at this.

I checked almost every day at the Company Office for news of the call to arms. After a couple of weeks and increasingly harsh words from the Company Sergeant Major, who by now had started to see me as nothing but a bloody pest, I managed to let the matter drift from my mind. You see, I did not want to have to face the possibility that I might not have been selected. I preferred my own version that they, the selection people, had found me too well qualified for what they had in mind.

Life reverted to me being the Provost Corporal. I eventually resumed my relentless task of trying to drop Silver in the fertilizer, at least deep enough to have him removed from the

Seat of authority which he currently held. This of course would allow the powers that be to promote the erstwhile Corporal Charles Hebden. R.E. and allow me to fill the boots of the Sergeant.

CHAPTER 2

"Corporal Hebden to the ships Orderly Room".

"Corporal Hebden to the ships Orderly Room".

The echoing of the ships public address system against the steel walls of the Troop deck gave the message a sense of urgency and made it carry the authority of it being an order, as indeed it was.

All messages broadcast throughout the ship were repeated just as this one had been. The reason for such efficiency was to

make sure that no mistake could possibly be made and the content of the message would be understood by all. The interpretation by the majority of soldiers on board was that the lazy sod in the Orderly Room who made these announcements, just liked hearing his voice, hence the repetition.

"That's you in it"?

This came from a spotty faced Private whose misfortune it had been to be allocated the Bunk, officially called a Standee, above the one intended for me. I made no response to his comment.

Spotty face tried again.

"They just said on the Tannoy that you was wanted in the Orderly Room. Your names 'Ebdon in it"?

I rounded on the Private.

"I can hear you know, nothing wrong with my bloody hearing. I can hear and don't need the likes of you to keep me on my toes. And, get your poxy feet together when you speak to me. I didn't get these for standing in NAAFI queue's you know", indicating the two stripes on the sleeves of my Battledress Blouse.

18

"Show some respect and call me Corporal when you address me you poxy faced bastard. Hear me" I bawled into his face.

"Yes Corporal" the timid little man said. "It's just that the Tannoy........."

Again I cut him short.

"Shut your gob lad, I know what the pigging Tannoy said, besides, it was me it was talking to, not you, OK?"

I had traveled by road the previous day from the Depot in Chatham to the docks in Southampton where I embarked on the Troopship Empire Orwell. This was the ship which would take me to Hong Kong. This was also my very first overseas posting since joining the Royal Engineers. My posting to Hong Kong had been quite a surprise. I was just called into the Company Office one morning and informed that I would be going to Hong Kong in three or four week's time. A quick couple of week's embarkation leave and here I was. Any lingering thoughts about the Malayan Scouts had conveniently been forgotten and I looked forward to my tour of duty in the Far East.

I was nineteen years of age and one of the youngest Corporals in the whole of the Royal Engineers. Oh yes, I had made the grade. My future was assured and I was destined for the top. There was nothing to stop my climb to the dizzy height of Company Sergeant Major or even Regimental Sergeant Major unless I did something stupid, or stepped out of line in some way or another.

My mind was fully occupied with these thoughts as I made my way to the ships Orderly Room, just as I had been instructed by the Tannoy only moments before. I knew exactly where I was going. As was my way, I had sussed out where each of the many gangways and sets of stairs would lead me. This I had done during the first couple of hours I had been on board last evening. In fact I had carried out a full recce of the ships layout even before unpacking my kitbag.

I marched along at a brisk pace and as usual, my mind started to build a fantasy of the reason I had been summoned to the Orderly Room. They must have some special job they want doing and need a reliable NCO to take charge of it for the duration of the forthcoming voyage.

Perhaps they want to put me in charge of a complete Troop Deck with all it's 150 souls who I would have the unquestionable right to issue them with whatever orders I was inclined to issue……? I suddenly found that I had arrived at my destination. It was something of a strain to resist coming to a halt with the stamping of feet and cutting the right arm sharply to my side with the subconscious calling out of "one – two" as I finally came to the halt position.

I stood facing a door on which, firmly kept in place by a pair of bolts, was a wooden sign. This was lettered in white paint and informed all and sundry that this was the Ships Orderly Room. The complete sign had been given two or three liberal coats of clear varnish, which I assumed was to protect it from damage by the sea salt air during the ships passage to Hong Kong. This to my mind smacked at organization and authority. However, on a second closer investigation of the sign, I was taken aback when I saw sellotaped to the bottom of it, an A4 sheet of paper on which was scrawled with a biro, knock and wait. Perhaps what went on behind the ships Orderly Room door was going to fall below the standard that would normally be expected from such an establishment?

I drew myself up to my full height and visually checked my general appearance. This was of course second nature to me. Then with stomach in and chest out, I knocked firmly on the door. No sound came from within .I waited a respectfully short time as instructed by the notice but I was now growing impatient. The waiting period seemed to last ages and ages but was in fact perhaps only twenty or thirty seconds or so. I began to contemplate whether I should repeat the knocking bit, just in case those within were so busy that they had not heard the first knock.

Being a trained soldier and therefore a disciplined person, I waited for a further twenty seconds or so before committing myself to such action. I considered that such a step, in my mind anyway, would be in complete disregard of the order which appeared sellotaped to the notice in front of me. After a few more seconds I resolved to knock again. Once I had made my decision, as was my way, I went in both feet first so to speak. Just as my fist was about to make contact with the door it suddenly burst open swinging inwards to the office. Out spewed three soldiers going hell for leather to the accompanying tirade of "eft – ite, eft – ite" from a bristling RSM.

"Alt, At on, Escort fall out", the RSM barked without even giving a sideways glance towards the two soldiers who had apparently been detailed as escort for the miserable little Private who stood rigidly to attention between the pair of them.

"I said At on the RSM screamed at the little man who now was the sole subject of his attention. The two escorts needed no second bidding and legged it just as fast as possible without breaking into a run.

The RSM was one of those unfortunate people who had a cast in his eye, which, to the casual observer anyway, it was difficult to decide just which eye was the offender. It appeared to change from eye to eye when viewed directly from the front.

The great man stood very close to the diminutive Private and attempted to fix him with his best Regimental stare. This only served to cause additional confusion to the poor man, who, being fascinated by the ever shifting eyeballs, was subjected to a tirade of abuse which was being issued from the RSM's gob in his efforts to point out the error of his ways to the poor little sod. Much of what was said only went to waste as the Private, according to the look on his face, failed to take in a single word.

"Don't let me see 'ide nor air' of youse for the rest of this trip, un'erstand me? Get out of my sight youse 'orrible little man youse, and get your bloody 'air cut, youse looks like a bloody wolligog, that's what youse looks like".

All this activity had taken me completely by surprise and I was forced to step backwards to avoid being trampled by the appearance of the escort and accused. The latter of this trio was now hightailing it to the comparative safety of his Troop deck having apparently got away with whatever misdemeanor he had been accused of.

The RSM turned and fixed his twin beady eyes on me. He seemed to be somewhat chuffed at having his next victim so conveniently close at hand. He very slowly looked me up and down and it was obvious to me that he was having some difficulty getting his brain into the right cog to deal with this new challenge and to assemble just what his approach was to be. He looked me up and down again, no doubt to gain a little extra time and of course, make sure that he had missed nothing on his first appraisal

"What do youse want Corporal"?

The ships Tannoy said I was to report here sir, Corporal Hebden. RE. sir".

He thought for a few seconds to digest what I had said and then, "Your initials are they, this RE malarkey"?

This was delivered at considerable volume as if I was on some other deck to him and he wished to make sure that the question was heard and fully understood by not only me, but any other person within a radius of a hundred yards or so.

"No sir, Corporal C. Hebden, the C standing for my Christian name and the RE meaning Royal Engineers which is the parent arm to which I belong, sir". I was feeling a little apprehensive as to what kind of reaction I would get from the ignorant sod in front of me. I was not to be disappointed.

"I knows what RE stands for laddie" he erupted. "Youse fink I'se fick or som'ink"?

By now my questioner had turned a bright crimson around his face and neck. There were little flecks of spittle forming at the corners of his mouth. All this went straight over my head, the tirade that is, and a fair amount of the spittle but not all of it. I managed to ignore for the main part, the animal that stood before me and pretended that he was a human being as well as the ships RSM. All the time this was going on I never moved my eyes from his face. I just watched and waited for the tantrum to finish as I knew it would. I had plenty of past experience when pretending to listen to Sergeant Silver in the Guard room at Chatham.

It wasn't the screaming that I minded so much; after all I had grow up with it in the past. No, it was about the word "laddie" which this buffoon had addressed me as during his performance. I was an NCO and carried two stripes on my sleeve to confirm such status. It was therefore not unreasonable, in my opinion, to expect to be addressed by my rank even by a Warrant Officer Class 1 who just happened to hold the temporary appointment of ships RSM. One day, just one day would surely come when I would be in a position where I could tell such ignorant bastards just how a proper soldier should behave.

With the barest of efforts the RSM indicated with a sideways motion of the head, that I should pass to the inner sanctum of the Orderly Room. Once inside I came face to face with a fat, sniveling Corporal who managed to smirk at me as I repeated the reason for my being there. He in return informed me that the Adjutant wanted to see me. This information he conveyed with an attitude that implied that he knew what it was all about but he was buggered if he was going to tell anyone, least of all me.

After a wait for some four or five minutes, which I spent doing my best to appear unconcerned about being there, it seemed that someone, somewhere, had touched a button which brought the RSM back into action. Once again he was at it with his "eft – ite, eft – iting" as he ushered me into the Adjutants presence. The obviously overworked, bespectacled Captain glanced up painfully at my arrival while he continued to search his desktop for the relevant paperwork. He winced once again as the RSM boomed out with great velocity the quite unnecessary announcement that he had tracked down the Corporal and what was more, he had spirited here, in the flesh, before the very eyes of the Adjutant.

The Adjutant thanked the RSM as politely as he seemed to be able to muster, while silently and secretly he was wishing the man would fall over the ships rail and disappear below the waters of Southampton Docks never to be seen again.

"I have some instructions here, somewhere, about you Corporal....... ah yes.......Hebden isn't it? Your last three is 112 is it not"? The last three did of course refer to the last three numbers of my full Army Number.

"Sir" I replied in confirmation.

"Ah here it is" he said holding aloft a piece of paper. This seemed to give him great pleasure at being so successful at finding it in such a relatively short time. He read from it direct as it appeared to be a Signal Message form. "21126112 Corporal C. Hebden. RE. to disembark Troopship Empire Orwell and proceed to Airborne Forces Depot, Aldershot with immediate effect.

My jaw sagged in utter amazement at what I had just heard. In fact, I was completely gob smacked.

"Are you sure you have the correct name, sir"? I queried almost boldly for a junior NCO addressing a Commissioned Officer. "My full Regimental Number is 21126112,sir".

"That is quite correct, there is no doubt that this signal refers to you Corporal".

"But sir" I started, only to be interrupted by his dismissal with a waive of the hand.

"See the clerk in the outer office; he will fix you up with a Movement Orders and Travel Warrant etc".

Again there was that gesture with his hand which signaled that the interview was at an end.

As if the underline the fact the Adjutant resumed the search of his desk, no doubt in the hope that he may come across some other scrap of evidence which would give him a clue as to what matter he should attend to next.

It was as if some unseen force had again switched the RSM on. He burst into activity and "eft, ited" me from the Adjutants office bringing me to an abrupt "'alt" thus narrowly avoiding a collision with the desk where the fat Corporal sat in an altogether un-soldierly manner. This slug of a man was, apparently, the Chief Clerk. It was he who informed me that I had all of twenty minutes to pack my kit and report back to the Orderly Room by which time the relevant documents would be ready for collection and I could be on my way to Aldershot. All futher attempts on my part to try to hlean a little further information proved to be futile. Off I went and packed my kit then re-presented myself at the Orderly Room. The fat Corporal managed to delay me as long as he possibly could but eventually I left the Empire Orwell and all the promise it had held for me.

It was late on Friday afternoon when I reported to the Regimental Policeman who seemed to be in charge of the Guardroom in Maida Barracks in Aldershot. The RP was a private soldier and had, apparently, been left in charge by some snotty NCO who no doubt had other things on his mind at the time. He gave me instructions as to how I would find my way to "A" Squadron Company Office where he had been told to send all new arrivals that afternoon. I left without a word of thanks for the information that I would be told what to do when I reported to the Squadron Office.

By now I was a weary man and my patience was growing thin as I reflected on the fact that it was only three days since I had been the all powerful Provost Corporal in full control of all matters Regimental in the Guardroom at Chatham. That of course was when Silver was not about. It crossed my mind that I could have given the RP a hard time and a bit of a bollocking but I was far too tired after my train journey from Southampton. My immediate need was for me to get myself settled in a Billet for the night and then I could go in search of information as to why I was here in Aldershot and not on the high seas, as it were, in the good old Troopship Empire Orwell?

The business of booking in and drawing my bedding from the Squadron Stores was soon attended to and I made my way to the Barrack Block to find a cavernous room in which I had been allocated a bed space. According to the instructions I had received on booking in, I was not to leave Barracks over the weekend and I was to report to "A" Squadron's Muster Parade at 0800hrs on the Monday morning. . Further questions by me had been to no avail as the clerk who had been left on duty knew nothing at all. At least if he did, he was saying nothing at all.

A quick shufti around the room disclosed that there were some twenty or so bodies in the accommodation which had originally been deigned to hold fifty men together with their bits and pieces of kit. The prospect of a long weekend in these surroundings held little appeal for me. I was however, quite surprised to find that there were two Sergeants who were billeted there as opposed to their usual accommodation in the Sergeants Mess. There were four Corporals and a couple of Lance Corporals the remainder being Private Soldiers as far as I could make out. A quick head count confirmed a total of twenty three bodies including myself.

The evening meal came and went with barely a single word being spoken by anyone. After queuing at the Hotplate in the Cookhouse I made my way to a place on a table which seemed to be mainly occupied by people from the same Billet as myself but again it seemed that no one wanted to talk.

Back in the Billet I made a further effort on no less that three occasions to strike up a conversation but this appeared to be a waste of time as no one was interested.

I began to have my doubts about my presence here in Aldershot and decided at 2130hrs to get between the sheets and scrutinize a copy of "Tit Bits" which I had found in the Rail Carriage on my way from Southampton.

Saturday passed slowly and Sunday was even worse as it passed even more slowly. By teatime on the Sunday afternoon I was thoroughly pissed off with it all. No one had told me anything, not even why I was here or how long I could expect to stay. From snatches of conversation that I managed to pick up, It seemed fairly certain that all the other guys in the room were on the same tack as myself and they were all here because of applications to join the Malayan Scouts. I consoled myself with the knowledge that the full picture would emerge on the morrow. Bloody well better I thought, I would see someone in authority. They couldn't piss about with Corporal C. Hebden. RE. like this, well not for long anyway.

The duty Bugler could have hardly drawn breath to issue the first note of Reveille when my feet hit the deck and I fumbled for the first Woodbine of the day. I had always been a "Good Getter Up" ever since my early childhood days in Yorkshire when, as the youngest member of the family I had quickly learned that to be late on the scene invariably there was little left to sustain one after everyone else had fed. I was quickly dressed and made up my bed before washing and being away to the Cookhouse to see what delicacies were available for breakfast.

By 0730hrs I was ready for the morning muster but thought I might try for information at the Squadron Office prior to going on parade at 0800hrs. I made my way smartly and found the Duty Clerk already at his labours. I bade him good morning and attempted to engage him in conversation mainly about what was happening about the Malayan

Scouts thing. The Clerk proved to be a cagey one gave nothing away, not even when I presented him with one of my prized Woodbines.

The Office door opened and in walked the Squadron Sergeant Major.

"What are you after Corporal" ? he asked.

"Just having a chat with the Duty Clerk sir"

"You one of the interviews for Malaya"?

I took the bull by the horns, as usual. "That's right sir, Corporal C. Hebden. RE. sir"

"Muster Parade 0800hrs as you was told I believe. Off you go and keep out of this Office, hear me"?

By the time I reached the Barrack Square most of the volunteers were already there. I fell in with them under the control of a Parachute Regiment Corporal who it seemed, had been detailed to gather us together and call the roll. When this had been completed the Corporal marched us off to the offices of "A" Squadron which was the self same place as I had been not many minutes earlier. We were left standing to attention on the road outside while he went into the Office to to reports that all was present and correct. After some minutes he reappeared and before instructing us to fall out, he said that we were to go round the back of the Office and wait but not to make a noise or wander off.

Our wait was not to be a short one and everyone began to get impatient at the lack of activity and indeed the lack of any sort of information about what was happening. Time hung heavy for us all. We had become very frustrated as our wait had now stretched to almost three hours.

At long last yet another Corporal appeared from the Squadron Office. He seemed to be a most officious type and obviously took great pleasure in what he was about to tell us as he seemed to think that he was the bearer of bad news. He informed us that the reason he was there was that a Major had been flown to the UK from Malaya and his purpose was to interview us individually as a result of our applications to join the Malayan Scouts. He, the Major, had intended to come to Aldershot that day, but unfortunately, in the last ten minutes or so he had informed the "A" Squadron Commander by phone that he was unable to make it that day. The same arrangements had been confirmed for the following

27

day which was Tuesday morning. We were told to fall out and report for Muster Parade the next day at 0800hrs.

Tuesday proved to be more or less the same as the previous day and we were yet again killing time on the grass at the rear of the Squadron Office. One of the Clerks appeared at something past 1000hrs with a sheet of paper which gave the order in which we were to be interviewed. He also told us that Major MacNabb had arrived and was presently having a cup of coffee. However, things would be getting underway very shortly.

This was better, things were now moving and the time had come to sort everything out. I lounged on the grass deep in thought as I waited my turn. This came about four Woodbines later when I made my way to the office which had the obligatory piece of paper pinned to the door. The notice confirmed that this was the office which had been reserved for interviews. I knocked and a voice from within bade me enter.

The Major was a Scott with bright red hair which seemed to be in urgent need of a Barber or something. He wore a faded cotton khaki shirt open at the neck and sleeves rolled up approximately to the elbow although the shirt sleeve order rig had finished sometime ago. He stood up as I entered the office. I threw up a very smart salute and as I did so, I noted that he sported a pair of Tartan Trews. In my book this labeled him as one of those Officers who cared little for the Parade Ground bullshit and the finer points of protocol so loved by many of his peers.

"Sit down young man" he said indicating the chair provided and then promptly took his own seat on the opposite side of the table.

"My name is MacNabb and I am "D" Squadron Commander of the Malayan Scouts. I am here to have a word with you chaps who have expressed a wish to join us in Malaya and sort of put you in the picture about what we do. At the same time, I shall run the rule over you to see what the chances are that you would fit in with the general run of things should you eventually join our small but elite unit in Malaya. Very important part of it, a very important part".

"Before we get started, I want you to know that if at any time you should think that you would like to change your mind about joining us, then you are free to say so without any recriminations whatsoever. If

28

this should be the case, you will be returned from whence you came. Is that perfectly clear"?

I replied in the affirmative but I didn't really understand what the Major was on about. Strange bugger this bloke. First he sparked me up by saying that I was just what they were looking for, then he puts me down with a stupid remark like this one about pissing off If I didn't think I would fit.

He continued, "You have some idea I take it of what we are about, eh"? He looked up and his eyes met mine full on in a sort of enquiring and somewhat piercing way. Something stirred inside me. I didn't quite know what to make of it. Was I jubilant or scarred or what? It was a very strange feeling that I was experiencing right at that moment. I had an urgent need to look away but fought it with all my might and managed to maintain the eye contact. It was as if he was looking right inside my very soul but I managed to maintain my determination. It had been an immediate thing that I was experiencing and I felt good inside. I had never met anyone quite like this bloke before, certainly not an Officer anyway. I liked him and what's more, I just knew straight away that I could trust him.

He was banging on about the famous Commanding Officer, Colonel Calvert who had been with Wingate's Chindits up in Burma knocking the shit out of the Japs who occupied the country up there during the Second World War.........many of the men had been in Force 136 and now had joined the Malayan Scouts. All experienced Jungle fighters, etc., etc., My mind began to wander. I was fighting the Bandits in the Jungle. My foot on a dead Terrorist who I had personally just seen off with a quick burst of my machine gun.

The Major was by this time in the middle of telling me what a joy it was to see a fine young soldier who was prepared to stand up for what he considered to be right etc., etc., "Patrols would be for extended periods and would be far from being comfortable" I drifted back to him from time to time......"with not a great deal to show for your efforts". He had quite a lot to say but I didn't pat all that much attention to the majority of what he said. This was later to prove to be a very grave error on my part. I should have listened carefully. If I had, things could have turned out far differently; perhaps I would not have joined the Malayan Scouts after all.

This I consider to be one of the major sins I committed, not only at this interview for entry to the Malayan Scouts, but time after time during the whole of my Military Service. I tended to hear only that which I wanted to hear. Of course that, combined with the fact that I always thought I knew what was best for me, led to my going down the wrong path from time to time. Fortunately I am still here to tell the tale. Nevertheless, I sat before Major MacNabb and made what I considered to be the appropriate noises as my interview went along.

I managed to bring the Major back into focus just in time to catch what I was sure I had heard somewhere before......."True soldiering, respect for your fellow man, much effort and above all reliability". He went on and on, by God he could Rabbit a bit could this one. That was one thing that all the Officers I had known were shit hot at anyway. He'll pause for breath in a minute I thought.

"So tell me Corporal, why does a young man like you with such an obviously promising future with the Royal Engineers, wish to pack all that behind you and become a Malayan Scout"?

Stupid bugger, I thought, what's he on about? It should be enough that I'm offering my services without having to answer questions like that. Anyway, wasn't it obvious that I applied when I did just to get out of that poxy job I was in. At least that was the reason when I first applied, but now, I could have done without it. I should be headed for Honkers (Hong Kong) and all those lovely slant eyed maidens who I had intended to capture and service by the bed full.

I gave some sort of corny reply, the sort that I considered would satisfy this mad Scots Major sitting opposite me. He was now telling me, in a quite pleasant manner I thought, that I should now go back to my Billet and reflect on what had passed between us. I was to return the next day to either confirm that I would accept a place with them or perhaps I might by then consider that I would not like to proceed any further. I now realize that the decision was entirely mine. There was no pressure put on me at any time.

I stood and saluted before turning for the door to leave.

"Oh by the way Corporal, you will loose your two stripes as is the case with everyone who joins us. All new entries, including Junior Officers revert to the rank of Trooper for the duration of the training period. What happens on completion of your training period, well, we would just have to wait and see".

Making my way to the Billet I was bloody fuming. Nobody had breathed a word about getting busted down to Trooper. Crafty Bastards, it was a con' that's what it was a bloody con'. They can stick it up their arse. Not me, I was not going to give up my hard earned stripes for anybody. No-sir-e-bob. I'd tell this MacNabb character in the morning, thank you but no thank you. He could go and play Boy Scouts with some other sucker not with me. Malayan Scouts, eh, I reckoned they were nothing but a gang of con' men.

And so it was. A ten minute interview which boiled down to nothing and failed to give me any firm idea what to expect should I agree to join them in Malaya. Nothing about what the unit did when they were in the Jungle, or who it was supposed to be that we would be hunting down. I assumed it was something to do with the Emergency which I had briefly read about in the Daily Newspapers, but there wasn't a bloody War going on so things couldn't be all that bad anyway. At the age of twenty, who gives a shit about such things? I was up for a spot of adventure and a trip out to Malaya wouldn't go amiss seeing as I had struck out on the Hong Kong thing.

The next morning found me at the Squadron Office ready to sign on the dotted line in agreement that I would become a Malayan Scout and do service in the Far East over the next two years.

It was just seven days later that I and nineteen of the other Volunteers were Singapore bound aboard the Troopship Empire Windrush. The remainder of the interviewees having declined the offer to join in this great adventure.

The sea journey was scheduled to last some seven weeks or so and on reflection, I did not enjoy it one bit. You see I had had the authority which came with my two stripes taken away from me. I was now but a

31

lowly Trooper enforced to work daily in the ships fish butchers preparation area.

What Had I done?

CHAPTER 3

We had spent the past seven weeks on the high seas aboard the old
Windrush as we made our way, ever so slowly, from Southampton to
Singapore. Much of that time had been excruciatingly boring and although I, at first found my duties in the fish butchers to be demeaning
I grew to look forward to the daily three or four hours I was required
to attend. It broke the monotony if nothing else. After just one night'
respite on dry land at the Transit Camp at Nee Soon, we were loaded the
very next morning onto one of the most uncomfortable Trains I ever had
the dubious pleasure of traveling on.

It was to take the best part of two whole days for us to travel up the
spine of Malaya to the Capital Kuala Lumpur.

The Train was indeed something to behold. It had sliding windows
to protect the passengers from the Monsoon rains, when they struck but
alas these suggested that they had not been used in a long time. They
steadfastly refused to budge and remained in the open position at all
times.

Now due to the terrain that the Rail Track had to negotiate it was standard practice to employ two locomotives to ensure that even the steepest
gradient could be adequately handled. One pulled at the front while the
other came into play, when required, by pushing from the rear. When
such steep gradients were encountered the speed of the Train could at
best be described as "Snails Pace". It was in such circumstances that the
Bandits would sit hidden in the Jungle undergrowth just off the rail track
and when the time was right; they would mount an attack on the soldiers traveling at such a leisurely pace as the Locomotives endeavored
to climb the incline. They would cling to the sides of the carriages and

fire into the compartment. They would lob Hand grenades through the ever open windows and in general create havoc.

To counter such surprises, the order of the day was that each Rail Carriage would be under the control of the senior soldier present and he would post sentries at each end of the carriage, not only to deter any of the enemy gaining access to it, but also to keep an eye out for any attack being mounted from the undergrowth. Each carriage had an observation platform situated at each end of the carriage and it meant that two men were required to mount guard at each end of the carriage. One would keep a lookout on the left side while the other kept a weather eye on the right side. With the temperature being what it was plus the humidity it was a devil of a job to remain awake and alert at all times. Thankfully for us new arrivals to the country, our journey from Singapore to Kuala Lumpur passed off with no nasty incidents.

The seating was constructed from strips of hard wood. Boy, were they uncomfortable; I reckon ones backside would have stripes across it for some time to come after the journey.

There was just one other feature of the Malayan Rail System which left an impression on me anyway. That was the essential facility of a Lavatory. Now due to the lack of maintenance of the track and the undulating nature of the terrain across which it traveled it would seem that it was here that the term "Rock and Roll" was first mentioned. What's that I hear you say, what has "Rock and Roll" got to do with Malayan Railway Lavatories? I'll tell you. A single facility was installed at the end of each carriage and was something of a novel design. This gave rise to the soldiers naming it the "Dart Board "type of crapper. It was nothing like the Water Closet design which we are all familiar with, although fashioned in a type of porcelain it was not the usual sit down type. It was merely a hole in the floor which was open to the rail line below. There were foot wells on both sides of the hole and what could only be described as "Grunting Bars" one situated on each side wall of the Lavatory. One would squat, feet in foot wells, one hand on each grunting bar to steady yourself and away you went. Due to the "Rocking and Rolling" of the carriage one was wise to time judge the time of "Bombs Away" to coincide with either the "Rock" or the "Roll" as any

34

misjudgment would inevitably end in tragedy. Due to the fact that there was no water facility in the establishment, this left the incumbent with something of a problem. Just thought I would tell you about that as it is something that sticks in my mind.

Having arrived at the magnificent Railway Station of Kuala Lumpur my traveling companions and myself were most grateful to have completed our journey without and serious incident occurring. We were all very tired indeed but our journey was not complete just yet. We were to travel by road to the Tented Camp which was the temporary home of the Malayan Scouts which lie some twenty miles or so from Kuala Lumpur and was between Port Sweetenham and the small township of Klang. We wearily climbed into an ancient Truck. I didn't know it at the time but it was an old Ford WOT6 which was the only vehicular workhorse that was available to the Regiment throughout my entire tour. It was ancient, broke down frequently and shook the living daylights out of it's passengers irrespective of the surface over which it traveled.

The driver who picked us up at K.L. Station, well he seemed to fall into the same category as the vehicle he drove. I think this must have been his maiden trip in a WOT6. I believe he changed gear only four or five time during the whole journey and yes, he made a bog of it every single time. Still the old truck didn't seem to mind too much. Perhaps it was used to such treatment.

We didn't understand that our lives could possibly be in danger as Terrorist ambushes were quite a regular thing along the Klang road at that time. We were too tired to worry and I am afraid just a group of new arrivals to the country who as far as I now know, we were the first replacements to arrive from the U.K. since the Regiment of the Malayan Scouts had been formed by Colonel (Mad) Mike Calvert in early 1950.

When we arrived at the Camp we found beds already made up in a couple of open-sided tents and turning down the offer of food, we turned in and were fast asleep in seconds, I would wager that to a man, the thought that our travels were over and we were now safe in the knowledge that here was the place that we could settle for the next two years at least, or so we may have thought. In fact we were destined to be on

35

the move, invariably on foot, for a great deal of the time during the next two years.

That old Army saying "Never Volunteer for anything" would ring hollow in our ears in the days to come.

We had all volunteered to serve in the Malayan Scouts (which was eventually re-mustered as the 22nd Special Air Service Regiment) and we would do so for the next two years. Our role would be to carry out Jungle Patrols seeking to find, and if possible destroy groups of Communist guerillas who had sought to shelter in the Jungle away from the constant aggressive attacks made on them by the British Forces right from the outset of the Malayan Emergency which was spawned in February 1948.

There were many vicious engagements between the two forces and in these initial encounters, the Communist were all but routed and collapse of their budding Army was widely believed to be imminent. They themselves had firmly believed that their struggle would be at an end by the turn of that year and the local population would have thrown the British out leaving themselves to be governed by a Communist Regime.

All went well at first for them and due to one thing and another, such as the lack of reinforcements from the U.K. and sadly the death of the British High Commissioner it seemed that their boast of victory by the end of that year was inevitable. The Communist Army now had a breathing space when they could re-assess their soldiers (both men and women) perhaps enhance their numbers and most of all instill a little discipline into them and generally improve their performance.

The local population, which comprised both Malay's and Chinese Malay's, were spread far and wide across the Malay Peninsula. They were easy pray for the Communists who either cajoled them to produce food for their troops, or alternatively, when sustenance was not forthcoming, they terrified them and abused them causing some horrific deaths amongst the Kampong dwellers. There was also a fairly large Indian population who were located in and around the main built up areas throughout the Federation and although they appeared to be a passive element in the community, it was also known that they too played a part in sustaining the Communists with both foodstuffs and in particular money.

The Malay Communist Party (MCP) now formed a secret alliance with the left wing Malay Nationalist Party (MNP). This alliance proved to be short lived as the Malay Police, under the guidance of both Ex British Police and former Palestine Police Officers was very quickly onto it and brought it to an end. In further efforts by the MCP to increase its strength, they brought even further and harsher methods to bear on the locals. This prompted the Government to move all who lived outside a certain area to be gathered in to live in an enclosed (fenced) Kampong Area with the entrance and exit gates being manned by the newly trained Home Guard. These guards were instructed in the basic use of ancient firearms and many were the tragic effects of arming such people whose only previous experience of a weapon was perhaps the Malayan Kris with which they had chopped firewood.

It was now 1952 and the Emergency was at its height with these "Bandits" as they became known, roaming the whole Peninsular blowing up roads and bridges. That was of course when they took time out from terrorizing the local Kampong dwellers. In truth the MCP Army was rapidly loosing faith in their leaders whose actions increasingly seemed to have neither rhyme nor reason to them. Food was becoming scarce, ammunition for their small arms was in very short supply, they were poorly clothed and shod, and they were invariably cold and wet, particularly during the Monsoon Season. In other words, perhaps the words used by most British soldiers describe how they felt, they were thoroughly pissed off.

To bring some variety to their somewhat mundane tasks, they would set up ambushes in order to destroy as many British Troops as possible and if they got very very lucky, a high ranking Military Officer or perhaps even a highly placed Politician in the Malayan Government.

When things got a little too hot for them, they would take to the Jungle. In many locations, there was a properly organized set up which was at their disposal. Bamboo built Camps had been established in deep Primary Jungle which was all but non approachable by the ground forces without them spending extended periods on Operations designed to root the enemy and destroy their Camps. This fact was the main reason why the Malayan Scouts came into being and were trained to sustain themselves for greatly extended periods in the Primary Jungle environment where they either managed to destroy the enemy or at least drive them out into Secondary Jungle where the conventional ground forces had the opportunity to destroy them.

By 1952 there was a good deal of Military Power to cope with the day to day problems as and when the situations arose throughout the whole Peninsula. These were mainly British Troops including those great little men The Brigade of Ghurkhas, The Malay Regiment and the Malay Police. The Malay Police Force also contributed in no small measure to light Jungle patrols and had made some real differences to certain areas of the Country.

I must not be remiss in my duties and must add to those already mentioned above, yet another often forgotten, additional arm of the Defense Forces. It is that of the Home Guard. They were certainly not the sharpest knife in the draw but they did their bit and very willingly too.

The Commanding Officer of the Malayan Scouts Regiment, Colonel (Mad) Mike Calvert, brought a wealth of experience with him when he founded them at the behest of General Sir John Harding, Commander-in-Chief Far East in 1950. He had of course learned his trade during the war against the Japanese where he served with distinction in Burma and in the Jungles beyond the Chindwin River. He was a brilliant leader who led by example and was much loved and respected by the faithful Troopers of "his" Malayan Scouts. He drew his founder members from whatever source he found available. Amongst these stalwarts were ex-members of Force 136 who had shown the Japanese occupiers of Malaya just what they were capable of and these men consequently brought a great deal of Jungle Warfare experience to the Regiment.

"Mad Mike" spread his net far and wide and managed to recruit men from the Australian Forces and many other National Forces including American, German and perhaps the most noteworthy was the Squadron formed entirely of Rhodesian Troops, who, like all the others, made a great contribution to the hard pushed soldiery in Malaya in the early 1950's. It is worthy of mention here that many of the Rhodesian Squadron were ex-Selous Scouts and proved to be very good soldiers indeed.

By the time I arrived on the scene with the rest of the volunteers who had been recruited from the British Army direct, things seemed to be at an all time low for the Regiment. I must say that the method of selection was just a few minutes interview with a serving Squadron Commander who had flown from Malaya especially for the job, and his prime objective was to "capture" as many bodies as was possible, irrespective of their qualities as soldiers or indeed the reason why they were volunteering. Such methods of selection, if this had been the way previously adopted, had inevitably thrown up some very dodgy characters indeed. They gained the name of being unruly and disrespectful to their Officers. They were also a heavy drinking set and not only fought amongst themselves but made themselves a thorough nuisance when sent on leave after a Jungle Operation.

It seemed that early in 1952 the Regiment, due to its general lack of success, which it must be said, was not entirely of its own making, and was under consideration for disbandment by the powers that be. With this new intake of men, which included me, the Malayan Scouts was given a final stay of execution and was given this last chance to prove its worth.

As history has shown us, it was a damned good job that this decision was taken for the poor performing handful of troops known at that time as the Malayan Scouts for they went on to become the 22nd Special Air Service Regiment.

Need I go on any further with this point?

The reasons, and there were many I am afraid, just why the Regiment was considered to be a spent force by higher authority, was entirely due to their lack of manpower and failure to attract more suitably qualified soldiers from all sources. By the middle of 1952, those men who had formed the basis of the Regiment had now reached the end of their promised two year tour of duty and were opting, in large numbers, to call it a day with the Regiment. The actual reason why that decision was being taken by the majority was based on a number of things. The prime reason seemed to be "Broken Promises". The main grouse of this being the promise that all members would be afforded a Parachute Training Course. The Regiment did not honor this. When the Rhodesians opted to leave for home en-bloc, some Parachuting did take place, including me. It took place at R.A.F Changi in Singapore but I am afraid it was a case of "Too little, Too late". The Rhodesians still went home and the drain of recourses continued.

My recruitment to the Regiment was due in the main to a fit of pique on my part. I disliked the way the Military Machine of the day treated their soldiers with what amounted to nothing short of contempt. This coupled with the fact that I was a young soldier fresh from my service as a Boy Soldier who simply craved for some excitement in my life. This was one of the prime reasons I had opted to join the Army. The Malayan Scouts seemed to offer all these things plus the fact that it entailed Active Service in an overseas location in the Far East.

At the time, I couldn't get my application in quick enough.

CHAPTER 4

Life now seemed to be taking on something akin to normality at last. We very soon recovered from our long journey and seemed to find plenty of opportunity to have a kip almost every afternoon. The long hot humid days were taken up as follows

Each morning before breakfast, we were gently exercised, initially anyway, by undergoing some light training. This usually took the form of a run with full kit. It was obvious that they were determined to get their new arrivals fully fit to the point of bursting. The afternoons after a somewhat heavy lunch (known as Tiffin), was invariably devoted to "Egyptian PT" which entailed lying on ones Charpoy (Bed) under a Mosquito Net, sweating profusely and dreaming of certain things which one wished were available but unfortunately, it was not.

The Cookhouse Staff tended to favour Pork Chops and they produced enormous meals for us. These so called Chops were indeed something to behold as each one could easily have been mistaken for either a Half Shoulder or even a Leg of Pork. It was a good man who could manage a brace of these at a single sitting. When you consider that the Tiffin menu was varied by an alternative fare perhaps only on two occasions each week, you found yourself conversing with your comrades in a series of grunts. There were cases where some men started to complain about curly tails but there appeared to be some doubt if this was due to the Pork alone.

The business of training was now gradually increased on a daily basis. This of course served to build up our strength again after such a long period of inactivity while on the high seas. It also enabled us to become

41

comfortably acclimatized with the local conditions. That is with the exception of one or two of us who had fibbed about our ability to swim when we filled in our application forms to become Malayan Scouts. I, unfortunately, was one of those who had told porkies about my ability to swim without the use of water wings and now was faced with the thought that I wished I had not been so deceitful.

Some evil sod that was responsible for getting us new arrivals fit and ready for a trip into the Ulu (Jungle), had increased the daily "Rodeo", which was the name by which it had become known. The increase had been to such an extent that it now led us to the River Bank which lye opposite our Camp. You've guessed it. There was now a stretch of fairly fast running water, which appeared to be very deep indeed, at least it did to a non swimmer, stretching out over some fifty yards to the opposite bank. Just picture the scenario. Two or three soldiers, each carrying a full complement of their personal kit fastened to their backs with webbing straps, they had just ran perhaps two miles and they were now faced with this obstacle before them. To complete their daily Rodeo they must now swim across the river to their camp. Sounds easy enough doesn't it? None of your pals know that you can't swim, you have never told them. What do you do? Panic and lose face with your buddies? Of course you don't. You have a quick shufti round to see if any of the others are hanging back. None are apparent so there is no alternative for you but to learn to swim right there and then.

There was just one other thing that was to be considered. The instructions were that should any Trooper be unlucky enough to get his Firearm wet and thus make it incapable of being fired, he was redirected, after stripping and cleaning his Firearm, round the course again bringing him back to the river a second time for another attempt at crossing it safely and correctly. The daily exercise was then rounded off by blasting off ten rounds of ammunition to prove the efficiency of the weapons and perhaps more importantly, to convince any secret onlookers that we could still show them a thing or two if they fancied their chances. After all this had been successfully completed we were then allowed to visit the trough, so to speak, where we would enjoy a hearty breakfast.

The moral here was of course "No Swim, No Eat".

I was not alone with the difficulties this presented; however, with the help of other members of my troop, it took me just three days to learn to swim, after a fashion. This pleased me no end and was to prove highly important at a later date when my life depended on my ability to keep afloat under extremely hazardous conditions.

The Tented Camp at Klang had been considered suitable as a temporary measure but when the Regiment was offered an alternative location, which boasted Atap Basha accommodation, (proper huts constructed from Bamboo and Palm Leaves), our leaders jumped at the chance. The whole kit and caboodle was loaded onto our aged Ford Three Toners and off we went to our new home. This camp was designated as the Regimental Depot of the Malayan Scouts. The new camp, which was some twelve miles East of Kuala Lumpur, was known as Sungai (River) Besi Camp. This was a much improved situation compared with what we had endured at Klang and it was very much appreciated even though it was somewhat remote from the bright lights of Kuala Lumpur. I mean this to be only a slight criticism as a Liberty Truck was made available at weekends. During the week, it was here in the river Besi that certain members of the Regiment, including myself, were able to improve their aquatic skills, which seemed to be a good thing to do.

The Camp had been built originally for use as a Malay Police Training Camp and to this end a Shooting Range had been established in a worked out Tin Mine which lay nearby. This facility was in use almost all the time as the soldiers could bang away to their hearts content at anything which would serve as a target. They were also able to familiarize themselves with such weapons as the Colt 45 Pistol and the 9mm Australian Owen Gun. Some of us had never even heard of these weapons and were all very keen to try them out. The two mentioned here were very popular indeed with the whole Regiment and the poor old lads in the Regimental Armoury were hard pushed to supply all that was in demand. I suppose that their popularity was mainly due to the fact that they were light and therefore easily carried in the Jungle. They were also very effective weapons at close quarters. It was to be here on the Sungai Besi Range that tragedy struck and the Regiment lost two of their most experienced Jungle Fighters.

A group of soldiers had spent the afternoon at the Range and as was usually the case, every round of ammunition had been expended by the end of the day. As they were packing up and preparing to make their way back to Camp, they came under Terrorist gunfire and unfortunately the two soldiers were killed. It was soon apparent that a small group of Terrorists must have watched, under cover of the scant Jungle under-growth close by. They must also have been familiar with the accepted procedure and knowing that there would be little chance of retaliation from the soldiers, as they would have used up all their ammunition. With this knowledge in mind, they very bravely came out and murdered them at their leisure. The mistake made by the soldiers was so basic and simple that the rules were changed immediately. A sentry was posted at all times when the Range was in use and he had his own supply of ammunition of course.

We lost no one further after this most unfortunate episode.

Training apart, there was a whole way of life that the soldiers of the FARELF (Far East Land Forces) were to accept and become familiar with. One example of this, not altogether new way of life, was that ones soled laundry (Dhobi) disappeared each morning as if by magic. It was spirited away, before you rose from your slumbers by some unknown, unseen Dhobi Wallah who had it washed and immaculately ironed, then back on the foot of your bed before nightfall. I never clapped eyes on the Dhobi Wallah, not that I was interested in him, being totally satis-fied with the service which incidentally, had just happened without any prompting from me, or anyone else come to that.

The day would start around 0600hrs when I would wake to find myself being lathered up for shaving. More often than not the Barber Wallah had almost finished his duties with a wicked looking cut throat razor when I returned to the land of the living and was fully awake. He would shave me while I slept.

I found this service somewhat disconcerting to start with. I was more than a little skeptical about allowing some unknown person to perform on my face and throat with a razor while I was still asleep. However, after two or three days my confidence in the Barber Wallah built and thereafter I remained in a sub-conscious state of mind while he carried out his daily task.

A Boot Wallah took care of my footwear. A comparatively easy task as the Black Leather Ammunition Boots, the forerunner of today's Boots DMS, were rarely worn. The Canvas topped Jungle Boots were preferred by the soldiers as they were soft and comfortable, at least when they were completely dry they were. When they were wet, well that was a differed matter altogether.

And then of course there was the Char Wallah. His establishment has been part of the British Army in the FARELF for as long as even the oldest soldier could remember.

It is a well known fact in Military Circles that all Char Walla's go by the name of "Mr. MacGregor" and the one that served us in the Malayan Scouts was no exception. It was he who controlled and directed all Camp Services no matter what they were. These could range from getting a shirt button sewn on, making beds, polishing shoes or simply washing a pair of socks. He not only directed the labour for all such chores, but even more importantly, he both set the rates for all services and collected the money due from each soldier immediately after Pay Parade each week. He truly was a sort of Managing Director without Suit, Rolls Royce or Posh Office Facilities. Added to all this was his personal duties of Bookkeeper, Accountant and Auditor. Only he knew his methods of keeping accounts. He kept his day to day records in a small A5 size notebook. The entries were made with a stub of indelible pencil which left a series of purple stripes on his tongue due to the constant licking prior to each entry which he made in some mystical form of code which was understood by MacGregor and MacGregor alone. The names of each soldier were not recorded but he had an uncanny skill in that he could quote the last four digits of any soldiers Regimental Number, from memory.

The reason for the lack of names was quite simple really. Over the many years he had served the British Army, as each new batch of soldiers arrived from the UK, the same names had been given time and time again for his records in his secret book. Tom Mix, Tarzan, Ginger Rogers, George Formby and of course the favourite of all time, Kilroy, were amongst the more flamboyant and ribald ones offered by the soldiers.

He visited each Tent or Basha at least twice each day when he would be accompanied by one of his assistants who carried the Tea Urn . A second assistant, invariably an Apprentice, would tote a basket which contained the infinite variations of the basic sandwich filling of Cheese, Tomato and Onion. Part of the Apprentices training was to swap any of these three commodities between the freshly baked rolls that they were served in. He would thus produce the combination requested by the customer. If a roll was made up of all three commodities and the customer stated Cheese and Onion, the Apprentice swiftly removed all traces of Tomato from the roll without the customer even noticing that this was being done. The item removed would, just as swiftly, be inserted in another roll in the basket. If the unfortunate Apprentice was seen by the customer to be working this oracle and mentioned it to MacGregor, he would reward the Apprentice with a smart clout round the lughole, not for doing it I might add, but for getting caught. The request for a Bacon Sandwich was of course standard practice, however, in view of MacGregor being a strict Moslem, he took it all in good part and informed the enquirer that he had run out of Bacon that very day, he would however, bring a Bacon Sandwich along just as soon as new supplies were to hand.

Yet another game enacted between Soldier and Char Wallah was that of disputing the weekly bill when Pay Day arrived. One would accuse the other of being a robber and a cheat. Each knew what was owed and the Soldier also knew that his funds were insufficient to clear his obligation in one go, credit would automatically be extended to the next Pay Day, however, it was Par for the Course to complain anyway.

The disputes were in the main quite amusing and in all cases the Char Wallah was accused of having no knowledge of who his father was. The Soldier would in turn be accused of having sprung from the loins of a woman had spent most of her waking hours lying on her back gazing

46

up at the sky in the Market Place or some such common location. Any serious complaint of non-payment was swiftly resolved. On the early morning tea round (Gunfire) of hot sweet tea, the errant Soldier received no service. Neither was he shaved nor his Dhobi taken care of. Result, the Soldier failed to function correctly without these essential services.

The ever present and very wise Mr. MacGregor would quickly bring him into line.

No Pay......No Services. It worked every time.

CHAPTER 5

Tomorrow, "A" Squadron was to undertake their first Jungle Training Operation. It was scheduled to take place in Primary Jungle between Kuala Lumpur and Ipoh in the North of the Country. We were to operate exactly as we would, had it been a "Puka" Operation. Each Operational Troop would comprise 12 to 14 men which would include a Troop Commander (Officer), Troop Sergeant, Troop Corporal and where possible, a Wireless Operator. There would also be approximately ten Troopers who would collectively have skills in the following fields. Medical, Explosives, Watercrafts, Rock Climbing and Rigging. This last one was another name for Knots and Lashings. Having such a variety of skills at the Troops disposal meant that it was most unlikely that no matter whatever was encountered, we would be able to cope with it ourselves.

The Squadron was split into 5 separate Troops as follows. H.Q. Troop, who would be responsible for all Administration and Transport requirements of the remainder of the Squadron which comprised No.1Troop, No.2 Troop, No.3 Troop and No.4 Troop. I was allocated to No.2 Troop.

In those early days Transportation by road was used exclusively to get men into and out of the Operational Areas. Later on in my tour of duty with the Regiment, movement matters became easier as we were ferried by Valetta Aircraft and Parachuted into our allotted area in exactly the same way as our Rations and other essentials were. However, at the time we were to make our first Trip into the Jungle we had to content ourselves with the aged 3ton Fords to get us into position.

Apart from transport, the H.Q. Troop dealt with Clothing, Footwear,

Food, Mail, Medical Supplies, Arms and Ammunition, Pay and Allowances, (Yes some of us were married and had dependants back in the UK, Medical Evacuations (by Helicopter) and the arrangement to have food and supplies Air Dropped to us in the Jungle by the RAF. Indeed the list was almost endless and it covered all the things necessary to keep the Operational Troops up to scratch. Not an easy job, believe me.

The other four Troops were all engaged in Jungle Operations each Troop being completely independent of each other. Their job was to march in from the drop off point to their particular Operational Area which would, initially, be an area which covered say, two map squares. The adjoining areas to the left and right, would be allocated to two of the other Troops and the fourth Troop would cover the rear and be kept in reserve should anyone bite off more that they could chew.

The task would be to sweep the area for signs of Terrorist activity. Search and destroy was the official name given to these type of Operations because there was nothing specific known about these areas and anyone loitering with intent, would be given short shrift and driven out into Secondary Jungle where other Forces could deal with them.

Each individual Troop would invariably be divided into three sections. This was, of course left to the Troop Commanders discretion. I am only able to describe what happened in No.2 Troop as that is the Troop I was a member of.

It is worthy of note at this point that each mans individual position in the order of march, was changed from day to day. This was, I believe, the Gaffers (Troop Commander) way of sharing the load and making sure that the worst of the heavy work was fairly distributed.

Two Troopers accompanied by the two Iban Trackers formed a Leading Scout Section. The Trackers were a permanent feature of the Leading Scout Section and would not have been happy to operate in anything other than the Leading Scout Section. We shall learn a little more about these small, but wildly ferocious men who were "Head Hunters", in the true sense. They came from Borneo and Lebuan to assist us in our hour of need.

The function of the Leading Scouts was to steer the rest of the Troop

49

on the course we were intended to travel. While doing this they would chop a way through the thickest of the undergrowth, meanwhile, they kept fully alert at all times for the presence of any Terrorist activity. The Ibans played a major role in this respect as they were not only able to detect that there had been human movement in the area, they could also give an indication of how many and how long since. They sometimes had a little difficulty in passing on their messages but seemed to get it across by drawing on a bare patch of earth. None of them spoke any English at all, but to a man, they could make themselves understood when they wanted a Woodbine from you. (Or should that read "State Express" or "5.5.5" which were issued to us in sealed tins of 50's). It was not a favourite place to be, up at the head of the Troop. It was bloody hard graft and always full of surprises of one kind of another the worst of these being that you would be covered with Leaches when ever a halt was called.

Following on behind this Section, a matter of five or six yards, which can be a long way in the Jungle, came the Main Fire Section. This Section was made up of the Troop Commander whose radio call sign was "Sunray", the Troop Sergeant, radio call sign "Sunray Minor", there was also the poor sod who had been allocated to carry the Bren Gun on any particular day. This too was not an enviable task as the thing weighed a ton and sometime felt even heavier. Finally in this Section came the Radio Operator. He was inevitably called "Sparks" by everyone, including the Gaffer. Poor old Sparks had a fair old load to carry as well. The old pattern, 62 Radio Set, plus a full set of Batteries was both cumbersome and heavy, but during my time on Operations, the faithful old thing never let us down.

Attached to the Fire Section there were usually a couple of Sakai Porters These chaps would be recruited from one of the many local groups who lived their lives in Jungle clearings. These little chaps, despite them being barely four feet tall when they were fully grown, were used to carry spare boxes of Bren Gun Magazines (loaded of course) and such items as spare Radio Batteries plus anything else that was a nuisance to cope with while the Troop was on the move.

The Sakai were not entirely trustworthy and would only stay with the Troop for a couple of weeks at the most. They were given an amount of Rice and Hard Tack Biscuits each day. They would eat about one half of what they were given and then squirrel the remainder away about their person. When they felt they had enough stored, they would hop it. They would be there at "Stand To" last thing at night, but the next morning they were history. Any Trooper who became careless with his ration packs and left food lying about, would be relieved of it by the departing Sakai Porter.

The final part of the Fire Section was made up of some 4 or 5 Troopers and these men would be detached as needed to aid either of the other two Sections.

Finally, situated behind the Fire Section, again some four or five yards behind came the Rear Section. This Section comprised two Troopers and the Troop Corporal who was always the last man in the Troop when it was on the move. He was always referred to as "Tail End Charlie". If were to say that he followed his two comrades closely, I would mean, very closely indeed.

In the Jungle it is perhaps only possible to see a few feet in any direction. With this in mind, it was not unknown for a Terrorist to allow the whole Troop to pass just a matter of feet away from him/her, only to slip a garrote round the neck of the Tail End Charlie and thus collect him quietly and very efficiently. If it did happen, and it had been known to , it could be that the unfortunate man would not be missed for the next half hour or so, it would be only then, when the Troop halted for a short breather that it became apparent that something had happened to him.

Everyone had a job to do in the daily order of things; however, the Troop Sergeant saw to it that no one suffered more than anyone else when it came to extra hard work. There was only one exception to the rule,. The Tail End Charlie was always the job of the Troop Corporal and that never changed.

Many different Orders of March had been tried out at various times, but it was finally decided that the one which we adopted in No.2 Troop, was as good as any that had gone before.

The role played by the Iban Trackers, although kept at a low key, was indeed one of the mainstays of the Troop when operating in the Jungle. They would be called upon to decipher any signs of human activity and were expert at reading how many men had been present at a "find" and how long ago it was that they had left the scene. I personally had difficulty in deciphering their idea of time. They would point in a certain direction and then, where possible, draw a number of stick men on the ground. They would then wipe it all out and replace it with a number of Sun's. This of course, to the European, had a number of interpretations. Did this mean (so many) men had gone (so many) days ago in the direction indicated? Did it mean that there had been two men here but one of them went one day and the other a day after? In fact the two days go bit could mean anything up to a week. There was little point in pursuing the matter, as the only reaction you would get from your friendly Iban was an enormous grin spread from ear to ear. This undoubtedly meant "don't believe me? Well please yourself".

Some of these chaps spoke just a smidgen of Pigeon English and this had been gleaned fro the soldiers with whom they had served. You can imagine the little diamonds they came out with from time to time. They were indeed a very happy band of men who insisted that they always worked in pairs the same two men always being in the same pair. They were easy to get along with and the Military, in their infinite wisdom, had taken to issuing them with a 303 Lea Enfield rifle each when they went out on Operations. I am afraid that without exception, they did not like the rifle and rather viewed it with some suspicion. In the event of a contact being made with the Enemy, they promptly disposed of it and drew their Parang (often called a Kris). Off they went in hot pursuit. It was no fairy story I'm afraid that back home in their native Borneo, when a kill was made, (often a human belonging to some rival Tribe), it was off with their head and then a portion of the unfortunate victims hair was wound round the handle of the killers Parang. The more hair on the Parang, the more successful the owner had been.

It was a popular belief within the troop membership that apart from reading the Jungle for signs of human movement or presence, these valuable little men from Borneo possessed a gift of smelling out a Bandit long before the Leading Scout had any inclination of heir presence.

Many a Leading Scout kept on breathing and kept on leading a somewhat comparatively happy life thank to a trusty Iban who rarely left his side while ever the Operation continued.

The pair who was attached to No2 Troop, cooked and fed themselves. They rarely made an overnight Bivouac as all we others did, (with the exception of the Sakai). When a call to halt for the night was made, they had a fire made and their cooking done before we poor souls, who had to rely on "Tommy Cooker's" and inflammable tablets to prepare our evening meal, had barely started the process and that would be prior to building our home for the night. Our Trackers slept up in the trees, which overlooked the rest of the Troop. They kept mainly to themselves but made no secret of the fact that they despised the Sakai Porters. I suppose they saw them as a lower breed in the social scale and therefore they had no time for them at all.

These fearsome looking men were covered in Tattoo's from head to foot, including the throat. They were applied by their fellow men. They were simply known as Iban Trackers and none that I knew ever seemed to have any other name. I suppose it was their lack of the English language that prevented them from informing us of their given names.

Although it was strictly against orders, many of the Troopers found that having the Iban's carry out a Tattoo on them, was a sign, as it was with the Trackers, that manhood was complete.

The method of application was primitive in the extreme. A piece of Bamboo stick was fitted with a four inch piece of hardwood inserted through a hole in the stick. This piece of hardwood would be cut to a point at one end and would perhaps be retained in the Bamboo stick by being bound in place with a suitable piece if vine. A further stick would be used as a sort of hammer, which, when the Bamboo was struck with it, it caused the hardwood point to cut into the flesh. The sharpened hardwood point would be dipped in a concoxion of Red Ochre (from Ant Hills) and spit, or perhaps boot polish and spit. The Boot polish would be carried as an extra by the person who wanted a Tattoo. Sometimes they would use certain leaves, pounded to a pulp and yes, again it would be mixed with the inevitable spit. Just one point here. It was always the Iban's spit that went into the mixture never the recipient's. It was many a

Trooper who regretted having such treatment applied whilst killing time in a grenade Ambush. They managed little or no sleep for two or three nights and absolute agony when on the move as the pack on their back rubbed the Tattoo and it's surrounding area, until it became a raw area which was no joke believe me.

Many suffered the pain to be able to boast an Iban Tattoo including myself. This I bear to this very day emblazoned on my back between my shoulder blades where it is away from curious eyes. After all these years, the Black Boot Polish has lost none of its luster. That says something for Cherry Blossom doesn't it?

The initial Training Exercise that we were about to undertake being scheduled for the very next day, I could sense a feeling of apprehension amongst my fellow men. It was obvious that we all had mixed feelings about the whole thing. After all, this was what we had volunteered for and who knows, perhaps we would be lucky and manage to have a dust up with these bad buggers who had been causing all the bother.

The Sergeant in charge of my Troop, known throughout the Regiment as "The Ox", had left us newcomers in no doubt as to what this Operation was about. It was to familiarize us with living in the Jungle on a day to day basis, and sustain ourselves for extended periods should circumstances warrant it. It would further teach us, not only how to look after ourselves, but how to look out for other members of our Troop as well.

We would live on the Army Issue 24hour Jungle, Man Pack Rations. These would be carried by each individual and we were to learn to spin out the contents and make them last for the period that they were intended to cover. There would be no popping down to the Corner Shop for a pound of Rice, or perhaps a Loaf of Bread just because you fancied a sandwich.

It was also hammered into us fairly comprehensively, that should there be any Terrorists either operating in the area, or perhaps even just passing through, they would be most unlikely to think "Oh hell, these lads are only learners, let's not shoot the poor sods, at least let's wait until they get a bit more practice in". It was now to be for real and I, together with the rest of the Troop were staring reality in the face, with

54

very little idea of how we would react should we meet up with any of these nasty little men.

Preparation was an important part here. What we packed, was what we would survive on during the next two weeks. Selection was paramount as that which was selected would have to be carried on your own back during the days that followed.

I had been issued with a Frame which went under the name of an Everest Frame. I was to strap a large Webbing Pack (37 Pattern), onto it and into this pack I was to load all my goods and chattels, including food, that I thought I would need during the first week of the Operation. What was to happen after that, I was not quite sure, but I would learn as I went along. All the Troopers hated the Everest Frame which, although made from the lightest Aluminum they were the most uncomfortable piece of equipment imaginable. They had bits sticking out where bits shouldn't stick out, and it was these bits that stuck into your back and made it sore. Apart from that, the Webbing Packs were far from being waterproof and this caused the contents to become very wet, very quickly. In the Jungle where drying facilities were somewhat few and far between, it only contributed to an already miserable existence.

This form of carrying ones kit was eventually replaced by issuing each man with a Bergen Rucksack which was a great improvement. How these Bergen's became available was something of a mystery, as they were not standard issue from recognized Military supplies. It didn't go unnoticed however, that every time any of the Regiments Transport was to go down to Singapore, (all Ordnance Corps Depots were located in Singapore,) on their return, a few more Bergen's became available. It didn't take all that many trips before we all had one.

The task of packing ready for the off in the morning, was indeed a test of skill. Each Trooper had been issued with seven, twenty four hour ration packs. The food issued for one day came in a cardboard box measuring some eight inches long by six inches wide and six inches deep. The contents were supposed to sustain one man for a twenty four hour period according to the Boffins who, I doubt had ever seen a picture of the inside of the Jungle let alone tried to exist in it on the meager rations supplied. I suppose it was just good enough to get by on but I did have my doubts when I found out later that I had lost some nine pounds in weight after completing just two weeks on the Training Operation. I came to the conclusion that such a loss of weight was not entirely due to worrying about Snakes, Animals (including Tigers), Leaches and of course Communist Terrorist's.

As I was busy with my packing it suddenly struck me that we were supposed to be going for two weeks, yet, there was only seven packs of grub for each man. What was to happen in the second week we were out there? Surely we were not supposed to diet during this most important part of our training.

The Troop Corporal, a very wise and experienced man, explained to us that after one week, we would receive an Air Drop courtesy of the RAF Dispatch Squadron who were based at Kuala Lumpur Airfield. That was of course subject to us Troopers cutting and marking out a Dropping Zone in the Jungle, big enough for the Pilots to see from above the solid green canopy of trees as they flew overhead at a speed of some two hundred and fifty knots.

The majority of the men struggled with the seven cardboard boxes of food, trying al ways to get them to fit into their packs with the contents still packed inside them. It didn't take us long before we realized that things would be a lot easier if we removed all items from the original packing (cardboard boxes) and stowed them in their loose state in the webbing pack. As the majority comprised tinned food, it greatly relieved the situation.

After we had solved this first problem, there came the business of how to accommodate such things as a spare set of underwear, socks, jocks, Poncho, Medical "J" Pack full of pills to cure all ills that may be visited upon me.What was I to do? Talk about a Pint in a Half Pint Pot. I sat on my bed surrounded by things which I considered to be absolutely essential for me to take. I slowly came to the conclusion that I would have to leave one days rations behind and maybe it would be two days rations.

While I was pondering the conundrum, "The Ox" made his rounds to see how we were coping and to inform each one of us that we would have to carry two Bren Gun Magazines filled with Ammunition of course, four Mk36 high explosive Hand Grenades, two Mk80 Phosphorous Smoke Grenades, two spare Magazines (filled) for our own personal Weapon, which in my case was a 9mm Australian Owen Gun. I was initially landed with a spare battery for the Radio but "The Ox" changed his mind at the last minute and lumbered someone else with it. Things like the Bren Gun Magazines would be passed on to the Sakai Porters when we had managed to secure the services of a couple as we were dropped off the Trucks close to where we would operate.

We, as a newly formed Troop, were very fortunate to have a couple of old sweats that had done it all many times before. They showed us how to cut down the load by getting rid of anything that was neither essential nor edible. Once this step had been completed, we were introduced to the bargaining session between all members of the Troop. This entailed giving away those items of food which just didn't appeal to you and in exchange you gathered up those items which had a certain attraction to you. Of course this, our first trip into the Jungle, we had no idea which things we would appreciate and which things we would want to get rid of next time. My tastes and dislikes changed a number of times as I gained experience. Things like a tube of condensed milk was just fine if you had sufficient time to let the hot tea dissolve the milk, (a good five minutes), but by hell, five or six tubes of the stuff was not only heavy, it took up quite a bit of room in your Pack as well.

The Pack seemed to be very heavy with all the necessities stowed away, however, the old sweats assured us that the weight would get less and less as the food was consumed on a daily basis.

By 2100hrs we seemed to be as ready for the morrow as we would ever be likely to be. It was time for us to retire to the NAAFI Tent to see off a few beers, remembering that an early start was called for the next day and we should not do the usual trick of trying to drink the place dry. As usual, the NAAFI was quite crowded but it soon became evident what the added attraction was, this being Tuesday Evening.

In the Regiment, there was a larger than average Trooper, who had an equally matching liking for Beer. It was his party piece, when suitably stoked up, to demonstrate how he could, with the aid of Plastic Explosive, blow the handle off a pint beer mug without cracking the beer mug itself. He would willingly demonstrate this after being treated to yet another bottle of Beck's Beer which was his favourite tipple. It was said he had arrived at the Regiment via the Royal Engineers in much the same way as I did myself. However, some of the feats performed by Fred, as he was widely known, were definitely in the Sappers Training Manual, at least not in the one that I had read when I was with the Sappers.

Another part of Fred's entertaining performance was that he would drop his trousers and invite any unsuspecting member of his audience, to come and hold a lighted match within the close proximity of his back passage. He would then let out a mighty "Fart" which would ignite as it contained a substantial quantity of inflammable gases.

Encouraged by his appreciative audience, he would follow this up by rolling a sheet of newspaper up and inserting it in his back passage. He then issued a challenge to all present, for anyone to be brave enough to do likewise. Anyone brave enough, or daft enough to take him on, would be invited to place a small wager on the outcome of the challenge. The wager never varied, it was inevitably a large bottle of Beck's Beer. The competitors would now line up and each protruding sheet of paper would be ignited at exactly the same instant. The winner would be the one who outstayed the rest by being the one who withdrew the lighted paper last of all. Needless to say, the winner was always Fred who seemed to be able to endure a singed rear with much more fortitude than any of his challengers.

It was a fact that most of the Regiment were a feared of Fred, especially when he had exceeded his enormous capacity for the German Lotion at which time he would invite any new arrival to compete with him. This was definitely a pleasure which they could definitely do without. However, the very size of the man left many new arrivals in no doubt whatsoever that they had little choice in the matter as their intention was that would not like to offend the man in any way.

It was my good fortune to never be challenged, but I did bear witness to many who had this misfortune.

CHAPTER 6

"A" Squadron was up at the crack of sparrows the next morning. Everyone ate an enormous breakfast knowing full well that they were about to experience a spot of self catering over the next two weeks.

After drawing our weapons from the Regimental Armoury, we spent some time cleaning and making minor adjustments here and there, just to make sure that the weapons would be ready for use should the need arise.

The old faithful Ford WOT6's were eventually coaxed into life and after loading, they set about transporting the complete Squadron, with the exception of HQ Troop, into what for the majority of us was unknown territory. The area allocated to the Squadron for the purpose of our Training Operation lay to the North of Kuala Lumpur but short of being as far north as Ipoh.

After the usual "hairy" ride, courtesy of the WOT6 drivers, who seemed to pilot their vehicles on the principle of one pert skill and nine parts good luck. We eventually came to a halt on the very edge of the Jungle, which at this point, came close to encroaching onto the road itself. We were all unloaded in double quick time and the trucks beat a hasty retreat.

Each of the four Troops disappeared into the Jungle with an equal amount of haste. I am sure that each one of us now realized that it was for real now. The practicing was a thing of the past and we were now faced with exactly what we had volunteered to do as soldiers of the Malayan Scouts.

We were keen to identify the Map Squares which had been assigned to us by the Squadron Commander, Major Westmorland, who was uni-

60

versally known as "The Poppy" (but more of him later). In this respect one Map Square was very much like another when the Map was consulted and thus our first steps in navigation under Jungle conditions became paramount. We would initially have to clarify what was physically on the ground and how such features could be related to it on the Map. This was to prove to be one of the most difficult tasks, not only on this my first Operation, but also throughout the full length of my service with the Malayan Scouts and latterly, the 22nd Special Air Service.

Close attention was paid to each man by "The Ox" and the Troop Commander in order to assess how we were performing and if we were learning by any mistakes we made. They were obviously interested how each man adapted to the surroundings. I knew that each member of my Troop was well pumped up during the first few days we were in the Jungle. Just let any of these Bandits cross our path. We would have 'em, quick as you like. We were nothing if not enthusiastic for the task in hand.

That first day went quite well but I found it to be hard work and I suspect, so did the rest of the Troop. We would move forward for some fifty minutes or so and then we would take a break for ten minutes. No smoking during the break. When we were on the move, we were fully employed chopping down the undergrowth in order that we could make some progress. The sky above us was only to be seen in short snatches as the tree canopy was almost total and the foliage was constantly wet.

The area had been specially selected I think as it was classified as Secondary Jungle. This type was much easier to handle than the Primary Jungle terrain which we would eventually have to handle. Believe me; I never considered anything could be worse than where I was at the time. My buddies and I had our hands full and no mistake.

Leeches were a real problem and they fell by the score onto us as we chopped at the wet trees and undergrowth. The trouble was that you never felt them bite you in the first instance, but when you did find them, they had burrowed their heads under your skin and were now bloated with blood which they had sucked out of your body. They seemed to concentrate on the soft areas of your body. Such places as the small of your neck, underneath each arm in the armpit and those I hated the most, in the groin area. They would make their way into the pipe of the Penis and if this were the case, you then had a serious problem when you came to get it out from its chosen spot. If the Leech was simply pulled out from its attacking point, the head would inevitably be left behind buried in the skin. Consequently under such hot and humid conditions, it went septic in the space of just a few hours. This condition in itself was not a minor thing as it could turn very nasty and lay a man low in a very short time. We soon learned the quickest and safest way to get rid of the loathsome creatures was to touch them with a lighted cigarette. This immediately caused them to abandon their feeding and they would drop off taking their head with them. This method, although efficient enough was not without its problems.

Smoking was strictly forbidden when we were either on the move or when we took a short break. The restriction on a fag at a short break was eventually relaxed, I suppose because it appeared to serve little or no purpose. If any Bandits were nearby, they would surely be aware of our presence from all the chopping that went on. In the main, nearly everyone waited for Bivouac time when they lit up and dropped their kecks before starting the nightly hunt for the black offenders.

The business of Leeches up the Penis proved to be a real problem. It was only when some of the old sweats, who had been at it for some time, suggested to us new boys that if a condom was to be worn throughout te day, we would suffer no further problem in this direction.

On that first day, by the time 1700hrs came round we were all knackered and just longed to lay down and go to sleep. It seemed that most of us would have been quite happy to roll up inside our Poncho (Waterproof Cape) and sleep. No food or even a mug of tea and certainly no wash or erection of any kind of shelter formed any part of our plans for the coming night. It was as if we had forgotten why we were there, certainly the possibility of Terrorists/Bandits being close at hand, waiting for their chance to have a go at us while we were at our most vulnerable, just didn't occur to any of us. We were very quickly put straight by the Troop NCOs. They checked out our pairings, which we had all agreed on before leaving the Depot, and then we had to set about building a two man sleeping Basha within the next ten minutes or so. These were then subjected to a rigorous inspection to assess their suitability for a one night stay. Some unfortunately didn't pass muster and they were pulled down by the inspecting NCO. The unfortunate (tired) Troopers were then encouraged to start from scratch and construct their sleeping quarters in a more soldier like manner. The lesson had been learned and we all became quite expert at whipping up a waterproof, windproof cover for the night.

The Troop Commander, Captain Taffy Williams, who was always referred to as "The Gaffer", visited each pair of men to check that they had indeed washed and made some sort of effort at preparing some food. All that remained now was to wait for nightfall when "Stand To" would take place before we hit the sack, or in our case the ground.

"Stand To" was something that happened at first light in the morning and again at last thing at night, when what daylight there was, was just about to switch off as it were. From previous experience, the Bandits were prepared to track a Troops movement all day long, but were loathe to attack when the soldiers were alert and ready to retaliate. They preferred to wait for the time when the daylight was just fading, or alternatively just about to break in the morning. They would then mount their attack hoping to catch out the sleepy men.

"Stand To" meant that the soldiers formed a protective ring about eight to ten yards outside their Bivouac Area. They then maintained a silence and listened intently for any signs of movement that could mean that the opposition was close by and would descend on them at any minute. This silent vigil would be maintained for approximately ten minutes until it was either pitch dark or alternatively fully daylight. It was then, and only then, that the whisper would be assed from man to man, "Stand Down". This had to be whispered, as it was not unknown for the Bandits to wait until they heard "Stand Down" and then they would launch their attack.

There was yet one other duty to be performed throughout the whole of the night. This was that every member of the Troop, including the Gaffer and both the NCOs, took their turn at standing guard during the night while the others slept. Although this was necessary mainly to guard against any enemy entering the Bivouac area and silently reducing

63

the number of Troop Members with the aid of a knife. There were other reasons also, wild Animals both great and small. They might just seize the opportunity to come amongst us in search of a succulent meal be that an open tin of beans or perhaps something even more substantial.

So came the end of our first day on Jungle Patrol. We were too tired to think about it but we had indeed learned a great deal about life at the sharp end and had gone a long way to being aware that self preservation and the well being of our comrades was of paramount importance.

Yet another important lesson we soon learned was that we should always make our Bivouac area within easy reach of water whenever it was possible. We became aware that "Easy Reach" meant just that. Not too far away, and yet not near enough to be woken during the night when a flash flood came about. Such an occurrence was capable of sweeping away both men and equipment in a matter of seconds. There were a number of other things for us to consider when choosing the area where we would spend the night. Never choose a place where there were any signs of animals going down to the water for their nightly drink. The couldn't care less who was sleeping there. It was their home and they had probably taken that route on numerous occasions. There was also the ever present Crocodile. They rarely stray more than 50 or 60 feet from the waters edge. I say rarely, but that doesn't mean that they never will. There is always the exception to the rule and a 10 to 12ft Crocodile is hardly a popular bed mate to have.

There was yet another reason why care should be taken. This was the fact that there were other creatures that were prone to acting to habit. The Bandits had the same basic needs as the soldiers and they too needed to Bivouac close to water. The area we chose was always checked for any signs that there had been, or indeed still had other Human visitors.

I was in the process of taking the Mess Tins belonging to me and Jack (my Bivouac mate), down to the water to wash them out and bring sufficient water back to make the pair of us a brew of tea. I had gone but a few steps, when "The Ox" spotted me.

"Where are you off to young feller"? He growled. "Decided to take a run into KL for a beer or two and perhaps a bit of Nookie down at the

Dance Hall have we"? He was not without humour and knew just how to apply it to a young soldier who was slightly out of his depth in the Jungle.

"Water" I replied thinking that should have been fairly obvious as I was carrying a pair of Mess Tins.

"Here listen to me and remember what I say. Never go to the water on your own, not even in the daylight let alone the dark. Always go in pairs. One of you have a wash down or do your utensils or whatever, while the other keeps his eyes open for unwanted visitors, human or otherwise. Then you can swap over and your mate can have a dip while you keep lookout. These Bandits are lazy bastards, they will sit for hours on end near a river bank waiting for just such an opportunity as you was just about to present to anyone who might be interested. Don't go shitting yourself about it. I'm not saying there is anyone out there right now but one day, just the once you fail to think about what I have said, "Bang" you are no more and very likely your mate as well. Now I ask you, who will we have to carry all those spare Bren Gun Magazines then"?

I thought the shooting and death bit to be so much bullshit which "The Ox" had thrown in just to put the wind up me. Nevertheless, I gave Jack the gist of what had been said. As was his way, he said nothing but I knew he would store it all away for future reference.

The Bivouac built by us was something to be admired, or so we thought. At first sight it appeared to be simply a Poncho laid on the ground and it was on this that the pair of us would lay. The second Poncho was placed above where we were to lay and this one was secured at each of its four corners to four convenient trees or Bamboo. That was all we had managed to do on our first night in the Jungle. The main problem seemed to be the same for all of us. That was deciding the height that the upper Poncho was to be tied above the ground so as to ensure that we had sufficient headroom when we were inside the Bivouac. All seemed fine while we were lying down, but in the event that either of us sat up or simply tried to leave, perhaps to answer the call of nature, or to simply get up to take their turn at Guard Duty, the result could be catastrophic in the pitch darkness. There was one occasion when the whole thing collapsed during a particularly heavy storm. It was bedlam. Not only was the whole Troop woken up, thinking the worst was about to happen, but Jack and I were completely soaked as indeed was our entire kit and weapons. If the upper Poncho was not securely tied, it could easily break free due to high winds and the incessant rain. There was nothing worse than trying to rebuild your Bivouac in the middle of the night.

Although these methods of providing cover for the night was, at best, far from comfortable on the back and shoulders, it was however, a quick and easy structure to make at the end of the days activities when we all felt knackered. Jack and I thought it was just about adequate as we couldn't care less how or where we slept, just as long as we could close our eyes immediately we were allowed to turn in.

All went well with the Bivouac building for the first week of the Operation and then disaster struck in the middle of the night. It must have been about 0400hrs when it seemed that all hell had been let loose. I woke to find myself lying in about two inches of water which had collected on the Poncho on which Jack and I lay. The upper Poncho bulged ominously down towards us and at its lowest point trickled a steady stream of water onto us below. Jack seemed to be oblivious that this was happening as he continued to snore away, no doubt dreaming of some flaxen haired beauty he had known at sometime or another.

This was yet another lesson we were to learn. The business of rigging the two Ponchos up and crashing out under them, proved to be not the way to do it. True, the old sweats could have pointed out the error of our ways but they were more inclined to let things take their natural course. The idea that slinging a Poncho tied to trees meant that it should be rigged at an angle and the slope of the thing was very important. If it rained heavily during the night, as it had when our tragedy struck, if it were allowed to collect in the upper Poncho, it was only a matter of time before the occupants below were soaked.

After this debacle, everyone adopted a more suitable arrangement. The Poncho's were fastened edge to edge with the heavy duty press studs which were fitted to them. One of the loose edges was then strung between two suitable trees at a height of about three feet above the ground. An envelope was thus fashioned and this provided something to lie on and in addition, provided cover from above in the event of rain which immediately ran off due to the angle of the upper Poncho. If time permitted, a further "comfort" could be provided by scrapping a small channel in the floor of the Jungle and this would extend all the way round the area you were to lay in. It provided your home for that evening with protection from water coming in from the immediate surrounding area.

It does sound very elementary doesn't it? However, any important lesson we leaned by making mistakes in the first place, was a lesson well learned.

I found the day to day slog very hard going indeed. Some days were worse than others depending on the terrain we covered, but none of them were easy. It was at this stage of the game that Jack proved what a stalwart he was, right at the time of my greatest need. Many were the times I would have crashed out and ignored the evening meal, replacing it with sleep. If it hadn't been for Jack preparing something after "Stand Down", and then insisting I eat it, goodness knows how long I would have lasted.

As the days went by, I, and no doubt many others too, found yet another task which we had to perform on a daily basis and most likely a number of times during any twenty four hour period. It was not only highly inconvenient, but an absolute bloody nuisance to boot.

On one particular occasion, when we were having a most excruciating, ball aching day, I broke a golden rule. I did it just the once and swore that never again would I do it. I was tempted on many occasions to ignore my promise to myself but, as you will see, it turned out to be a false promise anyway.

I was blessed with a dose of the galloping, screaming trots which lasted for two days. Now, this not only left me very weak, but I was also non too popular with the rest of the Troop. While we were on the move, it became necessary to call frequent stops in order that I could unload what proved to be mainly wind and water.

No matter how long you have been without water, and no matter how pressing was your need to slake your thirst, when water was taken from a river, it had to be purified before drinking. This was achieved by either boiling it when you prepared the evening meal, or if it was to replenish drinking water, the procedure was to pop a couple of little blue tablets into the Water Bottle prior to filling it. When these had fully dissolved, the drill was to add one of the little white tablets provided with the Water Purification Kit. The white one was supposed to remove the strong taste of chlorine left behind by the blue ones. Everyone, including the Gaffer I suspect, found this to be a long drawn out process and although it took only something like five minutes from start to finish, this could seem to be a very long time when you have been without water for a few hours in such hot and humid conditions.

One particular day after a hard climb to the crown of a Bukit (Hill), we were all exhausted and due to the efforts it had taken to make the climb, we were all short of water. In some cases some men had drained their water bottles long before reaching the top of the climb. This proved, yet again, to be a valuable lesson regarding the conservation of water and emphasized the point that Water Bottles should be maintained at full charge whenever the opportunity presented itself. This was particularly true when we were operating amongst the high peaks which do occur in the Jungles of Malaya. I know its obvious, but its highly unlikely that you are going to find a river at the top of a Bukit and it would just not be convenient to pop down to the bottom and refill your Water Bottle.

Jack and I had managed to get to the top and still have a small amount of water left; however, we had long finished that off during the decent to the floor of the Jungle. The decent seemed to take hours and hours and we were not only very tired, we were also beginning to suffer from the lack of water. It was turning out to be one of those days that you don't only think about from time to time, but you remember them for a hell of a long time afterwards. When, at long long last, we reached the banks of a fast flowing river, all caution was thrown to the wind. No check to see if we had any company to greet us. Our need for water overcame all else and we plunged into the river and immediately drank our fill. When our thirst was at last slaked, we suddenly came to our senses and sheepishly carried out the sterilization of the water we carried away with us in our Water Bottles.

The next couple of days gave rise to our thinking about what we had done. There had been no ill effects from the untreated water we had drunk. As a result, we concluded that the strict order about these blue and white tablets was nothing short of bullshit. The orders had probably been dished out to cover somebody's arse in the event of a Troop becoming inoperative due to bad guts. Hereafter, Jack and I, and I suspect a good number of others, drank our fill at every opportunity without messing about with blue and white tablets. This seemed to have little or no effect on our bodies, or so it seemed at the time.

Our new found freedom was to be short lived. I woke about 0200hrs one morning, and it was therefore pitch black. I urgently needed to dig a hole and dump the contents of my stomach in it. This was not as easy as one would first think for it was hard enough in the daylight when the rest of the Troop knew what it was that you were up to. However, in the dark with only a Machete (an eighteen inch long sort of chopping knife) to make the hole with, it was indeed a difficult matter.

My efforts brought the whole Troop to life and had them reaching for their weapons and making ready as they increasingly became convinced that they were about to come under enemy fire. It was the last thing in their minds that it would be one of their own comrades who was making such a racket in the middle of the night. I had of course drunk bad water and this was the cause of my dose of the screaming what not's., and we all know that when you've got to go, you've got to go. The rest of the Troop were, shall I say cross with me and let me know in no uncertain terms that they did not approve of such slovenly behavior with the water supplies. Strangely enough, Jack had none of the ill effects. He therefore felt at liberty to criticize his Bivouac Partner along with the rest of the Troop.

Along with our initial issue of Ration Packs we also received a separate item which went under the name of a "J" Pack. This little item proved its value time and time again during Operations. It comprised of a waterproof canvass wallet which housed some six or seven identical aluminum tubes. These tubes contained various kinds of pills and tablets. Apart from the usual Pauladrine, which had to be taken daily to combat

69

the effects of the Mosquito, there were tablets to make you go to the toilet if the need be. There were tablets to stop you going when you lost control of your bowel movements completely. The trouble was that the tubes were not marked in any way and many of the tablets looked the same. It was therefore a total lottery for the uninitiated when they were making their selection to administer medication to themselves.

Being of the resourceful types that we were, it didn't take long to learn the usefulness of marking the caps in some way to indicate what was within, prior to doctoring oneself.

On a lighter note, it has to be said that there was a game played by some of the more unscrupulous amongst us. It became something of a pastime when there was some of that rare idle moment to fill, when the caps of someone's tubes were swapped around. This meant of course that the owners just didn't know what the tube contained and in some cases quite serious problems arose as a result of such actions. The action of course was to mark the bottoms of the tubes in some way to indicate just what the contents were for. Any smart arse could change the caps round at their leisure and it wouldn't matter two hoots. There was also, in the early stages of the Emergency, a small pack of Morphine complete with a needle fitted. This was clearly marked that it was not to be administered to anyone with a stomach wound. This item was withdrawn within a few months of my arrival due to a very small number of soldiers misusing it for purposes other than what it was intended for.

This kind of medication was to prove to be so badly needed on one of the Operations that I was involved with. One of my closest friends suffered unnecessarily while waiting for the arrival of the Troop Commander who was the only person authorized to carry the Morphine shots.

So came the start of our second week of this Training Operation. This was to prove to be a very traumatic week for both the uninitiated and the fully trained soldiers.

By this time our food supplies were becoming a little sparse and many of the men were reduced to Hard Tack Biscuits and little else. This was of course due to the inexperience of spinning out the rations which would only come as second nature with time.

The first task in this second week was for us to practice the construction and laying out of a DZ (Dropping Zone). This was an area designated for an Air Drop to be delivered by the RAF using Parachutes. We set about it with great enthusiasm relishing the prospect of our food supplies being bolstered. A number of trees had to be felled, by hand of course, and an area which would be large enough for the Planes Crew to be able to pick it out as they flew past about 800ft above tree top level. It follows that this area would have to be large enough and marked out in some way that would give the Crew a chance to identify it as they passed over in the twinkling of an eye. Once the clearing had been made we set about identifying that we were indeed ,"A" Squadron of the Malayan Scouts and we were ready to take delivery. A large cross was laid out at the centre of the clearing and this was made up of brightly coloured panels which were Orange in this particular case. This had been agreed previously between our HQ Troop and the RAF Dispatchers. There we were then, having lost a lot of sweat chopping down trees and undergrowth and laying out our identification panels. All that was left now was for the Pilot and his Dispatchers to tip out our goods in the right place and that was all there was to it.

Many things can go wrong when you are taking your weekly Air Drop and should the delivery go wrong and you fail to receive it for whatever reason there would be many sad and hungry soldiers who had no option but to wait until the RAF found time to call on you again, which I must say they did so at the very first opportunity

Any Terrorists, who happened to be in the vicinity where an Air Drop was being prepared for, must have had little doubt about what was due to happen. The sound of trees being felled was an alien sound in the Jungle and could be heard some distance away. They would now make a Bee Line for the area in the hope that they may pick up a stray Parachute bearing all manner of foodstuffs, before the soldiers had a chance to get it themselves. There was of course always the possibility that a Parachute may become snagged up in a tree and may escape the notice of the soldiers The Terrorist's, whose need for supplies were every bit as urgent as our own, would in this event, wait patiently for the soldiers to move away from the area and then up one of them would go to recover the Parachute together with all that it carried. If they failed to get it by climbing, they would then, and only then, chop down the tree. If this was the case, they had to be quick about it because if the soldiers heard the sound of chopping, they would suspect what had happened and immediately send three or four men back to the DZ to investigate.

You will note that I say "three or four men", well there was a very good reason for this. It was not unknown that when an Air Drop had taken place and the soldiers, having recovered all their packages and gone on their way, the Terrorists would leave a couple of their men behind, while the main body followed the soldiers until they were some way away from the DZ. The two Terrorist's left behind would then begin to chop away pretending that they were recovering something which had become snagged up in the trees. This would be heard by the soldiers who had little option but to send men back to investigate. If they sent six or eight Troopers back, this would decrease the fire power of the Troop and they would be a much easier target for the Terrorists who were following them and whose sole object, now that the Troop was reduced to half strength, was to attack it and hopefully relieve it of the precious Foodstuffs they had received less than an hour before.

As this was a Training Operation and there was little likelihood of any Terrorists being in the Operational Area, the location having been chosen for this very reason I suppose, we nevertheless placed guards out in exactly the same way as we would on future Operations. Half of us stood guard to ensure that uninvited guests didn't come and poke their noses, while the other half felled the trees as if they had been Lumberjacks since they were knee high to a Grasshopper. When all was ready, and contact had been established between us and the Aircraft using the 62set and Morse Code, we took up our positions about eight to ten feet apart right around the DZ but just inside the perimeter of the surrounding Jungle. I found the next order very hard to obey. We were to face outwards and remain alert for any sign of visitors who may have designs on sharing our supplies. Under no circumstances were we to look inwards or upwards, to try to catch a glimpse of the Aircraft, this, it was said would break our concentration on the task we were supposed to be carrying out, acting as a guard.

At 1100hrs sharp we heard the engines of an Aircraft quartering the roof of the Jungle. It was not far from where we were and the sound said it was getting closer every second. The Crew would be searching for our DZ and its Orange panel confirming that they were at the correct address.

The Plane was right on time and the Troop Sparks was now tapping away at his Morse Key like a man demented. The Plane made its first pass over us and then turned into a wide arc to check such things as wind speed and height above the tree canopy and all those other things that the RAF Bods know about when they are doing an Air Drop. Swede (the Sparks) told us later, that the Dispatcher had quite humorously told him not to go away as they would be back shortly. We could now hear the Plane heading once more for us. In my minds eye I could visualize the Aircraft flying in a wide arc and then heading for our location while it barely skimmed the tree tops of the tallest trees in its path.

Just at the crucial moment when the Parachutes would spew out of the open door in the side of the Plane, "The Ox" appeared right by my side, as if by magic.

"Never mind looking up there for your bloody grub. Keep your eyes peeled for visitors like you were............".

There was what could only be described as an almighty screaming, tearing explosion and as it took place it seemed that it was all frozen in suspended animation before our very eyes as we gazed in wonderment and horror at what was taking place around us. The Aircraft sort of half dived into, at the same time half slewed out of the hole in the Jungle at the bottom of which laid the brightly coloured orange DZ Panels which had been spread there in welcome to the Pilot and Crew.

It all happened so quickly that my mind found it just too fast for me to comprehend what was actually going on. The Aircraft had plunged to the floor of the Jungle cutting a swathe of some 50 to 60 yards long through the tangled undergrowth and trees before coming to a halt and then spontaneously bursting into flame as it came to rest and setting off an almighty explosion.

On reflection afterwards, it seemed that the Planes Port Wing had dipped just enough for the tip of it to have dropped slightly inside the hole in the trees. This must have caused a large slice of the wing to have been torn away from the fuselage and the hell of it all happened in an instant. It was inevitable the Crew would have been killed on impact and this fact alone left members of our Troop in a state of complete and utter shock.

It was very noticeable that the more experienced men came into their own immediately. Their long experience was such that it ensured that they would act in a cool organized manner when such a tragedy as this took place. They went about their business in a very calm methodical way and it was these men who were the most help to both the Troop Commander and his Troop NCOs as they struggled to take in the enormity of the tragedy.

I, as a new member to the Troop, had never even seen a dead person before in my life. Not even someone who had died peacefully in their own bed. It suddenly struck me that I was perhaps about to be faced with someone, or perhaps more than one person, who had met their end in a most horrifically violent way.

My mind was racing rapidly and I felt very conscious that explosions were coming from what remained of the Plane. "The Ox" was bawling out orders to all in general and chaos seemed to prevail in all directions around what was left of the DZ. I gathered that most of the explosions were due to the fact that the Plane had been carrying ammunition and explosives for some other drop they were destined to make after dealing with us.

"Keep your heads down" came a bawled order. "Nobody must attempt to go near where the crashed Plane is. Come on all of you, gather round me here".

"The Ox" was standing beside the Gaffer who he himself was busy trying to pinpoint just where we were on the Map. This would of course be in order that he could report by Radio to our Headquarters in Sungai Besi and it would be of crucial importance that the information he sent was absolutely accurate. I cannot recall any orders being issued for anyone to approach the burning Plane to see if anyone had survived or not but I expect that this would have been one of the first things that was dealt with.

The "Sparks", with the aid of a couple of other Troopers, were busy trying to re-rig the wireless aerial. It had obviously been torn down and perhaps broken in places when the tragedy happened and it was now of the utmost importance that Radio contact was established without delay. After what seemed to be an interminable time, Sparks made contact with HQ and was doing his level best to deal with the numerous questions which were apparently being flung at him. The Gaffer was still consulting the Map and didn't seem at all sure what the exact Map Reference was even though it had only been the previous evening that he had given a Map Reference to facilitate the Air Drop.

It suddenly struck me again that violence in the extreme had manifested itself no more than 50yds from where I was standing. I admit that every explosion, and there were many taking place, I constantly ducked purely by reflex action. I was scared, I really was scared but I was far from being alone in my plight. After what seemed to be a long time, but in truth must have been between five and ten minutes, I collected my wits about me. I was conscious of "The Ox" shouting at what must have been intended for all Troop Members, but seemed, in my mind anyway, to be directed at me in particular. I was after all, the nearest person to the Troop Sergeant right at the time.

"Spread out, keep away from the Aircraft as much as you can but keep your eyes peeled for any signs of life anywhere".

We carried out a search of the area immediately around the remains of the fuselage which was still burning but the explosions were becoming less and less. I, and I am sure all the other Troopers found it most difficult to ignore the spectre of two horrendously charred skeletons which hung incongruously in the twisted metal framework that had obviously been the dispatch door of the Aircraft. It was through this doorway that they would have been about to dispatch the packages when the end came. They must have died instantly right there where they stood at their duty station.

As if in a dream I mooched around. I was of course in shock and my brain was racing like mad. I tried to take in just what it was that had happened in what seemed to be just a few minutes ago but in fact was now some thirty or forty minutes since the crash had occurred.

I must have been forty or fifty yards or so from where the main fuselage continued to burn furiously giving off frequent bangs when Ammunition or Grenades exploded. I moved forward in my search for something, anything, I knew not what. Suddenly, I stumbled on something which, on closer inspection seemed to be the body of a Human Being. There at my feet was what appeared to be a Sergeant in the RAF dressed in full uniform. He seemed to be sleeping and his features were quite serene.

Vivid memories of my find have returned to me from time to time ever since that day. These showed a corpse with no hat and the hairs on his arms and other parts of his exposed body which were between the bottom of his Shorts and the tops of his Hose tops were ginger and curled up at the ends where they had been singed. Strangely, the hair on his head showed no signs of being exposed to fire. This appeared to be confirmed by the fact that the hair at his temples was turning Grey. An extremely vivid picture indeed.

I of course registered nothing of this consciously at the time but in order that they came back to me again and again in the future, meant that my subconscious must have stored them away at the time.

The Sergeant lay as if sleeping and I showed no sign of being taken aback as I stooped to check for any signs of life. He was certainly dead and gave off an odor which reminded me of Roasting Pork. A smell which would remain with me for many a year to come.

"Put that in a Poncho and move it further back into the trees away from the Aircraft". This came from the Gaffer who was still making furtive glances at his Map at the same time trying his best to appear as if everything was well under control.

Jack and I being nearest assumed that this instruction was directed at us and accordingly, we set about moving the dead man. This was all being done with a burning Aircraft not a cockstride away, with Ammunition exploding at infrequent intervals, which caused us to duck every time it happened. As a result I found it most difficult to devote my undivided attention to the task in hand. A Poncho was laid alongside the body our intention being that we should roll it onto the Poncho in preparation for it to be carried away from the scene. The man was rather large and it was proving to be something of a problem when we set about moving him from where he lay. I placed my hands between his Shorts and Hose tops and lifted in an effort to move the body. Both my hands came away full of flesh that had come away from the leg bones. I knew immediately that the fire, which still burned furiously, must have cooked the poor soul. He must have been flung clear of the Aircraft as it struck the ground.

In spite of being rooted to the spot in sheer terror, I vomited violently and unashamedly all over the remains that lay at my feet.

I was barely past my nineteenth birthday on that day when I lost much more than the contents of my stomach.

CHAPTER 7

The usual order of things in the Regiment was that after completing an Operation which, under normal circumstances, would last approximately four to six weeks, when the Squadron had returned to their Headquarters, after a couple of days just to round up any loose ends, they were then sent on two weeks leave. These leave periods were usually a very boozy, riotous affair, so much so that the Scouts quickly earned a bad name and were criticized by all and sundry. Such activities were not conducive to a well trained Military Machine and it was in 1951 when Colonel Calvert returned to the UK for Medical Treatment, that the Regiment was taken over by Lieutenant Colonel John "Tod" Sloane.

Colonel Sloane was a Regular Argyll and Sutherland Highlander who unfortunately, had no background in the ways of Special Forces. His brief had undoubtedly been that the Malayan Scouts were close to becoming an unruly mob. He brought in a very strong measure of discipline and the more widely recognized day to day order of Military Standards was applied.

His first action was to withdraw all Squadrons who were out in the Jungle. He then set about a period of solid training for every member of the Regiment. Daily Muster Parades were held. Other Ranks were instructed to salute all Officers and the practice of using first names only had to cease immediately. He introduced a Reveille call every morning and, although this met with very little success, he endeavored to hold a Church Parade and Service every Sunday.

Towards the end of 1951 and early 1952, we were reduced to a role of backing up Police Patrols and this work entailed just skirmishes in Secondary Jungle in conjunction with the Malay Police. I suppose the word was, show us that you can act in a disciplined, soldierly manner and then, and only then will you be allowed back on deep penetration Operations in Primary Jungle which you are all so very proud of.

Many of the original members of the Scouts did not take kindly to the new regime and the methods being adopted by Colonel Sloane. He found that he now had a constant battle on his hands trying to persuade those he considered to be worthwhile material, to remain with the Regiment. It seemed the main reason why the Officers wanted out was because of their fear that their promotion prospects within their Parent Arm would be irretrievably damaged by their association with such a "Cowboy Outfit" as we were rapidly becoming known as.

The case of the Other Ranks was somewhat different. Many of them had been recruited in Mad Mikes day simply because there were no others available. Some of these men did leave a great deal to be desired as I have mentioned elsewhere in this book. The methods adopted to recruit them was, at the very best a slipshod affair. The Officers sent out by Mad Mike on recruiting missions were hardly out of the top drawer themselves and they were only interested in filling the quota they had been given.

By 1953 Colonel Sloane had completed his statuary two years with the Regiment which by now had been re-designated the 22nd Special Air Service Regiment. The Command of the Regiment was handed over to Lieutenant Colonel Oliver Brooke as Colonel Sloane, rather thankfully, I think, returned to the UK.

It was at this time that the Rhodesian Squadron called it a day and returned to Southern Rhodesia as already mentioned, and now "D" Squadron was formed from what recruits could be found amongst the British Forces currently serving in the Far East. The Squadron Commanders job was given to the ever popular Johnny Cooper who had been one of Colonel Stirlings Originals. He had left the Army for a little while at one stage but found the ever present pull to be a bit too strong and came out to Malaya to give us all a hand. I first met him when he was a Captain and was performing an almost impossible job. He was the Motor Transport Officer at Sungai Besi and he rather looked on his arthritic For WOT6's as a personal challenge to himself. They always seemed to respond to a few carefully chosen words from Captain Cooper.

.

CHAPTER 8

On the completion of the Training Operation where we had experienced the tragic loss of the Aircraft which was delivering our weekly Air Drop, we were kept reasonably busy with additional Training which entailed short excursions into the Jungle to learn how to handle explosives and lay Grenade Ambushes. We also learned how to construct a Raft on which two or three men together with a certain amount of kit could be transported down river fairly quickly and with comparative ease.

This later exercise was not without its lighter side. Many a man and the kit he was caretaking, had to endure an early bath as it were. Not only were there complex skills in the construction of a Raft, but the navigational expertise that was employed by the temporary Pilot's was something that was only entrusted to a handful of Troopers who showed promise in this direction.

During this period we acquired many new skills in the art of living and working in the Jungle. Some Troopers managed to knock up quite handsome meals from the basic foodstuffs we were provided with in the twenty four hour ration packs. Others, being a mite more adventurous, made use of items readily available growing wild in the Jungle. I must admit, I was not one of these. Not only because some of the stuff they ate looked a bit iffy to me and it did absolutely nothing for me when I smelt it being cooked.

One of the most useful things that Jack and I gleaned from this particular part of our Training was the skills that came to hand when building an overnight Basha. We found that the speed at which we could construct the shelter was greatly improved. We knew what bits to look for and exactly which the best way to put them together was. The result

81

was that we could have our Basha up and the grub on the go ahead of anyone else in our Troop. After a few weeks had passed, we new boys as we had become known were considered to be fully trained. At least we were thought to be good enough to become part of the Operational Force and play a full active part in Jungle Operations.

The Regimental routine was such that apart from HQ Squadron, there would under normal conditions, be only one Operational Squadron that was not actually engaged in some form of active Operation or other. This period when a Squadron was clear of any sort of commitment was regarded to be a time for rest and recuperation. It would generally last for about three weeks.

Almost without exception the Troopers would take off on leave in Singapore or Penang where the usual attractions of Oriental Nightlife would abound. This was just the thing to serve up to the troops after they had spent a period in the Jungle searching for and chasing those so elusive little men who sported a Red Star on their headdress, and that refers to those who managed to still sport a hat of any kind.

It was standard practice that the whole Troop, with the exception of the Gaffer, would pool their cash and in our case, "The Ox" became Paymaster. He would dole out so much to each man each day and that was it. No subs were allowed and he was stricter than any Bank Manager. Spend it all on one of the Dance girls (known as Taxi Dancers) at the local Jogget (Dance Hall) and no amount of pleading would shorten your wait until divi up the next day. This system worked very well indeed as it ensured that nobody became completely skint before the leave period was at an end.

All members of No2 Troop had decided, after much argument, that we would sample the delights of Singapore for this, our first spot of leave since our arrival in the Country. Accordingly we all traveled by Rail and on arrival we descended on the Union Jack Club. Ever eager to try something new, we set about sampling the famous Tiger Beer which we had heard so much about. Now I'm not saying it wasn't good stuff, it was, but when one got suitably stoked up on it, it tended to encourage many a stout man to get into trouble with the Military Police.

A popular pastime with the men was to compete in Trishaw races. These machines were a sort of three wheeled contraption with room to take two passengers at the front and the Operator, sat at the rear and pedaled along to the accompaniment of "faster Johnnie, faster". If the resulting effort allowed the Trishaw to be overtaken by one coming from behind, the Operator would be encouraged from his seat in the saddle, removed to the passenger position and one of the soldiers would take his place at the pedals.

The Trishaw was not necessarily owned by the Operator. He would in all likelihood be renting it from some rich Chinese who owned a number of them. Consequently if the machine were to suffer any damage, then the hirer was expected to pay for all repairs. Accidents did happen and damage was sustained, but I am proud to put on record that the soldiers responsible would press cash on the Operator to make sure that he was not out of pocket.

The races usually took the form of moving from one Bar to another. Players engaged a Trishaw and had to pay the Operator in advance. The saying "You don't catch old birds with Chaff" was as operative in Singapore in the 1950s as it was anywhere else in the world. Once the deal had been done and money changed hands, the Chinese guy would vacate the engine room and settle himself in the passenger compartment.

The soldier now took up position in the engine room. On the word go, the competing contraptions would be pedaled like hell at breakneck speed scattering all before them. The last one to arrive at the specified Bar would of course stand the cost of a round of beers for each of the competitors. This type of activity was very tiring due to overbearing heat and humidity and of course, as the night wore on, the intake of Tiger took its toll which resulted in the trips becoming of shorter and shorter duration

In the 1950s there were two streets in Singapore which proved to be a great pull to all servicemen whether they be Air Force Blue, Navy Blue or of course Khaki. These were Bugis Street and Lavender Street. Here you could buy almost anything you cared to mention. The street vendors offered goods and chattels covering a very wide range. You could have your haircut and a shave, a beer or breakfast, a full meal in most dishes of the World; you were not restricted to Chinese food. There were Jugglers, Singers, Acrobats, Escapologists and a host of other forms of entertainment such as the services of the oldest profession in the World. The place was a real magnet to the servicemen who had never seen the likes of it before. The local occupants of the two streets all had one skill in common which was over and above that of selling you anything. It was that they could guarantee that any serviceman who entered the area would leave without a single Cent in their pocket. Alas this was no idle boast, for he who did not spend all he had on goods and/or services, had his pocket picked of what remained by one of the many street urchins. After a couple of days, we managed to ignore the delights of these infamous streets and concentrated our efforts on consuming copious amounts of Tiger Beer and plaguing the lives out of the Trishaw Pilots until long into the night.

As we boarded the train, the one with the dartboard type toilets, which would carry us Northwards back to Kuala Lumpur, the whole Troop agreed that we had had our fill of Singapore. When we next were released on the local population we would make an attack on Penang Island. So much had been said about the service and entertainments on offer there. The general consensus was that the time was just about ripe for us to give it a whirl. A general discussion was held about what sort of Star Rating out of a total of ten we should award it, depending of course, which type of service we were assessing at the time.

Back in Sungai Besi we were soon into our stride and consequently we were very busy preparing for our next Operation. This was scheduled to be a quick affair as it was only just down the road at Seremban which was about twenty five miles south of Kuala Lumpur. It had been reported that some naughty Bandit chappies had been upsetting the Kampong dwellers and robbing them of what meager amounts of foodstuffs they had managed to scrape together for themselves. Our Squadron's aim was to round them up with the minimum of fuss and deliver them into the care of the Sikh Guards at Pudu Jail in Kuala Lumpur. The Warders there, renowned for meaning what they said to their Prisoners, would do their utmost to instill into them, "Thou shall not be a Bugger" and "Thou shall not steal", or something very much akin to that.

Life in Pudu Jail was not a soft option, nor was it supposed to be. Many of the Staff there were Sikh's and they had very good memories. Consequently most of them had old scores to be settled with the Chinese Malay community for the way they were treated by them when the Japanese were ruling the roost. They were enthusiastic about their jobs and appreciated the power that went with them. Their attention to detail was such that many of the Bandits who passed through their hands decided on a change of mind about believing in Communism, or any other "isms" come to that.

As time went by there became more and more Captured or Surrendered Enemy Personnel. (SEPs) After spending time in Pudu Jail they would express the wish that they would very much like to help the Malay Police and the Security Forces in anyway that they could. They meant of course that they had had enough and would now be prepared to disclose where Arms and Food dumps were located. All such information was worth its weight in gold, not only to the Security Forces and Police also to the Surrendered Enemy Personnel who knew full well that a bounty would be paid to them, in cash should their information be of value. Some of these people did very nicely thank you out of this scheme. From a soldiers point of view, I and many many others I might add, despised these creatures that were willing to sell their comrades down the river for just a few dollars. Still it was the Government who created the Band Wagon and these so called Communists jumped on it when the opportunity presented itself.

The Seremban affair was dealt with in no time at all. It proved to be no more than a little Local Politics being played. (Unfortunately Town Councilors the World over are the same I am afraid. In it for what they can get out of it). The trouble was not down to the Terrorists but was due to a few local bad lads who saw the opportunity to make a few bob and obviously thought "Well have some of that".

We dodged about and brushed up on our fitness and other skills while waiting for our next assignment. Fortunately it was not long in coming. We were to be engaged in one of the longest Operations we had been on since our arrival at the Regiment. Not only was it to be the duration of it that beat us down to a frazzle, but the very nature of it was to prove to be a most uncomfortable and depressing experience.

We were to operate in the Batu Luat Swamp on the Eastern side of the Peninsula. A Terrorist leader known as Ah Hoi was known to be hiding in the Swamp at this time with a reasonably large number of Terrorists. This same character also took to the Teluk Anson Swamp along the Tengi River North West of Kuala Lumpur at a later date in 1958. But this time he was again pursued by "D" Squadron of the Regiment. It seems that they drew a blank in just the same way as we were to suffer during our extended efforts in Batu Luat. Ah Hoi proved to be one of the more elusive Communist characters of the Malayan Emergency and proved himself to be an accomplished leader when it came to Swamp Warfare.

Our lack of success at Batu Luat was widely considered to be because the Operation was badly planned and grossly undermanned. We had no air support in any way shape or form. We did not receive our weekly issue of food and other supplies by Air Drop, we simply came out of the Swamp and either collected from a truck or alternatively, we would come out adjacent to where the Squadron HQ was located in a row of disused shops on the side of a row of what had previously been a Malay Village. Consequently, Ah Hoi and his merry men (and women) knew of our every move and simply kept out of our way.

The locals had abandoned their Village which they had built alongside the Swamp some considerable time back. They had to move under the ruling by General Sir Gerald Templar that all unprotected Kampongs were to be brought under the protection of the Home Guard and would be located in places which would make it difficult for the Terrorists to interfere with them. The interference referred to had become quite violent at times and was exclusively connected to the supply of food to the Terrorists by the Kampong dwellers.

The band which we were hunting was believed to be about 50 strong and was made up of both men and women. They lived in the Swamp but in the main they would be deep in. This would protect them from surprise attacks. Like all other Terrorists in Malaya, they moved location quite frequently in the hope that they would avoid detection by Ground Troops. Had even the smallest amount of Air support been available to us, we would have been onto them like a shot as there are not many places you can hide 50 or so personnel in a Swamp, well not from the Air anyway.

By this time in 1953, the Terrorists main function seemed to be to just stay alive and avoid capture. They preyed on the local Kampong Dwellers for food and would infiltrate just sufficient personnel, men and women, to destabilize the locals and frighten them into giving up what foodstuffs they were able to muster. Refusal by the locals to cooperate often resulted in some atrocious and barbarous attacks on the women in the Compound and more often than not the death of Males who were considered to be anti the Communist cause.

General Templars orders to relocate those who lived far from any main community seemed to work to some extent but after a short period of time, it seemed that the fear the Terrorists spread in the Kampong Dwellers, worked in the favour of the Terrorists.

One of the most hideous things which it was my unfortunate duty to behold was when they ripped open the belly of a young woman who was at lest six months pregnant. They nailed her corpse to a long table, with her entrails hanging from her, they paraded the whole ghastly thing around the Kampongs which lie adjacent to the one where the poor unfortunate woman herself had lived.

The Home Guard, who were recruited to combat such atrocities were themselves singled out for attention by the Terrorists and soon after their formation they became less and less effective and this was entirely due to the fear that the Terrorists were able to instill. The regular Malay Police Forces just couldn't spare the manpower to guard the Kampong Dwellers; consequently it was what remained of the Home Guard who had to continue to bear the brunt of things.

The Malay Police were at the time, fairly heavily criticized by the Regular Forces who had been drafted in from overseas countries in an effort to contain the uprising of Communism within the country. This criticism was quite unnecessary and totally misplaced I think. With the limited resources at their disposal they played their part in the full sense of the word including Light Jungle Patrols under the command of their own Officers. There were reports of some quite heroic feats performed by them. Unfortunately in those days when it was all "Hey Lads Hey" no one paid much attention to the performance of anyone other than the more well known fighting men who came from the more popular Regiments.

The problem became increasingly urgent for the Local Population. The Government would punish Villagers by sending them to Prison if they supported the Terrorists with food, while the Terrorists would punish them if they did not provide them with the food.

"A" Squadron were meanwhile still trying to cope with the Batu Luat Swamp in their search for the ever elusive Ah Hoi and his band of vagabonds.

Life was pretty miserable for the soldiers. Up to their thighs in green slimy water most of the day and not much of a dry spot on which to Bivouac for the night. It was also one hell of a job to get a "Tommy Cooker" (Emergency one man Field Cooker) going in order to brew a mug of tea at night when all the Stand To and Guard duties had been attended to. As was usual, Leeches were the biggest bug bear, however, here in the Swamp they seemed to much more prolific than they were in the Forests and Jungle. In addition to this, the place seemed to be crawling with all manner of species of Snake. Some of these seemed to have little or no fear of Human Beings as they would go for you at the least provocation. It was also rumored throughout the Squadron that Crocodiles had been seen but fortunately it was not to be my lot to have to deal with this as I never actually did see a Croc'.

The Terrorists left few traces of where they had been and always seemed to have moved away from the area well in advance of our arrival. Even when we received good firm information from our HQ in Sungai

Besi, it seemed that the message could just as well have been sent to the enemy at the same time as they were long gone when we got there.

After a further few more week's morale was at an all time low. Operating in this unspeakable terrain week after week and no contact with the enemy, started to allow a feeling of dismal failure to creep in. It was most unfortunate but it was at this time that we lost our first Trooper to the enemy.

The Troop Commander had just called a halt in order that we could all take a breather for ten minutes or so. We were right at that moment on a fairly raised bit of ground which came above the water level and it seemed like a choice place for us to have a break. There were also quite a number of real trees growing there in addition to the usual Mangrove Swamp Bush. We took up our usual positions as was the drill whenever a halt was called. The men would move off the track and then they would lay alternately either side of the track as it was not advisable to sit all together in a tightly knit bunch. If you sat in a group, the whole Troop, in theory anyway, could be wiped out by just one Hand Grenade being lobbed in by some nasty little Terrorist prior to him making a very hasty departure. As I have mentioned previously, the ban on smoking had now been lifted while we were on this Swamp Operation. One of our Troopers was to take advantage of this easing of the regulations and prepared to indulge himself on a State Express cigarette. Finding that his matches had become wet and were therefore useless, he stood up and made to move across to the opposite side of the track to get a light from his buddy who was already puffing away. He made the trip across to get his light but when he stood up to return to his allotted position, a single shot rang out and he fell where he stood having been shot clean in the head. His killer must have been watching us from the safety of the trees and seeing his opportunity, killed our man with a single shot. The unfortunate Trooper must have died instantly.

There were very strict rules about moving around when a halt was called and it seemed that the dead man had either completely forgotten about them or perhaps he was so pissed off with what he was engaged in, that he simply threw caution to the wind. This tragedy was remembered throughout the Regiment as a standard lesson in Jungle Craft. Needless to say, our Troop made a very comprehensive search for the Terrorist but there was no sign of him, or her to be found. Whoever had done the deed either found refuge up in the trees or even left the area in one hell of a hurry.

Things were not all bad for "A" Squadron during this awful Operation. No3 Troop had the good fortune to bag five Terrorists all at one single contact. Strangely, they had been down in the dumps, as we were at the lack of contacts with the enemy, then suddenly, their chance to shine came at last. The Troop carted their kills back to the row of old shops where they stacked them on the Veranda laid out head to foot for all to see.

Members of my Troop, although a bit miffed, merely said "Lucky Bastards" and then quickly pointed out to the men of No3 Troop that two of their kills were women and the other three were fairly old men who couldn't run fast enough to get away. Nevertheless, we all joined in the celebrations that took place that night.

A few days later "A" Squadron was ordered to return to Sungai Besi. Our Troop, apart from our tragic loss, had had not a single contact with the Terrorists throughout the whole of our period of involvement. This of course gave rise to certain ribald comments from the rest of the Squadron. The most popular seemed to be, "when are you lot going to get used to Jungle Warfare"? "When are you lot going to start contributing to the Squadrons record of kills"? I think that which caused us the most pain was when the Governor said he was considering sending out HQ Troop in our place next time and leave us to dish out rations and mail etc., Still it was all given, and accepted, in the manner in which it was meant.

Although it all tended to rankle a bit, No2 Troop pretended to ignore it on the whole and we all hoped that we would have the opportunity shortly to even up the scores just a little anyway.

CHAPTER 9

It was leave time again and the Troop decided that we would all go to Penang. This would be our first visit to the Island and it would be the start of a very serious problem later in the year for me personally, but of course I was not to know that at the time. It was also a very well kept secret that the next Operation we would undertake, would be on Penang itself, but we were not aware of that at the time of course. However, it was leave time now and we all went off together. As was our normal practice we pooled our resources and handed it to "The Ox" for safe keeping.

We had all been booked in to the Sandicroft Leave Centre for our two weeks stay. The Centre was about fifteen miles north of Georgetown which formed the main built up area of the Island and it was in Georgetown that all the attractions that may be of interest to the soldiers existed in profusion.

Sandicroft itself was a very comfortable establishment indeed with soft beds and good food in abundance. Of course there was a lively Bar which opened at 1100hrs and remained in action until late at night. The adjoining beach had sand which was of a similar quality to Self Raising Flour, which used to be advertised as being examined grain by grain and graded by funny little men in Bowler Hats (on TV of course). It was the ideal spot for snoozing after feeding and boozing sessions.

We took full advantage of all the facilities but of course after two or three days our thoughts began to turn towards Georgetown and all that it was supposed to offer a young fit soldier who was on leave. This of course seemed to be a much more pressing matter once the Sun had gone down and the bright twinkling Neon Lights fired up the imagination and created thoughts about just might be hiding behind them.

It quickly became apparent that the local Almond Eyed Ladies, who were rarely seen during daylight hours, were out in force once nightfall was upon the streets and Bars of Georgetown. They had, apparently, had a very good tutor, as from a soldier's point of view anyway, they seemed to know exactly what to put on their menu's for us soldiers seeking Rest and Recuperation.

The odd hundred or so, I never did count them, of these magnetic creatures acted as Loose Cannons as it were and moved freely from one Coffee Shop cum Bar to another in what appeared to be a strictly controlled rotation system. In this way it was ensured that the whole district was covered and no potential customer would inadvertently slip through the net. Business was indeed, brisk. All these ladies seemed to be self employed as there appeared to be no fixed charge for their services. They charged each customer just what they thought the market would stand at any particular juncture. Of course there was a special rate for drunks and the like and these shrewd ladies seemed to be fully capable of judging the extent of the inebriation of any potential client. They were without a doubt, under the protection of some enterprising Male person (or Triad Gang), who of course demanded a percentage of the ladies takings in return for the protection they offered whether it was called upon or not.

By far and away the "City Lights" and the "Piccadilly" employed the majority of the Ladies of the Night, if employed is the correct term. These establishments operated under the guise of being Dance Halls and although dancing did take place on these premises the Triad Gangs who controlled them were far more interested in selling Booze and Sex.

Both places operated in the same way. A Band comprising three embers, a Drummer, a Saxophone player come Trumpet player and a Pianist come Accordion player attempted to keep the Dance Halls and their clientele jumping in a sort of local dance which went under the name of The Jogget. Now none of these so called musicians were ever likely to be snatched up by Billy Cotton or the James Last outfit but a combination of any three of the five instruments mentioned could dish out the decibels non-stop from around 2130hrs until first light the next day.

When on Jungle Operations, first light was greeted with the soldiers on "Stand To". Here in Penang when we were on leave, things were slightly different. Those soldiers who had managed to Jogget this far were now propositioned by the "Taxi Dancers". Negotiations took place with the lady of your choice and the bargain was struck. Needless to say the soldiers were always the losers for as the night had progressed and the intake of Beer had reached a certain level, the lady in question had become more alluringly beautiful and invariably desirable to the point where he would declare his never ending love and devotion and would frequently promise to take the little lady away from all this.

Perhaps the word "Jogget" mentioned above would bear a little explanation. Use your imagination and picture a large expanse of Dance Floor with fifty to sixty ladies, of varying grades of course, all lined up on one side of the floor. They sat on chairs in a most provocative manner in order that the split in their Cheong Sam (Chinese type Dress) displayed a large expanse of thigh. This of course was designed to heighten the desire of the customers who lined up (no chairs) on the opposite side of the floor. The idea was that the customer crossed the floor and proffered a Dance Ticket to the lady of his choice. The couple then swayed and moved roughly in time with the output of the Band all the time circling ones partner but having no physical contact between them whatsoever. This performance was known locally as the Jogget and the proceedings lasted anything from one minute to something like three minutes. This period was of course dependant on what type of support was being given to the Band. In general as the night wore on, the length of each Jogget depended to a great extent on the ability of the customers to maintain their footing despite the number of bottles of Tiger Beer they had managed to consume.

The Dance Tickets were available the entrance to the Dance Hall. These were sold at ten cents for a single ticket however; they were only sold in blocks of twenty five at a time. The ladies traded their tickets in to the Management at the end of the night's business, hence the more tickets they collected, the more cash they earned. It must be added here that a great number of these ladies were experts at scrounging quite a number of tickets and there were many a customer who found that his supply had disappeared after just a single encounter on the Dance Floor.

Another ploy used by the Management was that the ladies would beg the customers to buy them a drink. They could put on quite a creditable performance to convince the unfortunate customer that they were in mortal danger of drawing their last breath if they did not receive a glass of liquid within the next minute or so. The drink was ordered and supplied in one of the smallest glasses you have ever seen. Before the dying Taxi Dancer was allowed to even hold the drink, the waiter demanded payment of $2.50 which he pocketed with great alacrity and disappeared into the heaving sweating throng who were apparently enjoying being robbed on a regular basis.

When closing time arrived, this being decided according to the flow of Dollars being received, those ladies wishing to increase their nightly takings even further, and I think this would be most of them, would sort out the more sober of the customers and negotiate a price for Roof and Bed for what remained of the night. Unused Dance Tickets were in no way acceptable as payment for such facilities, however, ready cash was highly prized. In this way their masters would be unaware of what the lady had charged for her services and would therefore be in a relatively weaker position when the matter of commission (protection) was discussed.

Military Police, known as Red Caps, became particularly active at closing time and were hell bent on spoiling the happy and probably drunk soldiers wishes to seal the bargain he had struck earlier in the Dance Hall. They would wait some fifteen minutes after the Dance Hall had closed its doors and then carry out a sweep of the Kampongs where the ladies lived. In this way they stood a fair chance of catching anyone engaged on night maneuvers. Perhaps those who were about to go into action would be scared off and put to flight with nothing but a pair of socks. The sight of two or three hairy Troopers in full flight, some booted and suited with others making good their escape clutching a pair of trousers which apparently, there had been little time to put on, it was indeed a sight to behold.

It was during this particular trip to Penang that something occurred which was to cause me much grief before many more months were passed and what at first appeared to be a heaven sent opportunity proved to be one of my most glaring sins.

A Dance was arranged to take place at the Sandicroft Leave Centre and the Management decided it might not be a bad idea if they were to invite along some of the British Nurses and whatever other European females they could scout out. After all it was the early 1950s and the British Army was sufficiently snobbish to believe that their soldiers would prefer to mix with their own kind as opposed to the Almond Eyed sorts of Chinese or Malay origins. If only they had known of the full extent of the delights of Georgetown, perhaps things might have been different. It is true nevertheless, that there are none so wise as those who profess to know it all.

Great excitement abounded at the prospect of being able to hold ones dance partner close to you, as was the practice back in the UK, and what a super change it would be from the Jogget where we were forbidden to touch any part of your dance partner, while actually pretending to dance I hastily add.

It was at this dance that I made the acquaintance of a really charming girl who was of Irish origin. She worked as a Nursemaid for a German family who lived in a rather posh house about two miles along the Coast Road, north of Sandicroft Leave Centre. I must confess, I was very impressed by her and immediately made up my mind that she was far and away the best looking woman amongst those who were present. Accordingly I treated her with the utmost respect and put on a display of charm which I was more than capable of doing. Even when we went for a stroll in the moonlight under the long string of Palm Trees, I made no untoward advances with the exception of one or two fleeting kisses which I placed tenderly on her check. She appeared to enjoy this every bit as much as I did. It was not that I didn't have the urge to make a move and take things further and I sensed that she was fighting her own battle

95

in this respect. It seemed that both of us were trying hard to control our feelings, which was not an easy thing to do given the highly provocative circumstances presented by the whisper of the sea on the sands and the gentle breeze stirring the Palms under a huge Moon which lit up the scene with a near daylight effect.

We talked about a lot of things, such things as where I lived in England and what a fine job she considered we soldiers were doing in Malaya and exactly what was my job with the Malayan Scouts? And many other things besides. I was only too pleased to talk of such things as it never crossed my mind that I was doing anything wrong and in fact, in my estimation of her went up even more as I thought it was nice of her to think so much about her fellow countrymen and just what they were doing here in the Far East which is such a long way from home.

We seemed to get on very well indeed, so much so that she invited me to visit her at the place where she worked with the children either during my present leave or perhaps at some future date when I again came to Penang. She assured me that her employers would make me most welcome.

When it was just a few minutes before midnight a car arrived to pick her up and in true Cinderella fashion, she was whisked away leaving me not just a little sad at the conclusion of the whole evening.

My memories of her lasted at least a full couple of days afterwards but these were soon ousted by the offerings of the "City Lights" and the "Piccadilly" coupled with the Bars of Georgetown which seemed to act as magnets to a soldier on leave from Jungle Operations. Eventually the leave period came to an end and it was back to business on the Mainland.

"A" Squadron were now assembled at Sungai Besi. Everyone seemed to be revived and refreshed as a result of our recent leave period. Without fail, we were all straining at the leash to be off into the Jungle and seek out some of these bloody Bandits. After all, we had something to prove to the rest of the Regiment after the Batu Luat escapade.

CHAPTER 10

It was about this time that the Malayan Scouts ceased to exist and the Regiment took the title of 22nd Special Air Service Regiment. The new title meant little to those of us who were serving the statuary two year stint. It made no difference to the pay we received and knowing little about the activities of the famous Special Air Service in the past, the rebirth of the 22nd Special Air Service Regiment took place without any fuss or bother. Things did not alter on a day to day basis and we just carried on as we had done previously.

It was widely thought throughout the Regiment that due to the lack of success in the various recruiting campaigns, it had been decided that as opposed to the Regiment closing down due to the lack of manpower and therefore its viability as a fighting force, the change of title might just have the effect required and inspire a much needed influx of soldiers of the right caliber to the Regiment. I suppose it did have some effect but the fact remained that forays as far a field as Korea was undertaken and we did indeed manage to glean a few men from the Gloucester Regiment who were apparently fed up with life in Korea and saw the offer to revert to the Jungles of Malaya as a welcome change to their existence.

There was an arrangement which had been in force long before we became known as the 22nd Special Air Service Regiment. All new members to the Regiment were obliged to sign the agreement on joining. The prime content was that all new members must have at least two years of their current Military commitment still to run when they arrived in Malaya. On completion of their two year stint they were free to return to their own Parent Unit from whence they came, or as an alternative, they were given a choice. They were free to apply to serve with any other British Army Unit and should they be accepted, then that is where they went.

They were of course at liberty to sign up for a further two year stint but the takers of this option were few and far between. Recruits, either new ones or re-signings were hard to come by, as what was on offer didn't amount to much at all. The daily work was extremely hard going and there was no additional pay to be had unless, and until a Parachute Course had been successfully completed. This became one of the biggest gripes we had. It was not so much thee pay as the fact that most of us had been attracted in the first place because of the promise that we would get a Para' Course reasonably quickly. Nothing much was being done in this direction in early 1952 as it meant that we would have to travel down to the Changi Parachute Training School in Singapore in order to qualify. With the number of bodies being barely sufficient to cover the Regiments Operational Requirements, there was little wonder that the men could be spared to undertake this training which, at that particular time, was not considered to be part of the Regiments role.

Yet another thing which deterred soldiers from joining, or re-joining, was this business of all Other Ranks, without exception, having to revert to the rank of Trooper which was a bit of a sickener. In some cases they held the rank of Sergeant with much service to their credit. It is true that all Commissioned Officers were required to serve as Troopers during their first few weeks with the Regiment. However, they had the comparative life of comfort as they were accommodated in the Officers Mess and were fed to a much higher standard than was the lot of the Other Ranks. After a suitable period of time, usually lasting anything from a fortnight to a month or five weeks, they assumed their original rank and received the pay associated with that rank for the remainder of their tour with the Regiment. A further perk they benefited from was that they went back to their Parent Arm with the rank they held when they left. This was not the case with the Other Ranks. We lost our rank and the pay that went with it when we joined the Regiment. We did not assume that rank when we returned to our Parent Arm. This seemed to be a kick in the guts of many of us and when we became familiar with the way the Officers were treated in comparison to us, well what would you expect? Unrest prevailed and the Rank and File earned the name of being an unruly rabble that drank heavily and paid scant attention to Military Regulations.

The Powers that be had only themselves to blame for this state of affairs as none of these anomalies were revealed until after you had signed up and in most cases had made the journey to Malaya to take up the post. This was most certainly true of those recruited in the UK but whether this was the case for those recruited in Korea, Australia and Rhodesia is not clear by a long chalk. Experience tempts me to believe there was little difference in the way that these recruits were treated. The contingent recruited from Rhodesia stayed barely two years in Malaya before returning to their own country. Their main gripe was that they had been promised a Parachute Course and it had just not materialized. With regards those who were recruited in Korea, amongst them was a soldier who had received a very prominent award for bravery while under enemy fire. He didn't stay with us very long as he found the prospect of launching himself into space through the open door of a Valletta Aircraft much more daunting than facing hundreds of North Korean Soldiers in the dead of night.

The Rhodesian Soldiers had arrived in Malaya all at the same time and consequently were formed into their own Squadron ("C" Squadron). It was widely thought that they were receiving Special Forces Pay and Allowances which made the British Soldiers pay seem like that of the poor relations. They had the advantage of being allowed to retain any rank they had on joining and they were commanded by their own Officers from their own country. They proved themselves to be outstanding soldiers and many acts of bravery, which was legend throughout our Regiment, but was unfortunately very rarely recognized by the British Government. The Rhodies, as they were known, kept themselves to themselves and were not exactly the flavour of the month with the rest of the Regiment.

It was widely believed that the two year rule was not without its benefits.

Back in 1952, National Service was still in force and this effectively excluded National Servicemen from the Regiment. Consequently this meant that everyone was a Regular Soldier who was serving as a career man and had something to prove. The reasons why these men had volunteered for such a small and virtually unknown outfit were many and varied. Some were in search of adventure while others were running away from something or perhaps someone. Life in the SAS in Malaya was the ideal place to disappear from view and perhaps even get lost altogether.

When their two year point was reached, many of the soldiers opted to return to the UK for a spot of leave. They promised that such leave would be regarded as inter-tour leave and after a couple of months they would be back to start another tour of duty. Alas there were many who did not return, having said they would in order to get back to the UK as opposed to being posted to another unit in the FARELF and made to serve out a further full year before returning home. This attitude only went to prove that the real commitment of some of the members of the Regiment was not all that it was cracked up to be. As a result of such attitudes, the rules were altered just as soon as it was discovered what was going on.

If it was the genuine intention of the soldier to return for a further tour, he was obliged to commit his promise to paper before leaving for his spell in the UK. He then had no option but to return to Malaya. Should he decide that enough was enough on completion of his two year stint, he would then be required to serve for a further one year in the FARELF thus making a three year tour (known as a Python) in all. This extra year was spent with the Unit of his choice just as his initial contract had stated.

Perhaps the thing which surprised us all more than anything else was the standards of recruit selection and the subsequent training given to all new members to the Regiment. It became painfully apparent that selection standards were practically non existent and any old Tom, Dick or Harry just had to sign on the dotted line and they were in. This was hardly conducive with the standards set by the majority of existing members whose lives may depend on the actions carried out by another Troop member when the Fertilizer hit the Fan, so to speak. Consequently there were a number of men who became members who should have been weeded out at an early stage and not been entertained for entry to such a close knit group of men.

Morale in the regiment took many severe blows and it became obvious that even the most experienced Jungle Fighters were leaving the Regiment when they came to the end of their contract. Numbers fell dramatically and after the withdrawal of the Rhodesians, the Regiment seemed doomed to being disbanded. A number of incentives were offered to the more seasoned men who wanted to leave but it seemed it was too little too late for nothing seemed to stop the rot.

In spite of the low morale, demands on the Rank and File seemed to carry on unabated. The rewards received by these very brave men were meager indeed. All were expected to maintain peak fitness and be fully proficient in all field crafts in addition to being capable of handling a wide selection of arms and other assorted weaponry. It is true that these were not superman requirements from the physical point of view but they were nevertheless of a very high standard. The conditions that these soldiers were expected to operate under was very demanding indeed and should have been recognized by the Military Authorities, but there you go, isn't it always difficult to recognize any hazardous situation when you sit in a nice cozy office in Whitehall between the hours of 0900hrs and 1600hrs (Approximately)?

Jungle Craft was something that could be taught during training but although there was a Jungle Training School in the State of Johore in the south of Malaya, not many members of the Regiment ever saw it. The large majority of us were sent out on so called Training Operations as I have described elsewhere in the book. We did cope, but only just. We fended for ourselves but it is doubtful if we could have managed if we had run into a sizeable Terrorist Gang. Well, not in the initial stages anyway.

CHAPTER 11

It was towards the end of 1952 when "A" Squadron were chosen to carry out an Operation on Penang Island itself. It was suspected that there were people from the Terrorist Organization who were indulging in Rest and Recuperation just as we the British soldiers did. They were apparently becoming a nuisance to many of the local population particularly the coastal dwellers that as Fishermen, had plenty of good food which the Terrorists were taking advantage f. There was a problem however, on how to get full Squadron of SAS men in amongst them without them suspecting anything.

It was fairly obvious that all entries and exits to and from the Island could be monitored by observing what was going on at the Ferry Jetty in Georgetown. It was almost certain that they kept a watching brief on all comings and goings. Fifty or so men with Red Berets and the Winged Dagger proudly displayed on them would certainly have sounded some sort of a warning note to them and they would be off, back to the Mainland before you could say 22nd Special Air Service.

The brains department back at Sungai Besi must have thought long and hard to come up with what they considered to be a foolproof solution to the dilemma. On reflection, we all thought that a pack of Brownies would not have been fooled by the plan, but there we are, there are none so wise as them that know it all.

It so came about that just at that time a Battalion of the Manchester Regiment had arrived in Singapore from the UK. They were obviously not familiar with the ways of the Jungle and therefore presented little or no threat to any Terrorists who were experts in this type of warfare. The plan was that the whole of "A" Squadron would be sent to Penang under the guise of being members of the Manchester Regiment. We were to be decked out in Blue Berets suitably badged with the Manchester Regimental cap badge. Once on the ground we could spread across the area where the Terrorists were known to be and Bingo, we would wipe them out of existence in just a few days. Fiendishly good plan, what? That would fool them.

Not so I'm afraid.

We put on our fancy dress at the Sungai Besi Headquarters. The Bandits wouldn't know what we were up to, would they?

We were transported to the Station at Kuala Lumpur in the SAS Ford WOT6's which had the winged dagger emblazoned on both their front and back. Perhaps the Terrorist lookouts would believe that we had been kind hearted and lent the Manchester' our transport.

We were, on arrival in Penang, greeted at the ferry Terminal by our Squadron Commander who arrived sitting up in the Gun Turret of his Scout Car resplendent with his Red Beret, and of course a large painting of the Winged Dagger and those famous words "Who Dares Wins" emblazoned across the front plating of his Humber Scout Car.

Our Squadron Commander was a real flamboyant character who had spent a good deal of his service in India. He went under the name of El-Supremo when we were not in the jungle but when we were deep in the Jungle on Operations; he was always referred to as "The Poppy". This was the obvious title for him and he always led his soldiers from the front but in no way would he bear fools gladly. Without fail he wore his Red Beret when we were on Operations but he always insisted that members of his Squadron wore the prescribed Jungle Green Hat with the yellow band around it. This was to ensure that other members of the British contingent would not under any circumstances mistake them for the enemy which, given the conditions we were operating under, could have been very tragic indeed. There was no mistaking who the Boss was at any time. I imagine that a number of Terrorists had probably laid an egg in the arse of their pants when catching sight of a Red Poppy swanning around in the Ulu (Jungle).

There seemed to be no point in delaying the start of the Operation on Penang. After all it seemed that speed of action would play a part in the outcome of things. The Terrorists were surely in no doubt what was coming and would make their own plans accordingly. The complete Squadron was transported out from Minden Barracks and was dropped off at various points along the east coast of the Island. The plan was that each Troop would work a specified sector of the coastline and link up with the Troop which was allocated to patch north of where they were established. A search of all Kampongs together with an area extending about one Map Square inland was given the once over in an effort to discover any people living there who was not considered to be a local person.

What a problem this turned out to be. Firstly we hadn't a clue who was entitled to be there and those locals that were approached were much too afraid to point out to us anybody who was a visitor, either a welcome one or perhaps an unwanted one. There was a road which ran north to south for the whole length of the island and this, in places, came within some two to three hundred yards from the waters edge. It was the seaward side of this road that we tended to concentrate on.

There were many Kampongs built close to the sea as would be expected, for almost all who lived there earned their living from the local fishing industry. Our Troop visited each one in turn and after a day or so just showing ourselves and taking stock in general regarding the number of people living there, we moved on to the next Kampong to repeat the exercise. It was not at all surprising that we saw no identifiable Terrorists either holidaying or working. No one came up to us and said they were a Terrorist on holiday, but there again even if they were they probably wouldn't have had the time for such niceties. This coupled with the fact that they were hardly likely to be wearing their Jungle Greens or Khaki Drills which made it all the more difficult even if they did exist

On occasions we backtracked and revisited a Kampong which we had left only a few days before. This action seemed to be a little more promising as we quite often twigged that certain people present there had not been present when we last visited. They had probably known that we were coming in the first instance and moved off northwards prior to our arrival. When we as a Troop moved on to the next Kampong they simply skirted around us and went back to the place we had just left. Any such suspects that we encountered were sent back to Georgetown for interrogation but we never heard whether our efforts had been fruitful or not.

This badly planned and poorly executed Operation seemed to drag on and on and we all felt that we had been sent on this wild goose chase just to say that the Regiment was fully active and doing their bit. It was a most soul destroying effort but as the saying goes, "it's an ill wind which blows nobody any good" and it had one very good advantage for "A" Squadron.

Our Troop would "Patrol" for some two weeks and then we were lifted by Regimental Transport and taken back to Minden Barracks in Georgetown. Here we would spend the next week clearing up after our two weeks work and getting ready for the next time the Transport would once again ferry us to the same spot on the coast where we would do exactly as we had done a number of times before.

There was one big plus for me personally with this very slow way of life. I had many opportunities to improve my aquatic skills which had been dismal up to this point as I have described elsewhere in the book. A change of procedure was implemented and we were split up into just four man patrols. Although this was persisted with, it proved to be just as hopeless as patrolling with a full Troop. There was not a shot fired in anger by any of us and of course we all became very disillusioned with it all but we did enjoy the frequent breaks we had which meant that we got to spend a fair amount of time plumbing the depths of the facilities in Georgetown.

It was early one evening while I was taking in a sample of the Bars, that I was quite suddenly greeted in the street by the girl I had met when I attended the Dance at Sandicroft Leave Centre. She appeared to be delighted to see me again and suggested that we find a Coffee House where we could have a chat and bring ourselves up to date.

I readily admit that I too was more than a little pleased at meeting her again and we spent the best part of the next half hour talking about anything in general. She said that she still worked as a nursemaid for the same people who lived out on the Coast Road. She went on to tell me that her name was Bridie and how she spent many evening sitting alone in her rooms with no one to talk to after she had put the children to bed.

She said that she had mentioned to her employers that she had previously met me and she had asked me to visit her at her place of employment. They in turn had seemed to think that that would be a good idea. We talked on a little further and then agreed that I should visit her the very next evening and she hoped that I would be able to meet her employers.

The following day was spent by No2 Troop cleaning and oiling what seemed to be every weapon that the British Forces had ever possessed. Thoroughly bored, I could hardly wait for 1600hrs when we would knock off for the night when I would spruce myself up and set off for my rendezvous with the gorgeous Bridie. I had let my imagination run just a little bit wild a couple of times during the afternoon. I had told her that I would be there around 1900hrs and she in return had told me that she would have finished with the children around that time.

I knew that the house was not far from Georgetown and by the time I was ready to leave Barracks I had made up my mind that perhaps it was better if I were to take a short walk as in this way I would be sure to be there on time.

I must have been walking for something less than ten minutes when the heavens opened up and I was soaked to the skin by one of those tropical downpours which are renowned for their intensity. I had spived myself up in my best gear and applied lashings of after shave in order to impress, but alas, all this had now changed and I feared that I cut a very sad picture just when I had seemed to have cracked it.

Bridie was on the lookout for me and welcomed me enthusiastically in spite of my bedraggled appearance. She showed a good deal of concern at my plight and started to peel off my outer clothing just as soon as she was able. It was right at this time that her employer, at least I took it to be him, arrived in the annex where the Nanny lived and she hurriedly introduced me to him. She went on to add that I was the young man she had told him about earlier that day. Her employer in turn showed great concern for the plight of her guest and insisted that I take a hot shower and put on a spare bathrobe until such times as my own clothes had been dried and ironed by a member of his staff. I was highly embarrassed because of the condition that I had arrived in but had little option but to comply with his instructions.

I was very soon sitting on Bridies Veranda with a large Whisky and Soda to fight off the fear of a cold, or so I was informed. She sat beside me and we talked of many things including how long I had been in the Services and just what my ambitions were. We were sitting on a swing lounger and she constantly, albeit barely perceptibly moved ever closer to me. By the time I was on my second Whisky she was kissing me which put me in a bit of a stew because her hand lingered on my thigh which seemed to be readily available because I wore nothing else but the bathrobe.

Things had just progressed to where I was handling her ample breasts and my passion was beginning to get the better of me when she suddenly jumped up from the lounger and this could not have been a moment too soon as her employer came round the corner of the Veranda. He politely asked if all was in order and asked how my clothing was coming along. Little did he know, or perhaps he suspected, that my clothing was the last thing on my mind right at that time and I was doing my very best to disguise what was happening to me beneath the bathrobe which surely was by now fairly obvious. I managed to tell him that all was going well and with this assurance, he disappeared back from whence he he had come. I am convinced even to this very day that he was fully aware of what was going on.

A Houseboy appeared with my freshly washed and pressed clothing and I took myself off to the Bathroom to dress. When I returned to the Veranda, Bridie had tidied herself up and although I was pretty keen to take up where we had left off, she hinted that it was time for me to leave. Although this came rather suddenly she gave me the impression that she was keen to see me again and it was at her suggestion that if I were free the coming Saturday, perhaps we could take a trip to a beautiful little beach which she knew of across the other side of the Island. Of course I jumped at the offer and quickly added that I would hire a car to take us there. She in turn offered to pack a picnic and we would make a day of it.

Back in Barracks things seemed to drag like hell. Would the weekend never come? To a man the whole squadron was of the opinion that we were wasting our time with this ill thought out plan, but it seemed that we were destined to see it through to the very end. I personally even now, have little doubt that there were some wry smiles on the faces of certain leaders of the Communist Terrorist Organization.

The brains department arrived from Sungai Besi to re-assess the situation and put us, the foot soldiers on the right track. Perhaps they liked the idea of a couple of weeks here in Penang where they could take advantage of the many tourist facilities and have a jolly good time at the expense of the Military. They did come up with one quite brilliant suggestion however. We should try to form smaller patrol numbers.

"You know, cover more ground, spread yourselves much more thinly".

When we told them that we had done that a couple of weeks back they went into one of their secret conferences as they inevitably did and we heard not another thing from them.

The whole affair was a complete and utter cock up from start to finish. The only action the brains department had neglected to take, was to send copies of their all important briefing plans to Communist Headquarters, where ever they might be, with a covering letter expressing their wish that they would appreciate the fact if they would kindly co-operate in the future, as far as was possible.

The Terrorists and the Emergency were far from my mind and Saturday couldn't come quick enough for me to see Bridie again and this time, perhaps.........Well anything might happen on a small secluded beach couldn't it? I said nothing to anyone about the arrangements I had made. I didn't even tell my best mate Jack who was obviously wondering where it was that I had disappeared to on the odd occasion. It had to be a woman, it just had to be.

I must admit that it bothered me somewhat in as much as I was about to pop off to the eastern side of the Island with this young succulent female who had tempted me to this so called secluded beach and she had kindly thrown in the promise of a sumptuous lunch, apart fro all the other activity which I anticipated, but would agree, it was my imagination running wild at the time. After all I had only met her two or three times before, once at the dance and then in the street and of course when I got pissing wet through going to see her where she worked.

The though came into my mind that I didn't really know her at all, she was a relative stranger. AS it has been written numerous times before, I will not bore you with the reservations I had but will simply say Bridie was lovely and the unspoken promise of the possibilities on offer set me off like a Stag in the Rutting Season. It never even crossed my mind once, that the area she intended to show me was purported to be well known for Terrorists and it was highly foolish, nay stupid, let alone a dangerous thing which I was about to do.

Saturday came and off I went to hire a car. I found this to be quite a simple thing to do and was soon on my way to where Bridie lived. I felt very proud as I drove up to her house and found that she was waiting for me with a large basket with goodies for the picnic. She carried an additional shoulder bag which I assumed contained such things as a swimming costume and towels etc., which was of course if she intended to wear a costume. The thought nearly drove me wild and I almost knocked a Chinese fellow of his bike.

She gave me all the necessary directions and eventually we came to a place where she said it would be safe to leave the car. As we were unloading or goods and chattels she explained that the beach we were heading for was some 15 minutes walk from the road. However she assured me that the track we would follow was indeed a very well worn track and the going would be quite straight forward as it was quite wide in some places.

I couldn't have cared less what kind of track it was, I would have willingly chopped down heavy Primary Jungle to clear our way to the beach which she said held much promise. If only we could get cracking and get on with it.

It took all of the 15 minutes she had mentioned but the walk had been pleasant and my first sight of the beach confirmed in my mind that it was truly a beautiful spot. I was immediately into my trunks and headed for the water. Bridie showed no signs of reluctance or shyness as she changed into a stunning two piece swim suit. She lay on the beach and made no effort to join me in the water. On seeing this I was smartly out of the water and plonked myself down beside her on the beach. I just couldn't resist her and I kissed her as we fell into each others arms.

The place had been totally deserted when we arrived and for this I was extremely grateful. It was not very long either before I was even more grateful as we made love under the hot tropical sun. Even if the beach had been crowded it was doubtful whether either of us would have noticed as we consumed each other and then we eventually just lay there completely drained of our passion, at least for the time being anyway.

I must have fallen asleep, for quite suddenly I was aware of two Chinese gentlemen who were standing close to me and this brought my surroundings sharply into focus. Bridie was standing and was partly dressed having wrapped a Sarong round her body. She appeared to be taking little notice of the two men who were now looking down at me and speaking to each other in what I assumed was Cantonese.

On seeing that I was now fully awake as I sat up but did not rise to my feet at this point, the taller one of the two spoke to me in what can only be described as the Kings English which held the barest of an inflection proving that indeed, he was not of English origin. The facial feature of course confirmed this at a single glance.

He spoke mainly of the beautiful weather we were enjoying, in true English fashion. This he followed up with an appraisal of the lovely beach we had found to while away our leisure time on a Saturday afternoon.

At first I rather thought that he was one of those people who took a great deal of pleasure in practicing their English at every opportunity that came their way. He then, quite surprisingly I thought, went on to say how pleased he was that he had met me.

Still no warning bells.

How long did I expect to be staying on the Island? He then asked me where I would be going when I eventually left the Island.

I started to feel very uncomfortable and glanced at Bridie a couple of times while all this was going on. She didn't join in any of the conversation and nor did the short fat man who was the other half of the pair who had suddenly appeared. In fact Bridie stood a short distance away from where I sat and she seemed to be busying herself with unpacking the picnic basket and laying out the goodies.

She called me when the food was ready and to my utter amazement the two Orientals came and sat next to us and got stuck into the food as well. Bridie seemed to accept this as being the most natural thing in the world that this should happen and began extolling the merits of some pie or other to all three of her picnic guests while meanwhile lashing out the Chardonnay as if it was going out of fashion.

Still no warning bells, but I started to become very angry at what was developing around me and I seemed to have no control whatsoever of the circumstances. She seemed to be fully at ease about these two blokes being here and them scoffing our picnic as well. I suddenly realized that I was not fully switched on. I was letting something else do my thinking when I should have had my mind at red alert as per the way I had been trained.

In a flash it occurred to me that Bridie had produced four beakers for wine. Why? Was she expecting company? Another thing, why had she packed so much food? Surely she didn't think that we two would be able to eat that amount.

I was now fully alert to everything around me and the two Orientals in particular. I stood up and immediately felt a little better as the two men remained seated on the ground.

The taller man was speaking again and he suggested that I might like to meet him in Georgetown and perhaps we could go for a typical Chinese meal before I left Penang, whenever that may be.

The old warning bells were in full swing now. However I was somewhat relieved to hear him involve Bridie in the invitation which gave my mind something of a rest for I was beginning to think that perhaps he was a Sausage Jockey or something akin to that.

I was now thoroughly embarrassed about the whole situation but as Bridie was now involved and she readily agreed to go along with it, I reluctantly muttered a grudging acceptance.

It struck me as most strange that a total stranger should meet me on a beach and issue me with an invitation to eat with him back in Georgetown. What was more; he had asked me when this meeting would be convenient for me. He had gone on to say that Bridie could let him know and he would check if he would be available on the date I chose. I was now even more confused at what was seemed to be happening to me, it was rapidly becoming something that was far beyond my control.

It suddenly occurred to me that Bridie must know these men and I gradually turned to the fact that she must have known that they would be there at the beach. She must also know where to get in touch with them in Georgetown for had not the man said she would contact him when I had given her a date.

I had fleeting thoughts that I must report what had gone on to one of my superiors when I eventually arrived back at my Barracks.

When the two men stood and bade us farewell, they disappeared round the Headland that seemed to form the end of the beach. Bridie moved close to me and made those googly eyes as if to signal that a matinee performance was well overdue. I was very soon lost in passion once more and temporarily forgot all about the two men and everything else for that matter.

I never did report the incident to my superiors which was a grave mistake. A mistake for which I was to be suitably reprimanded at a date not too far into the future.

The dinner never did take place as "A" Squadron left Penang and returned to Sungai Besi just a few days later.

CHAPTER 12

We were preparing for our next Operation back in Sungai Besi and were therefore very busy from morning to night. From dawn to dusk we were fully occupied checking Arms and Ammunition, Radio and spare parts, DZ Panels and LZ (Landing Zone) Panels and of course our one-man twenty four hour Ration Packs. As was usual at this stage of an impending Operation all members of our Troop took part in a swap and barter session of the contents of the Ration Packs. The usual exchanges of Tinned Mixed Vegetables for Foil Wrapped Oatmeal Blocks and Tubes of Condensed Milk for wrapped Fruit Gums went on as usual. The object of all this swapping and changing was not only governed by an individual's likes or dislikes, there were other considerations to be taken into account.

Weight was a considerable factor. For instance, If you kept all your tins of mixed vegetables you may have say, six or seven tins of the stuff. Now mixed veg' was not a popular choice with most of us as it had to be heated prior to consumption and if this task was not carried out, it sure was something of a queer choice to have for your evening meal. On the other hand Oatmeal Blocks could be dissolved in a little hot water in no time at all and if anything, they were just as nourishing as, and certainly more palatable than mixed vegetables. Besides, the tins the veg' came in was far heavier than two weeks supply of Oatmeal blocks. Wine Gums in rolls, just as they were bought in the UK were a favourite. Firstly they could be sucked while you on the move during the day and tended to slake your thirst as you went along. Secondly, on the rare occasion, usually on the night you had taken your Air Drop, the Gaffer would dole out a liberal drop of Army Issue Rum to all and sundry. The enterprising soldier could dilute the strong rum with a drop of water and then add two or three Wine Gums and let them dissolve into the Rum over a very low heat with the result being almost enough to convince you that you had had a damn good night on the "Piss". Anyway this potion tended to allow you to get very good nights sleep without worrying what strange livestock might enter your Poncho while you lay slumbering in it. Jack, my bivouac partner and I took no part took no part in this exchange business, that is unless there was a particular very good deal being offered by someone then we would snap it up in a jiffy. Other than that it seemed that what he liked, I didn't and the reverse seemed to also be true. Anything he was not partial to seemed to find favour with me.

In the last few days run up to starting the Operation, we were informed that this one was likely to be the longest one we had done to date. This little snippet of information gave rise to much speculation as to where we were headed and just what our objective would be when we got there. Although we didn't know it at the time, it was to be 113 days before we returned to civilisation once more.

Had "A" Squadron been Parachute trained at the time, we would undoubtedly have made one of those daring Tree Jumps that the 22nd SAS became famous for. Unfortunately our Squadron had, so far, not been selected to attend the RAF Parachute Course which was held at Changi in Singapore. It was therefore necessary to transport us by road to the Operational Zone which was somewhere to the north west of Ipoh. As was the usual form, we were told nothing else at this stage. It was however a foregone conclusion that our means of transport would be the old WOT 6's, what else? What a thrill that would be.

The old sweats put two and two together as they had many times in the past with an almost uncanny accuracy. Up past Ipoh? Operation to last longer than usual? It could only mean one thing. We were taking over from "B" Squadron who had kept themselves busy in that area for some time now. Rumour had it, and rumour in the SAS was invariably close to the real thing, that a Jungle Fort was being built by the Regiment and it was almost certain that "A" Squadron was about to play their part in it.

The ride from Sungai Besi was the usual thrilling affair as the "drivers", if that name could be applied to them; drove hell for leather hoping against hope that any ambush laid for them by the Terrorists would be hard pushed to catch them out. They were frequently described by a number of their passengers as carrying on like a Badger with its arse on fire as they travelled the highways and byways of Malaya. Nevertheless they invariably completed their task with some style and the occasions they were caught out were indeed few and far between.

I must just record an incident here which came my way one day when we were resting in the camp at Sungai Besi. I was detailed to drive to Kuala Lumpur Railway Station to pick up a dozen or so new recruits who had just arrived from the UK. Nothing strange about that you may think, but here is how it all came about. I was mooching around the Motor Transport lines where a chap that I had served with as a boy soldier was now employed to keep the Regiments transport in some sort of running order. The Officer in charge of the Transport Section at that time was none other than a very famous SAS man (Captain Johnny Cooper). Well the Captain spotted me and called me over to ask what I was about. When I told him that I had served as a Boy Soldier with his ace mechanic and all I wanted was to have a natter, he suddenly asked me if I had any experience driving a Ford WOT 6. I of course didn't exactly say that I had but I do admit that I must have given him the impression that I was pretty clued up in this respect. "Right" said the Captain, "Take that one over there", indicating with a waive of the hand in the general direction of a number of trucks, "and go and pick up the new bods from KL Station". Now I had never driven upon the public highway. In fact I had once had a go on a Scooter in a field but never anything like a Ford WOT 6 but pride would not let me admit it, not even to someone as important as the famous Johnny Cooper.

In I get and had the old girl started almost straight away. This of course gave me the added confidence I needed. Johnny Cooper would no doubt be casting an eye on me to see just how proficient I was at this driving lark. As I went along the track which would take me to the metal road which would eventually lead me to Kuala Lumpur I gained confidence with every few yards I travelled. Very soon I became aware that I didn't need to remain in bottom gear all the time and that changing into a higher gear was soon learned after my first few attempts. Of course with this came a proportional increase in speed and by the time I arrived at Kuala Lumpur Railway Station it would have been hard to distinguish me from any person who in fact was in possession of a bona fide Driving Licence.

Having easily found the new guys, I invited them to mount the truck and prepare to take the ride of their lives out to our depot at Sungai Besi. We were home in record time and I was quite pleased with myself because I hadn't hit a single thing either going out or coming back.

As a result of my efforts I became the proud possessor of a Pink Slip which qualified me to drive any Military Vehicle on the Public Highway.

I end this little story by telling you that this was the one and only Driving Test I ever took or ever passed to this very day. Perhaps all the Drivers in the SAS managed to qualify in the same way.

Now it is back to the Operation we were involved in which took place to the north of Ipoh.

After arriving at the drop off point, thankfully still in one piece, the Squadron were keen to get into the Jungle. To hang around at the drop off point was not recommended as there had been a number of occasions when troops had been engaged while they were either hanging around on an open road or perhaps just on the peripheral area of the Jungle. It was recommended that we were away from the area just as quick as was possible. I must say that Jungle Operations were always preferred by the soldiers as opposed to riding on the highway with our Hells Angel's Drivers.

We set off in buoyant mood and full of expectation for we now knew just where we were going. Just before we hit the road after loading at Sungai Besi we were told that we were headed for the Jungle Fort which "B" Squadron had been building and we were to take over where they had left off. Of course we would maintain our system of patrols in the area but this was something that still had to be worked out when we arrived at our destination.

117

There was an overall plan whereby a series of these Jungle Forts, perhaps three or even four in all were to be built. These would be strategically placed across the country where the Terrorists were the most active. They were to be constructed from solid timber which seemed to be a sensible thing to do when the locations were considered. They were to be enclosed in a strong (probably Teak) high perimeter stockade fence with a pair stout pair of entrance gates similar to those seen in Wild West films. I suppose the powers that be considered that if this design of gate hed kept hordes of Redskins at bay for so long, they would provide ample protection against the Communist Terrorists.

The basis of the whole concept was that troops would be able to stay out on Operations for extended periods. This would reduce the many comings and goings by road between the Depot at Sungai Besi and the nearest point to the Operational area. The Terrorist had many spies on the look out for them and it was a certainty that they would be informed as to which way we were headed just soon as the old WOT 6's were started up. Likewise they would be told exactly where the drop off point was by their lookouts and if their leaders considered it to be the prudent thing to do, they would scaper well clear of the area immediately thus ensuring that we, who were dead keen to meet these "Gentlemen", would be unlikely to make their acquaintance on our daily walks in the forests of Malaya.

The Fort where we were now located seemed to us that it was going to be a rather swish affair when it was fully completed. The overall compound was large enough to accommodate a semi-permanent Landing Zone for a Helicopter. This could alternatively be laid out as a Dropping Zone to allow the RAF to make their deliveries of Foodstuffs and Ammunition direct to a known location without the bother of searching the Jungle for a DZ prepared by the Troopers.

Our Squadron, "A" Squadron, was divided into five Troops and were designated as follows. HQ Troop, which was the smallest, always stayed in a Base Camp, wherever that may be. It could be back at Sungai Besi or at a place selected by the Squadron Commander which would be nearer to where the four Operational Troops were actively operating. This Troop was made up of such personnel as the Sparks (Radio Operator), Medic and perhaps a Demolitions expert. These men could be called upon to augment the strength of any of the Operational Troops should the need arise. The remainder of HQ Troop was made up of Trackers. These men came from Borneo and were from a tribe of head-hunters and went under the name of Iban's. They spoke little English but proved themselves time and again to be a great asset to the Troopers that they accompanied into the Jungle on Operations. Their skills at tracking and reading Jungle signs were second to none. Their hearing was really phenomenal and they would hold their hand aloft to demand absolute silence while they deciphered some far off alien sound that they had detected.

They were truly ferocious people and they adorned their bodies with Tattoo's which were not only on their arms and chest but boasted a series of flower like emblems on each side of their back. They started quite large at the shoulder and gradually diminished in size as they came close to their waist. What was about the most amazing thing about they chaps was that they Tattooed each others throats from collar bone right up under the chin. This must have been a very painful thing to have applied when the method they employed to do it was one of the most primitive things I had ever seen.

They would first sharpen a four inch piece of Bamboo to a needle point at each end. They then selected a second piece of Bamboo which was about one inch in diameter and about eighteen inches long. The needle pointed piece was then tied to this second piece and secured firmly in place about four inches from the end. They would then acquire a fairly heave piece of timber (perhaps a piece of Teak) which they would use as a sort of hammer like instrument when they started work on their comrades Tattoo. All that was now required was some sort of colouring die, which when hammered into the human skin would leave an imprint in it. Black Boot Polish was a much preferred medium, as this mixed marvellously with a drop of spit. In view of the fact that Boot Polish was not readily available in the Jungles of Malaya an alternative concoction was used. The Iban's would take a portion of Latex Rubber from one of the many trees that grew there. Into this they would combine anything handy which would give it colour. This could be the scrapings of a piece of Charcoal or perhaps the ground up dirt from an Ant Hill or even the Red Soldier Ants themselves which, as the name implies, they were coloured red and came in abundance in the Jungle. The needle pointed Bamboo was dipped into the colouring concoction and then the stick to which it was attached was struck firmly with the Hammer/Striker which caused the needle point to be forced into the skin and leave a small deposit of the colouring agent in the skin every time it was pierced by the needle pointed piece of Bamboo.

It was indeed a long drawn out job; nevertheless many of the soldiers did have an Iban Tattoo etched into their flesh on their back. Here it was out of sight but not without the pain when they hoisted their pack onto their back to continue their journey through the trees and undergrowth of the Jungle. A scab that one could only describe as bloody awful would form over the Tattoo and due to this being constantly being rubbed of with your pack, it took weeks before it began to heal. It did make life miserable but true to fashion of the time, we still had them done. I still bear mine to this very day and will take it to my grave with me.

The Iban's always worked in pairs and although they were issued with the old Lee Enfield 303 Rifle, they had little use for it. They carried a Kris in a home made wooden scabbard which they tied to their waste with suitable plaited vines. The Kris was honed to a razor sharpness and had tufts of hair wrapped around both the handle and scabbard. The story went that this was human hair which had been removed from their victim's heads. Some of these "Fighting Knives" for that is what they really were, had been handed down from Father to Son over quite a long period. Although Head Hunting is not quite so prevalent in Borneo and Sarawak today, there is still the odd report that a feud has broken out and when this happens, to use a modern saying......."Head will roll".

Whenever a contact was made with the Terrorists, or even if contact seemed to be imminent, away went the Rifle and out came the Kris and off they went in search of their prey. They were in fact very nice chaps but we all were always just that bit wary of them.

There was yet another set of people who came under the care of HQ Troop and these people also were attached to the Operational Troops as and when required. They were members of the Sakai race who were indigenous to Malaya. They acted as Porters to the heavily laden Troopers.

Some of these people who lived their lives entirely in the deep Jungle well away from civilisation. They had suffered awful atrocities at the hands of the Terrorists mainly over the issue of food which these little men had grown to keep their families alive. The Terrorists would demand all that they had and when they did manage to rustle up enough courage to refuse, they were subjected to severe beatings and sometimes even worse. The whole race were virtually Pigmy's and as a fully grown man would be hard pushed to be taller than four or five foot. They were enormously strong and could carry prodigious loads; however, they were far from being either honest or reliable. They would stay with the Troopers for perhaps two or three weeks only. During this time they would hoard the food given to them and then they would suddenly disappear. It was however miraculous that the vacancy they created was immediately filled by another Sakai who happened to be near at hand just when he was required. The Sakai would eat almost anything at all. Monkey, Tree Rat, Snakes or anything. The Rice which was issued to them on a day to day basis was indeed a delicacy and was highly prized. I never saw one of them eating Rice. Presumably they saved it to take back to their tribe where it would be perhaps eaten or more likely saved as seed for a proposed crop of their own.

"B" Squadron seemed to have been very busy during their stay and had completed the man structure. It was now to be "A" Squadrons task to build living accommodation and other additions such as a Cookhouse etc., There was to be a Radio Shack and of course a Stores Block where all the goodies would be kept away from the thieving hands of the Sakai Porters who had the peculiar knack of letting things stick to their hands. The final building was to be a Tactical Headquarters Building where the brains of the outfit could be housed and plan their Operations and pour over many maps at their leisure.

It had been established at the outset that the entire facility would have running water which would be available from a conventional tap and this would be purified prior to entering into the system. The plumbing pipe work would of course be made from suitably adapted Bamboo which grew in abundance in the area. Permanent living and sleeping accommodation was to be provided which would be an enormous advantage over sleeping under a Poncho with a buddy by your side. In fact it was intended that the Fort would be as near a duplicate of the facilities back at base in Sungai Besi. That was of course less the transport facilities as all movement would as usual be by Shank's Pony.

Now that "A" Squadron was fully installed at this, the first Jungle Fort to be built, a new strategy was developed as to the deployment of the four Operational Troops. Each Troop would take a turn at remaining in the Fort while the other three would be engaged on Jungle Patrols. These Patrols would be of something like five or six days duration and on completion of the cycle, it would begin again with a different Troop staying back in the Fort to continue the building process while the other three Troops continued to look for the baddies. By rotating the Troops in this way it meant that none of them would carry out Patrols for more than about eighteen days at a stretch before having the comparative luxury of a period in the Fort in a proper bed.

The arrangement was very flexible as indeed it had to be to cover all manner of eventualities that cropped up from time to time. It was however, very popular with the majority of the Squadron. There were exceptions of course as was nearly always the case. Some of the men would have preferred a full five or six weeks on continuous Operations and then back to Sungai Besi where they would have a spot of leave when they could sample the delights that they had perhaps missed the last time round.

There was yet another system which was in operation which did bear fruit to some extent. This system way devised and controlled by both the Military Headquarters in Kuala Lumpur who were ably assisted in the matter by the Malay Police Force. It was called the SEP Programme which stood for Surrendered Enemy Personnel Programme. A thorough Interrogation of such people was carried out in Kuala Lumpur to find out about Food and Ammunition Dumps etc., It was however sometimes the case that anyone who was either captured or voluntarily gave themselves up to the Squadron who were in situ at the Fort at the time, would be checked out and immediate action taken on any information obtained in this way. Some good finds were made as a result of this quick action.

When a Terrorist decided that he or she had had enough of the Jungle life with all its hardships and restrictions, they would wait for an opportunity and then leg it to the nearest Police or Security Force Post where they would give themselves up. There was a jolly good reason why they should wait for the opportune moment to get away as should their Gang Leader get any hint whatsoever that to bail out was in their mind, bang, the gang had one less mouth to feed. Apart from that, such swift action by the leader served to put the frighteners on other members of the Gang and thus deterred them from going walk about. When they did manage to surrender they were usually in very poor physical condition having lived on starvation rations for a considerable time. Hunger was not their only concern as many of them had a variety of illnesses for which they needed urgent medical treatment.

It soon became widely known that they preferred to surrender direct to the Malayan Police as opposed to the Security Forces. They apparently thought that should they surrender to the Military, it was more than likely that they would have to traipse around the Jungle for some time before the soldiers finally returned to their Base. Apart from that, they were sure that they would go onto good grub with the Police straight away but with the Military they would be given the bare minimum and that would be made up from the old twenty four Ration Packs which was hardly called popular by either us or the surrendered Terrorists.

Apart from the food consideration, there was another reason why they preferred to surrender to the Police. I would be the first man to agree that it something of a pain to have one of your enemies travelling with you as you earned your daily bread. It was damned hard graft looking out for yourself and your buddy without having to keep an eye on any passengers. You were never quite sure that their intention was indeed to surrender or perhaps they were playing along and would, in the middle of the night, cut the throat of one or two Troop members before disappearing back to where they had come from.

The soldiers made no secret of the fact that they detested them and treated (or mistreated) them accordingly. The ones who did make it back to civilisation, and I am afraid there were some that did not, were first questioned very closely about their past experiences in the Jungle. They were then handed on to the famous Pudu Jail in Kuala Lumpur or occasionally to the main jail in Ipoh. Whichever was the case, it was much of a much ness as the period spent there was jokingly referred to as a Rest and Recuperation period. They were re-interrogated from time to time to see which things they had told about were porkies and which were genuine. If any of them came up with the goods and disclosed something useful, such as the location of an ammunition or food dump for example, they were handsomely rewarded with a cash payment from the Government of Malaya. The cash payment was only forthcoming of course after the Security Forces had investigated and proven that the information was genuine.

In the initial stages the reports that the SEP's made were in the main pure fiction. This ruse was fairly short lived however as the soldiers did not like being used in this way (accompanying them to a spot in the Jungle) by the authorities who hoped against hope that the story they had been told might just have a grain of truth in it. The fact that someone who you had classed as an enemy in the not too distant past, and he/she was now trying to cop a fair sized wedge from the Government while under the protection of the Security Forces did not sit too well with the soldiers. There was little wonder that those that we called "chancers" were keen to return to the relative comfort of their Jail Cell as any disgruntled soldier can be a very hard taskmaster, especially in the middle of the Jungle when they are wet, hungry and generally pissed off with life anyway.

The Terrorist movement was highly organised and tried to operate, administratively that is, in a similar manner to that which the Security Forces employed. By its very nature this meant that a series Couriers were installed and they travelled from State to State covering the whole of the country. They carried orders and sometimes cash between the many groups and gangs that existed at that time. All the directives and orders from their hierarchy to the troops on the ground were distributed in this way and the Couriers tended to use set routes where the going was comparatively easy as the Jungle tracks were well defined and simple to follow with the aid of such things as a map.

One such route had been pointed out by an SEP to the authorities. This information had been passed on to "A" Squadron to investigate as we were the nearest Military outfit to where it was supposed to be. It was decided that Jack and I together with two other members of No1 Troop would make our way to the designated spot and we would weigh up the possibilities when we got there. Our Troop Governor suggested that we take along two of the Iban Trackers who would know in a jiffy if there had been any local foot traffic lately and should this be the case, a Grenade Ambush should be laid in the hope that some of those country gentlemen should decide to stroll down the track which we would keep a beady eye on.

I prime target was that we should capture a Courier with all the paperwork that he may be carrying at the time. This would indeed prove to be a great coup as the Intelligence Section back in Sungai Besi could learn a great deal from such material if it came to hand in time for something to be done about it. This would normally have been a two man job but the SEP giving this information, had also said that a movement of personnel from one State to another was imminent and he thought that the track mentioned might just be the route that they would take. On being pushed further, he had confirmed that a group of some twenty or so personnel would be travelling. It was this last bit of information which had convinced the Governor that two extra men should come along as well as the two Trackers.

I took the decision to lay the Grenade Ambush and decided that it would cover some thirty yards of the track with live fire cover at each end to catch any stragglers and to sweep up any who managed to avoid the initial impact and attempted to leg it out of the area. It was also decided that we would not involve the two Trackers in the observation of the track while we waited patiently for visitors to arrive. Although they were quiet men they were easily bored and would perhaps wander off leaving us a little exposed. We also decided that once we had laid out the Grenade Ambush, we would then work it with two men on and two men off changing every two hours. In this way nobody would get cheesed off or perhaps nod off while on sentry duty. With this arrangement firmly established we considered that we stood a good chance of either capturing a Courier or killing twenty Bandits or perhaps even making a clean sweep of the lot.

125

It crossed my mind at the time that the Squadron success figure would improve greatly if we did make a clean sweep in this comparatively easy task. The kill rate could certainly do with a boost.

· The construction of the Ambush was quite a simple affair really and the activation of it was even easier. The basic principle was that a number of High Explosive Hand Grenades were placed at suitable intervals alternating along each side of the track. These were spread some six to eight feet between them. By distributing them in this manner, the actual killing area was made as large as possible. All the Grenades were connected by means of a Ring Main made up from Detonating Cord which would be activated by a single Pull Switch. When the Switch was pulled, all the Grenades would explode almost instantaneously. This would not only make life difficult for anyone within range on the track but there was a strong possibility that his/her Communist Membership would come to an abrupt end at that time. The person who had to pull the Switch to set the whole thing off, had to judge to exact moment when he would do this in order to make sure that as many Terrorists as possible had passed into the killing zone. The second man on watch with him would, by prior arrangement, be covering the entry point to the killing area and once the balloon had gone up, so to speak, he would have a show down with anyone why didn't get as far as being actually in the killing area or perhaps had been one of the lucky ones and was beating a hasty retreat as fast as his little legs could carry him. This arrangement gave the Switch puller the opportunity to initially count the men who had passed the entry point to the killing field before he sent them off to meet their maker as it were. There were no set procedures for this type of action and the methods adopted by other members of the Regiment were many and varied, however I personally liked to have a Phosphorous Grenade (80G SMOKE) at each end of an ambush in order to cause maximum panic and general confusion amongst the unfortunates who were being attacked.

This particular type of action, Grenade Ambushes, was not a popular activity with the soldiers. After the initial laying of the Ambush, the waiting in complete silence was, to say the least, very trying indeed. We had to maintain absolute silence as the as at the first sign of any strange (alien) noise that was detected, meant that the Terrorists would high tail it back the way they had come. For my part, being a realist, I always considered it to be highly unlikely that they might make another attempt to pass the same way with the next twenty four or even forty eight hours and we may as well call it a day and pack up and go home.

Apart from the boredom of waiting hours on end in absolute silence, we were waiting for something that may, or may not happen. This was a soul destroying job for us. When it did become apparent that the Ambush was a failure, either because the Terrorists had twigged that we were around or perhaps we may think that we had waited long enough for them to show, there was the problem of us disarming and recovering the Grenades, Fuses and Cordtex etc., this was much easier said than done. The Grenades may have been on the ground covered with leaves etc., long enough for the fuses to become unstable through dampness. If this was the case they could possibly blow up in your face as you lifted them either off the ground or perhaps withdraw them fro the Grenade itself. I was keenly aware of the dangers here and being a firm believer that discression is definitely the better part of valour, I invariably left our Ambush position with an almighty bang. In this way I was never responsible for any of my comrades being short of a hand or even a finger or two.

This practice was frowned upon by the powers that be as they, not only considered it to be a waste of explosives, but it would deter the Terrorists from visiting that particular venue again if they could possibly help it. Shame? But there we are, who would be looking in the early morning, in the State of Perak, to see who was making all that noise. It was certainly not those still in their cosy beds in Kuala Lumpur who were stupid enough to issue such orders in the first place.

We had laid our Ambush on this particular occasion and had made provision for some twenty or so souls to be accommodated. The waiting game had started but we were not to wait long for in something less than four hours, the main object of our attention came into the killing area seemingly without a care in the world and he was entirely alone. The Courier had arrived and it seemed to waste to spoil it all and blow up all those Grenades just for one happy little man who after all, was moving at such a leisurely pace. Apart from that, he may be carrying some valuable paper work, or even cash and it would be a crying shame to destroy anything like that. We nabbed him without a single shot being fired and I swear that he couldn't have cared less. In fact he seemed to be quite cheerful about the fact that his duties as a Jungle Courier appeared to be on the point of termination. He was carrying a webbing satchel (British Army Pattern 37), in which there were documents giving instructions for attacks on Kampongs and Road Ambushes of Military Vehicles. The content caused quite a stir back at the Sungai Besi base and a helicopter was sent to the Fort to pick up the booty. What Headquarters didn't know was that there had been a few thousand Straits Dollars in the Couriers Satchel. Strangely, these somehow got mislaid as the documents were passed from hand to hand during the trip back to civilisation. The soldiers were not stupid, any bits of paper which referred in any way to money, was also removed from the Satchel, just in case.

It was during this extended Operation that something happened which caused a great deal of distress to the men who were involved. Subsequently a ray of sunshine fell on them as one of those involved received recognition for the bravery he had displayed under extreme enemy fire. It must also be said at this point that there were many acts of bravery which went unnoticed due to the fact that in the main, they were never reported by the people involved as they were considered to be carried out in the normal line of duty.

It was standard practice that in the event that anyone became a casualty during a contact with the enemy; all efforts would be made to recover the casualty as quickly as possible. The reason for this was not only to give aid to the soldier affected, but also because it was known that the Terrorists were likely to chop up the body whether it be dead or alive if they could get to it before the soldiers were able to. They were sometimes quite determined to fight over a casualty in order to carry out their gruesome act and it was just such a case that happened during one of the patrols out from the Fort.

I was leading a four man patrol and we were carrying out a sweep of a large flat area. This must have been a Sakai Kampong at sometime in the non too distant past. It was believed that it had been closed and the occupants moved to a more secure area under the Emergency regulations. The whole area was covered with tall Lalang (grass) which in parts extended above the level of our heads making it impossible to see just where we were going. We were following what had previously been a footpath but was now was hardly recognisable as such due to the lack of use it now attracted. As usual we were line astern and about three to four yards between each man. We were abruptly thrown into contact with the enemy.

A burst of fire brought down the leading scout with the rest of us diving for cover on alternating sides of the path we were following. All fell quiet after the initial burst. Even the Birds and the Beasts of the forest held their hush as if in anticipation that was yet more to come. In spite of the quiet none of us moved an inch. We were far too well trained and we knew that as the Terrorists had seen our leading scout before he saw them, they would be waiting for the rest of us to give away our positions by moving. Some minutes passed with things being at stalemate as it were. We could hear our injured comrade calling to us for help which convinced me that his injuries must be pretty serious otherwise he would not be calling out for us as he was trained to maintain silence and wait for assistance. It was fairly certain that the Terrorists had a pretty good view of where he lay and would most likely be playing the waiting game to see if anyone was to go forward to the mans aid. They would then be in a position to pick us off at their leisure or perhaps, even worse, maybe we would have withdrawn back along the path and they would have a free go at doing horrible things to their victim and take the opportunity to relieve him of anything he had that was of use to them.

This was bad enough but there was an even more pressing reason (depending on how you looked at the situation), why we should get moving and recover the casualty. Each of us had taken turns acting as the leading scout and it just happened that the guy, who was now a casualty, was also carrying the Bren Gun. This was a highly desirable piece of weaponry and if the Terrorists were to manage to secure one of these, it would be a great prize for them all and a sad loss for the soldiers. As I was Patrol Leader, I took it upon myself to make an effort and try to reach the casualty or at least to get within earshot of him without exposing myself. At least I would be able to give him reassurance and should the Terrorists show themselves closer to the casualty I may well be in a position to bring fire to bear. Although I told myself that there was of a secondary reason, I must retrieve the Bren Gun if at all possible.

I edged forward crawling on my stomach but had barely made two yards progress when there was a sharp burst of automatic fire. Although the bullets showered all around me, I was fortunate not to be hit. From this surprise effort on their behalf I drew the conclusion that they didn't have a very clear view of exactly where I lay but had obviously sensed, rather than saw some kind of movement which they would surely be expecting of us as one of our party had been hit. I was now only about five or six yards from the casualty but each time I tried to move closer, the bastards opened up again and sprayed the area all around me. It was rather sad that I was completely unscathed but the poor old casualty suffered yet another couple of shots to his legs.

I turned away and crawled back to the rest of the patrol members who lay, one either side of the path, and a good twelve to twenty yards away from the casualty. We all agreed that we must get away from the path we had been following and then try to approach the casualty from a completely different angle. We were all agreed that the stricken man was our first priority and we should get to him as swiftly as possible but we also were all well aware that the Terrorists must by now be fully aware that there was a Bren Gun to be had if they could get to it. It was logical that they would attempt to keep us at bay until last light when they would attempt to snatch the prize and be away with it. As the light began to fail, their chances of success would increase. Nevertheless, as we had always been schooled to believe that the Jungle was neutral, it followed that our chances of success increased on a par with theirs as the light failed.

It was by now late afternoon when all this took place and after attempting, and failing to get any closer, it was now becoming increasingly urgent that we came up with something, anything to break the deadlock. It was going to be very difficult to see any movement that the enemy made if they decided to advance on the casualty under the cover of darkness.

We then all agreed that some form of deterrent should be set up in an effort to deter them from doing so. Now as the casualty was within earshot of where we now lay, I called him in as low a voice as was possible. He responded right away and gave me the impression that although badly injured, he could understand what I was saying to him and he had sussed out the situation he was in by himself. I asked him if it was possible for him to get the gun up onto its bipod legs at the front end and then cock the gun ready for action. If this could be done, then the gun would re-cock itself every time it was fired. With a bit of luck the mechanism would be set already to single shot firing which meant that the casualty would have to pull the trigger every now and again to keep the Terrorists with their heads down. If we could set this up it meant that they would not be comfortable about getting any nearer to the casualty as they would think his injuries were such that he could still fight them off should they decide to approach him.

His reply was that he was not at all sure if he could manage this but he would have a bloody good try. I had to help with lots and lots of encouragement but at last he had the gun up, cocked and ready to fire. It was unfortunate but the poor man had found himself unable to get the bipod legs down and the gun up on them into the firing position. He had however, managed to cock the gun and push the safety catch to the firing position. If the casualty managed to fire one or two rounds at oddly spaced intervals that would suffice. At least that was the plan. I passed these instructions in a very low whisper to the casualty who somehow managed to convince me that he understood but he was obviously in considerable pain by this time.

Quite suddenly and much to my surprise there were two or three rounds fired from the Bren Gun which, due to it not being elevated by its bipod legs, it sent up a shower of debris just in front of the injured man. This of course brought an immediate response from the Terrorists who returned the fire but it was in a most haphazard fashion and I drew the conclusion that they were just letting off rounds at random because they just did not know what to do about the situation.

A period of quiet followed and then came a repeat from the Bren Gun. This brought return fire from the Terrorists once again but it was still very haphazard. There was then a further quiet period followed by the good old Bren Gun with the now familiar response from the enemy.

All the time this was taking place I managed to whisper guidance to the injured man and tried to build up a little confidence in himself. I was well aware that a change of magazine would be called for at some stage quite soon. For my part, the enemy pinned me down. They sprayed the Lalang on all sides of me every time I attempted to move in any direction. My luck held and I escaped injury.

The two patrol members who were further back and consequently out of the immediate line of fire, racked their brains for some sort of solution to the dilemma we found ourselves in. If they were to leap up and make a charge at where they thought the enemy position was, they may end up in deeper water than they already appeared to be. They didn't know how many of them there were and it was a certainty that after such a period between their first contact and now, they would surely have dispersed over a wider area. One thing was certain however, they were sure to have a damn good view of the injured man and the Bren Gun which by now they would be drooling over. They would wait it out until an opportunity presented itself for them to make an approach and not only seize the gun but to perhaps mutilate the injured man as well. They were undoubtedly clever enough to have realised by now that their opposition comprised just a small patrol and if they outnumbered them by any considerable amount of men, they would have had a walk over if they carried out a full frontal attack. I thought this most unlikely as that was not their style at all. They would prefer toile up and play the waiting game when they would sneak upon their opponents as opposed to facing us man to man and toe to toe as it were.

The wounded man rallied himself somewhat at this stage and with what must have been a super human effort on his part, ha managed to get the bipod legs down and locked into the firing position. This meant that it would now be much easier for him to fire the gun and when it came to changing the magazine, which must be very soon now, well he may find this task just that little bit easier than he would have in the previous situation.

I pondered the thought about just how many magazines he may have been carrying when he was attacked? Where they readily available to him as he was surely now in a lying position and if they were in his back pack, would he manage to get them out when they were needed? If he could possibly get just one magazine change then with careful use of the gun by using short bursts and the period between bursts were of a slightly longer duration, then the enemy could be kept at bay for some considerable time. This of course was entirely dependant on the injured mans ability to continue to play his part in the action. Of course there was the additional factor about the situation with the magazine and ammunition availability. This was causing me to have serious concern about the whole situation.

The two other men of the patrol had made what movement forward they had been able to and were now somewhat closer to the casualty and myself. This they did every time there was an exchange of fire as it provided good cover for them. The enemy would have their heads down out of sight and that was for sure. However, the two of them realised that they would be unable to get near to the injured man before nightfall and even now the light was just beginning to fail. This lack of daylight came all of a sudden as it always does in the Tropics and very soon it was dark.

The exchange of fire continued but I wondered about just how long this would be possible. The two men contemplated splitting up and then carrying out an assault from two different directions both at the same time. The Terrorists had somehow anticipated such a move as they had put up a really big, widespread barrage just as the light was failing. This put paid to the plan and eventually abandoned it. During the extended barrage the two men had been extremely fortunate as neither of them were injured in any way. That is with the exception of their pride. They did not like being forced to take cover and could do nothing in their own defence let alone defending both the casualty and myself.

Time marched on and the injured man, ever aware what his fate would be if the enemy got to him before his buddies did, was also very conscious that it was not only himself but the gun that was making him such a tempting target. Consequently he continued to rally himself time and time again and deterred his enemies right throughout the hours of darkness by sending off a few rounds now and again. I didn't sleep all night my brain searching for a solution to the dilemma which would still be there when first light came at daybreak The casualty did indeed do a sterling job right throughout the night letting off the few precious rounds at intervals just to let both his buddies and the Terrorists that he was still there and was still in business.

It was a long night for all concerned, but the two men of our patrol, who were free to do so, did not sit by idly snatching forty winks when they were able to. As quietly as was humanly possible they advanced on the position where they knew that at least some of the Terrorists would be present. They had been in this assumed position from the time of the first contact right up to last light. It was now just about first light and the two of them decided that they had moved as far forward as they aught. After all it sure would be un-nerving if they were to make any further movement forward only to find themselves staring into the face of some little oriental gentleman. They both very briefly considered the position and decided that as the time had come, with first light, they would both lob a 36Grenade directly at the spot that they considered they enemy most likely to be. Before they could attempt this, it followed that they should inform me, as patrol leader, what they were going to do and I, in turn would try to tell the casualty to expect the ensuing explosions when it all took place. I hoped against hope that he would still be in a suitable state to absorb at least some of the information. We all trusted that this action might solve the dilemma providing it was delayed just long enough to take the necessary aim with the Grenades.

It was suddenly light enough to see what we needed to see and two Grenades were lobbed into the desired area.

The Bren Gun had been silent for some time now as indeed had the return fire from the Terrorists. The two men's nerves screamed with tension. They had been very anxious to be rid of the fully armed and primed Grenades which they clutched in their sweating hands. Where they were to throw them was an entirely different matter.

Eyes and ears straining for the slightest sign of exactly where the enemy was, but this was to no avail. There was no sign of them at all. Advancing most cautiously , they quickly found the spot where the enemy had spent most of the previous afternoon and evening keeping our patrol pinned down and at the same time having a good view of the man they had shot.

They must have legged it under cover of darkness just before first light either as a result of fear that we would surprise them or perhaps they had other orders that they must attend to. Whatever the reason, they were gone and our injured buddy could at long last be attended to.

The wounds he had sustained proved to be most serious and just how he had managed to keep firing bursts throughout the night showed extreme courage on his part. Not only had he kept the Terrorists away from himself and the rest of us, but he had also deprived them of the much valued Bren Gun.

Our patrol carried no Radio and I immediately sent a man off to the Fort to get us some help and to arrange for a Helicopter to evacuate our buddy. It still took us a few hours to get him to the Fort where he was picked up and taken to the British Military Hospital at Kinrara near Kuala Lumpur.

It proved to not matter that Morphine was not available on this occasion. The wounds that our man had suffered would have precluded the use of it anyway.

CHAPTER 13

The Operation which was based on the Fort, went on for some sixteen weeks and we found that life was much more comfortable for us all in "A" Squadron. This undoubtedly was due to the relief we felt from being in the safety of the Fort as opposed to virtually having to remain semi-conscious all the time when we slept in the open. There was of course the added bonus of us having properly cooked meals every day that we spent in the Fort. The food was plentiful and varied, which in turn was due mainly to the enhancement of Squadron funds as a direct result of the capture of the Courier which was covered in the last chapter. Everyone concerned with the Operation agreed that it was a resounding success but there was still that little cloud over the Squadron, we so badly needed to improve our kill record. The Poppy told us that we must not loose heart about this. If we were destined to bag a few Terrorists then we would do so. If it was not on the cards for this, then we should comfort ourselves by thinking that they were bloody scarred to death to come in to contact with "A" Squadron which he knew were a first class bunch of Jungle Fighters. I, and many others, thought this to be so much Bullshit but if it pleased him to think that this was the case, well let him think so.

The time came when we were to make our exit from the Fort and re-turn to Sungai Besi. Rumours abounded that we were to be air lifted by Helicopter back to civilisation but it proved that they were just that, Rumours. We would of course make our way out of the Jungle in the same way that we came in. On foot of course. The majority of the Squadron didn't seem to mind this at all as the homeward journey always seemed to be easier than the outward one. At least that was the theory in force at the time. However, this proved to be not the case when the Squadron had been on the move for less than a full day.

The time was around 1300hrs and as was the usual practice, when circumstances permitted, a mid-day Sitrep (Situation Report) was sent via the 62 Radio set back to Headquarters in Sungai Besi. Accordingly, the Sparks (Radio Operator) slung his Ariel rigging up in the trees and set about making contact with the Headquarters Operations Room. This standard procedure took place just to let the brains of the outfit know exactly where we were and to confirm that everything was going along OK. The transmission was on this occasion abruptly interrupted by HQ who demanded immediate air clearance in order to send a message to "A" Squadron Sunray. (This was the call sign of our Squadron Commander). The instructions were that he must take the transmission personally and he was to confirm when he was in a position to do so. "The Poppy" was informed and he at once took on the role of a Sparks and confirmed with HQ that they were clear to go ahead.

It must be remembered that all Radio traffic was by Morse code. Any attempt to transmit in clear (normal speech) just wouldn't get through if the distance was in excess of a few miles. Apart from that, the old Communist Terrorists were smart enough to try and monitor Radio contacts whenever they were able. They may not have been very clever at reading a good standard of Morse which was sent at a reasonable speed, but they certainly understood the English language.

The versatility of the SAS Officer was proven beyond any doubt when "The Poppy" took all this in his stride as if he never did anything other than operating a 62 set in the middle of the Jungle in northern Malaya.

We knew something was cooking as the break we were having at the time was now well past the normal time we would have if it was just a normal break. The word was soon passed from mouth to mouth that the Squadron was not going home just yet after all.

It seemed that the brains at HQ had obtained some information from an SEP, and the Squadron, being nearest to the target at the time, was to investigate and report back to HQ. Apparently this SEP wallah had really spilled the beans against the promise of a handsome cash reward and safe passage to a different part of the country. All his hopes and dreams hung by a thread and depended on how accurate his information proved to be.

There was supposed to be a very large cache of food and other goods plus an amount of ammunition that had been deposited in a dump and was meant for future use by the Terrorists. He said he knew the exact location of the dump as he himself had been in the party who had laid it down. He said it was buried below ground in the side of a Bukit (Hill) and the area was heavily covered with Bamboo.

Now this guy stood to make a few bob out of this and he insisted that if the soldiers were unable to find the dump, he would willingly go back into the Jungle to show them exactly where it was located. That offer was of course made, providing the soldiers would escort him, for should he be exposed to any of his former comrades, he would be dead meat for sure. It was therefore decided that he would be flown into the Fort by Helicopter and a small party from "A" Squadron would retrace their tracks back to the Fort and collect him. They would then escort him back to the place where the Squadron were bivouacked waiting for all this to take place. A four man escort were sent off before nightfall and they were expected to be back sometime around mid-day on the following day.

That evening "The Poppy" called an "O" Group (Orders Group) of all Troop Commanders. He gave them a run down of all the information that he had received and then they worked out the details of who would do what as they searched for the dump. Some of them were openly sceptical about all the fuss that was being made for what appeared to be just another simple task. After all, it was going to be something of a treat for them to be searching for something that everybody was fairly sure would be there for the finding. This of course was as opposed to making a soulless search for non-existent Terrorists who by now was becoming fewer and further between contacts.

"The Poppy" was shrewd enough to detect something in the general attitude of the Troop Commanders which indicated a certain cavalier approach was establishing itself in their minds. He scotched this right away by disclosing that although the SEP seemed to be honest about the dump and what was stored there, HQ had given a warning that all may not be what it at first appeared to be. It had certainly been known in the past that an SEP had come up with good solid information about certain things, and the Military had both bitten and swallowed it hook line and sinker as it were. What a surprise it had turned out to be when the soldiers had been led into a trap and were greeted by a large number of Terrorists who were of course expecting them. It was quite possible that this type of scam may be in the process of being played out right now with "A" Squadron 22nd Special Air Service, being cast as the fall guys. This gave the Sunray Minors (call sign for Troop Commanders) food for thought. Consequently they passed on to the Troop Members every word that "The Poppy" had said to them.

This was not the first dump that "A" Squadron had unearthed and they were all looking forward to the next day. If the last dump was anything like a yardstick to go by, there could indeed be some rich pickings to be had. There had been some quite amazing finds made by th soldiers, as the Terrorists seemed to have a thing about burying those things they either didn't quite know what they were, or perhaps thought the sale of such items might prove beneficial if they were kept for a while. Whatever the reason, they squirreled away many amazing things ranging from Artefacts to Janet and John books wrapped in a protective wrapping to preserve them while they were in store.

The SEP and his escort arrived just on noon the next day. He proved to be quite a young man who spoke excellent English and contrary to common belief that all Terrorists were undernourished and skinny, he was quite a healthy looking specimen. Perhaps this fact alone had given rise to the doubt that he was the genuine article. He was quite talkative and passed among the soldiers as if he had known them for some time and was indeed their friend. In all, he seemed to be a decent bloke and tried to make a good impression on all he came into contact with.

"The Poppy" did not approve of this fraternisation and quickly put a stop to it. In fact, he had the man tied by the legs and tethered to a tree, just in case I suppose.

A Sergeant from "B" Squadron who had a fair smattering of the Malay language had interviewed the SEP. This task proved to be much easier than had been expected, and it transpired that the Terrorist had an excellent grasp of Map Reading, which was more than could be said of some of my comrades. He readily pointed out the general area that he believed the dump to be located in and then suddenly became even more enthusiastic when the Sergeant pointed out a Bukit (Hill) which the map indicated that it was quite steep and also heavily clad in mature Bamboo. He became increasingly sure that this was the spot where he and his colleagues had laid the dump. He was them fed and quickly returned to his tether at the tree.

It was decision time for the men of "A" Squadron. They went over the general situation and discussed their plans and the possibility that they may be facing being trapped at the base of a Bukit. This would seriously restrict their means of escape should they suddenly be surrounded by a large number of Terrorists. After thinking it out thoroughly it became obvious that the soundest plan would be that we operate as a complete Squadron as opposed to any individual Troop taking on the task of checking out the location. One never could tell, caution was always the watchword as it was possible that we were under observation right at that very moment if it were a set up job.

Plans were re-appraised and maps closely scrutinised. It was finally agreed that the Squadron would approach the target from three different directions. One Troop would keep the back door covered, just in case anyone tried to leg it up the Bukit and attempt to make an escape down the other side. It was also agreed that we should all leave our current location with immediate effect. We were to move in the general direction of the target without giving away any clue what our intentions were, or even that we had in mind to attack the target area the next day. We needed to be as close as possible without giving the game away.

All this was part of our planned strategy to cater for the eventuality that the SEP had been telling "Porkies" and his pals were right now laying down a Grenade Ambush, or maybe even two or three for all the men of "A" Squadron knew.

We started out about mid-afternoon and moved as we had previously agreed. An early halt was called to the daily activities in the hope that this might indicate to the enemy, if they were present, that we were in no particular hurry to go anywhere and what was more, we didn't have much of an objective in mind right at that time.

The Squadron attitude was somewhat laid back at this stage but no one was kidding themselves. This was a serious bit of work we were about to undertake. The bivouac for that night was a rather hurried affair as we had become accustomed to sleeping on Charpoys (Wooden and Rope plaited beds) while living in the fort.

The SEP showed distinct signs of being nervousness, which became even more pronounced when he was tied up for the night. The presence of our two Iban Trackers sleeping close by him must surely have eliminated any thought of escape during the night. Whether his nervousness was because he feared that some of his former Comrades may decide to pay a visit, or perhaps he feared what the soldiers might do to him in the event that he was unable to point out the exact spot where the loot lay. He may have been having thoughts that the dump may have been cleared out while he had been in custody in Pudu Jail. Whatever the reason, it certainly seemed that the cat had got his tongue for he made no attempt to converse with anyone which was unusual for him.

Just after first light the next morning, the four individual Troops moved off and began to converge on the target area as had been previously been agreed. This was of course the most likely spot where the dump would be found if in fact it did exist. This movement of course, had all the added dangers of them coming too close to each other and mistakenly shooting up one another thinking that the movement in the Jungle signalled an imminent attack by some hidden Terrorist force.

It should be remembered that each individual Troop was highly trained to operate as an individual force, and it was alien to the way they thought for them to now be acting as part of a larger force. It was not that they were trigger happy but they had always been told that it was highly desirable that they got off the first shot, in any possible situation that may be a live contact. They were now faced with the instant question, "is it one of ours, or is it one of theirs"? I must admit that my nerves began to jangle a bit and I am certain so did those of my buddies.

The whole area was covered with Baluka (very tall Fern like plants) and extremely thick Bamboo which together made it extremely hard going. The SEP indicated that we were very close to the place and within a short time he signalled that we had arrived at the spot where the goodies were buried.

We didn't pitch in and start digging right away but we did carry out a thorough search of the immediate area, and after making contact with the other three Troops of the Squadron, we posted lookouts around the complete area. This we considered to be an added precaution as we would make sure that we would be warned if any unexpected visitors decided to call.

Under the guidance of the SEP we began digging wherever he indicated and it seems that no one was more surprised that he was when the first item was uncovered. In fact he visibly showed signs of relief as a broad smile spread across his face as if to say "I told you so".

The general area showed no signs of the ground being disturbed for some time and the dump had been made some two feet below the surface. Whenever it was possible to do so, goods had been placed in empty Kerosene Tins. These would be about fourteen inches square and perhaps some two feet deep. Each one had been individually sealed with a piece of rubberised sheeting which looked suspiciously like a bit of an Army Poncho.

We continued to excavate the immediate area and after a couple of hours or so we managed to unearth almost twenty tins and various other bits and pieces. The contents proved to be a sight to behold. There were about thirty Army 24hr Ration Packs, all unopened. Numerous boxes of Army Compo ration packs the contents of each box being intended to feed three men for four days. It was something of a surprise to fine three bolts of Khaki Drill Cloth. This was all brand new material and boldly printed on each bolt was the name of the firm who had manufactured it, the date that it had been manufactured and the address (in Liverpool) where it had been made. The date of manufacture was only about one year prior to us finding the stuff. It is truly amazing how the Terrorist Organisation managed to come by such things. There was something like ten or a dozen tins which were packed with Rice. This of course was the staple diet of the Terrorists. There were such things as Baseball Boots, Woollen Socks and a large amount of Tea, Sugar and Tubes of Condensed Milk, but perhaps the prize find was about five thousand rounds of 9mm ammunition. This was in very poor condition the entire amount being badly covered in verdigris or some such form of green mould. It was so poor that if it was to be used it could possibly be very dangerous to the person using it. There were some twenty four HE 36 Grenades and about ten or a dozen British Army 80 Grenades that gave off phosphorous smoke when discharged. All the Grenades appeared to be in fairly good condition and together with the two cans of detonators that were there, they would have caused someone some heartache oneday.

We finally unearthed what indeed was the strangest find of all and it was the last thing that anyone would have expected. Wrapped very carefully in a piece of the protective covering was a full set of Janet and John reading books together with many coloured pencils. What use these could have been to the bloodthirsty Terrorists, the Lord only knows.

Whoever had been their leader when this dump was laid down had been a man (or woman) who knew what they were about. They had chosen the dumpsite well and it had been prepared with much thought going in to it. It was most unlikely that any patrol would choose to linger very long if it were to pass close to the dump area as it was covered thickly with Baluka and Bamboo and was on the side of a Bukit which would be avoided at all cost by any patrol passing through the area. The tins had been laid separately with no more than three tins in any cluster. Clusters or individual Tins had been dotted around at random. This was of course a precaution against total discovery even if just one or even two clusters were discovered by the Security Forces.

It must be said that although the find was of great importance to us, it would most certainly be a great blow to the Terrorist Organisation and without the aid of the SEP it was most unlikely that anyone would have found it. Still as I have said before, he would be handsomely rewarded for his efforts and would also be shipped to a different part of Malaya to start a new life where his chances of being recognised by anyone was just a remote possibility.

There were a number of Sakai Porters who were kept at the Fort. This was mainly to cover any emergency portering jobs but it was also that they had nowhere else to go as the Terrorists had destroyed their villages and robbed them of all that they could, which wasn't much in the first place. These happy little guys were occasionally pressed into service. A number of them were now taken to the dump site for the purpose of carrying the goods found to the nearest point where they were to be collected by the Regiments transport and taken all the way back to Sungai Besi. Why this was so, I failed to understand, as they could have just as well been recovered to the Fort where they would be available for all to see. The poor old Sakai's were of course transported back to Sungai Besi along with the loot. This proved to be a rare treat for them for most of them had never been out of the Jungle where they lived, until now.

It was at this precise moment that my world seemed to have been tipped upside-down.

At the end of the Operation the Squadron was, as usual, picked up by the WOT 6's and returned by road to Sungai Besi. The trucks had barely rolled to a halt on the Transport Car Park at Sungai Besi, when the Orderly Room Sergeant appeared and was calling for Trooper Hebden to make himself known. I identified myself and was informed that I was to report to the Adjutants office immediately. I of course complied for after all, I was a good soldier who had never been in any sort of trouble throughout the whole of my service to date. Well, maybe I had suffered a small brush or two with the Redcaps (Military Police) on the odd occasion, which was only to be expected I suppose.

Reporting as instructed, I was ushered into the presence of the Adjutant. I stood mouth agape at what the officer was saying to me. A telephone call had been received apparently from the Mother Superior of a Convent in Penang. She had requested that Trooper Charles Hebden be sent to Penang with all speed to collect the woman he was to marry.

It appeared that the Convent, for whatever reason, had accommodated some female or other who had informed the Mother Superior that she was engaged to be married to a member of the Special Air Service. That member was apparently none other than me. I was resident at Sungai Besi Camp and the Mother Superior, anxious to be rid of the female I suppose, now wanted me to collect her and bring her back to Kuala Lumpur where she had said this coming marriage was going to take place.

I was completely and utterly gob smacked by the tale the Adjutant unfolded before me and I was fully prepared to deny any knowledge of a female in Penang. After all, how could I have said I would marry someone when I was already married and my wife was back there in the UK living with her parents?

It was obvious to me just who this female was in Penang. It could be none other than Bridie. But why oh why was she now in a Convent and not in the classy house where I visited her on a couple of occasions while the Squadron was in Penang? Apart from that, how or why had she involved me in a tale of marriage, which I certainly knew had not even been mentioned by either her or myself?

The Adjutant wanted this item cleared from his desk as quickly as possible and with just the bare minimum of words, he told me to get my arse into gear and get up to Penang and sort it out.

I really didn't have any option but to go up to Butterworth by train where I changed and took the ferry over to Penang.

I eventually arrived at the gates of Convent where I was eyed closely by a very old Nun. I stated the nature of my business which was very carefully considered by the Nun. She thought about it for some minutes it seemed, then she opened a side entrance and without a word being said, motioned that I should go in. Here a different Nun indicated that

145

I should follow her which I did, mainly because she spoke not a word but she did keep glancing round behind herself to make sure that I was keeping up. Perhaps she also wanted to make sure that I didn't slide off into some other part of the complex and commit some dastardly act that was forbidden to all residents let alone a visitor.

I eventually arrived at the door that bore the sign that this was the office of the Mother Superior. My escort gave me hand signals that I should stay where I stood, and then she disappeared after having first knocked and then waiting what was a respectable period of time before entering. She was back out almost immediately and waived me into the presence of yet another ancient Nun, but this one was different. She had a tongue and spoke with an Irish accent.

The old girl greeted me coldly and went straight into the questions which she had obviously pre-prepared as she kept checking on a hand written list, which I was unable to read from where I was sitting.

She asked me a variety of questions about Bridie, and myself. I told her nothing of any consequence thinking all the time that the best person I could talk to was Bridie herself. Perhaps that way I could get a clearer picture as to the state of the game, whatever that was. What on earth did she think she was playing at? Marriage indeed. I knew that I had never mentioned that word to her or anyone else for that matter. I loved my wife and missed her very much, but no, I would never have mentioned marriage to Bridie no matter how pressing was the urgency to have a romp between the sheets.

The old girl plied me with tea and biscuits but to no avail. I was saying very little in reply to her questions. All that I wanted right then was to meet Bridie head on and then I would be able to decide just what I should or should not say after I had heard her.

After almost an hour had passed since my arrival, Bridie was finally brought in and the Mother Superior stated that it was perhaps best if Bridie and I went into a small side room and discussed the situation together and then it could be decided what the best course of action would be. To my surprise she added that we must have lots to talk about as she fully expected that I would be taking Bridie back to Kuala Lumpur with me when I returned.

We moved to the side room which ran off from the Mother Superiors office. We were instructed that we should leave the door open while we talked. I knew that this was not only to let the old girl eavesdrop on what was being said, and there was no hanky panky, and she would make sure of that. I looked closely at Bridie now and the state of her shocked me. She looked to have aged ten years since I had last seen her.

She wore no makeup at all and her dress was not the usual fashionable thing she was used to. I thought that this was probably because she was here in the Convent and not outside in the real world. She told me that her German employer had attempted to rape her on more than one occasion and after his last effort, she had decided that enough was enough and she would leave her employment. She had very little money and the Convent was just about the only place she could turn to.

She said that she had tried to telephone my Regimental Headquarters but had been told that Trooper Hebden was away on Jungle Operations and it was just not possible to contact him. Apparently I had been her immediate thought when she had fled from her employer's house; she said she was absolutely certain that I would take care of her.

All this of course was delivered amidst floods of tears and many coy looks from behind her handkerchief. When I thought it all through later, I realised that this had been part of her ploy and she wanted to keep check on how things were going for her and how I appeared to be taking it. I explained to her as gently as I could that I was already a married man and consequently there was no question that I could marry her, not now, not ever. When I asked her what had given her the idea that I would do such a thing, she very quietly said that she thought I was married and she had made up the story just to get the Convent to take her in. She further put it to me that if I would take her to Kuala Lumpur, she could get herself a job and a flat and would be no trouble to me whatsoever. She shyly added that I would always be more than welcome to visit her whenever I wanted.

Memories of a picnic on a beach came flooding back to me at this point, and without any further thought on the subject, I agreed that I would take her with me the very next day.

On hearing this news the Mother Superior was delighted. She obviously wanted rid of the potential problem that had so suddenly been thrust upon her and she had indeed hoped that the matter would be resolved quickly. It mattered little that this young woman had told a pack of lies in order to be taken in, the end of the matter was now in sight as far as she was concerned and she just hoped that this nice young man was able to cope with the situation.

Bridie had obviously spun her the same story about her previous employer and this was the reason why all her personal belongings were still up at the house where she had been employed. The old girl agreed that she would recover the belongings and arrange to have them forwarded to Kuala Lumpur when Bridie had provided her with an address.

With all those details having been agreed, she discussed briefly with Bridie the position on finance which resulted in a cash advance being made to her, the sum of which was not disclosed to me.

I now found myself with a young woman in tow who I had promised to take away but not until the next day which was when the daily train would leave for Kuala Lumpur. She readily suggested that we take a room in a hotel for the night and it would be necessary that I attend to these arrangements as she had just one other thing to attend to before she left Penang. She said that she would be gone for something like one hour and that I should get settled in the room at the hotel.

When she had gone, doubts began to form in my mind. She had proved to be a skilful liar to the Mother Superior. How did I know if it were true about her employer and his amorous intentions? Perhaps this also was a complete lie and just an excuse to get away from Penang and down to Kuala Lumpur.

She was back within the hour and now that we were at last alone, all my doubts were dispelled by her as she used her womanly skills on me as we rolled on the bed provided in this, a second class hotel, or at least that's what it called itself.

The following morning we made our way to the Ferry Terminal in Georgetown at the start of our journey southward. To my surprise, as we waited to board, the two men who had shared our picnic that day on the beach came and spoke to us. The one who had suggested that I meet him and have a meal, apologised for not doing so and assured me that when he visited Kuala Lumpur he would make contact,(he didn't say how), and we could renew our plans as he put it. It wasn't until much later in the day as the train made it's excruciatingly slow way southward towards the capital of Malaya, that it occurred to me that there was something odd about them being at the Ferry Terminal and yet made no effort to board the Ferry. They seemed to have waited until Bridie and I had boarded and the Ferry had slipped its moorings at which point they had disappeared.

I didn't mention this to Bridie who seemed to have taken it all in her stride, almost to the point where she had expected a visit from them.

I was beginning to have grave doubts about my decision to take her to Kuala Lumpur. There was something that didn't feel right about it all. How come she knew these Chinese blokes? She certainly seemed to be at ease with them and it bothered me to think that there was definitely something between them and her. I decided that I must ask her about them, but not right now. I had more than enough on my plate wondering about accommodation for her and how very handy it would be for me to visit her, frequently if I wished.

I tried very hard to put all such thoughts of making love to her out of my mind, for the immediate future anyway. I also tried hard to console myself with the thought that I would install her in one of the many hotels in Batu Road and then she could sort herself out a job and perhaps even a little flat somewhere handy.

Having temporarily solved the immediate problem of Bridie, I tried to loose myself in my work with the Squadron. When I returned to Sungai Besi after my trip to Penang no one sent for me to ask how I had got on, it seemed that all had been forgotten. Accordingly I tried to put it from my mind but with little success I might add. The facts would come to my mind at the least provocation and that was when my mind was not fully absorbed by some task or other which temporarily commanded my full attention.

The days seemed to drag by for the whole Squadron as we were making ready for yet another Operation. At least this time we seemed to have drawn a decent one. We were to go to the Boh Tea Estate in the northern part of Malaya where rumour had it, there were quite a large collection of Terrorists who were apparently ruling the roost and making life thoroughly miserable for the whole of the Estate Staff who happened to live on the Estate. The Operation was not scheduled to start immediately as the Monsoon was almost upon us. To say that life in the Jungle was a bitch at this time of the year was indeed an understatement. Operations during the Monsoon season were avoided if circumstances permitted.

The Squadron was granted an extra two weeks R&R (Rest and Recuperation) and as was usual, the men decided that Penang was the place to be, yet again. After all everyone seemed to have enjoyed the delights of both the City Lights and the Piccadilly in addition to the home comforts of the Sandicroft Leave Centre. I decided that I would spend the two weeks in Kuala Lumpur in the company of a certain young lady who still lived in a seedy hotel in Batu Road. It had rather surprised me from time to time, when she was not available to see me on some of these occasions. When this occurred I tended to seek solace in the many Bars along the Batu Road. I was naive enough at that time to believe, in my own mind anyway, that she was putting in a little time searching for a job and perhaps a flat as well.

Consequently, I spent most of the two weeks period either miserable, or drunk, or even both of them at the same time, depending on what time of the day it was. I frequently went back to Sungai Besi but it was just not the same with all my pals being away. I invariably returned to Kuala Lumpur the same day as I had arrived and if not, it would be the very next day after that.

I was glad to see the end of the two weeks period and the return of the rest of my Troop who came with tales of great piss-ups and absolutely glorious dolly birds in the Dance Halls. I was not impressed and remained down in the dumps and not a little worried about the situation down Batu Road. I felt I was responsible for her being there and also that she had no visible means of support. I was giving her a sum of money each week, supposedly as a loan just to see her over. When I gave some extra thought to this, she never seemed to be short of cash which was apparent every time she opened her handbag. I began to feel that I was a bit of a chump who had got myself into a fix. I just didn't know what I could do about it.

The Squadron had only been back three days from their unexpected R&R when we were given some great news. We were all to go down to Singapore for a Parachute Training Course at the RAF Training School in Changi. Our turn had come at last and the spirit of the Squadron showed a marked improvement. We were once again to be split into four groups, which would of course be based on the four Operational Troops and all the odds and sods such as Store men and Cooks etc., would be absorbed by each individual Troop.

Being a member of No2 Troop I was in the first batch to be sent to Singapore which for me provided a good diversion not only from the Jungle bashing, but also the other matter which seemed to occupy my mind for the majority of the time.

All the basics of being a Paratrooper were taught at Changi. How to strap on your Parachute Harness. How to be responsible for the man in front of you in the "Stick" as you moved down the Plane to the exit door. How you should carry the Static Line of the man in front of you and cast it aside so that it did not become a hazard to the man behind you. We were shown a mock up of the Dispatch Controllers lights, which were operated by the Pilot at the appropriate time.

Next we were shown how the PJI (Parachute Jump Instructor) would stand at the Planes exit to see us on our way back to earth and how he would use the orders "Red On" (get ready to go) and "Green On (you should by now be on your way) and finaly "Go". If you heard this last order it meant that you were too slow into action. We were also told time and time again that we should always keep our feet and knees together both on exit and on landing. The theory behind this piece of information was that it protected all that was near and dear to you and it would be somewhat protected. There were also special instructions on how we should land, these we were encouraged to practice whenever the opportunity presented itself. In real life terms it invariably turned out to

151

be Heels, Arse and back of the Head when once more we made contact with terra firma.

Each man did of course collect all eight of the final White Nylon ties which was the very last link between Static Line attached to the Plane and the extreme top of the Parachute Canopy. These bits of Nylon were saved by a great number of the men who kept them for many years as a special good luck charm and a reminder of those first eight Parachute Jumps which each man must complete in order to qualify for their coveted Parachute Wings. They were something that was unique to them which also served as a reminder of days gone long ago, when to a man, their hearts went into their mouths and not infrequently I might add, the plug came out of the other end.

On completion of the eight descents we were considered to be proficient in the art of parachuting, however to satisfy the requirements of the Regiment, we were to undergo further training. We were to learn the art of jumping into the Trees of the Jungle. This was not possible in Singapore and we had to wait until we returned to the Highlands of Malaya to practice the art. We would report to Kuala Lumpur Airport each morning and draw Parachutes from the Packing Shed. We were then loaded onto an ancient Valetta Transport Plane which was fitted out for Parachuting. We would be accompanied by a Parachute Jumping Instructor (PJI) who I remember was not always at his best in the early morning. Off we would go to an area where the Trees we of a suitable height (bloody great big ones) and at the behest of the PJI we would step out from the Plane and experience the most appalling and terrifying crash landings amongst the branches of these hugely tall trees. On coming to rest, probably hanging by the unmentionables high in the tree tops, we would do a quick check mainly to see that we still had the prescribed two arms and two legs and that they were still attached to ones, by now, very sore body and they appeared to be still in reasonable working order.

If all appeared to be in working order we would then set about lowering ourselves to ground level by using a variety of different rigs which ranged from Webbing Strops to Canvass Briefs. (None of these worked very well and some of these caused a great deal of pain to some of the

Troopers). I am very pleased to say that things did improve as new methods were tried but the progress in this direction was very slow indeed.

After we had patched up any damage such as abrasions and cuts, this being just a training exercise, we marched out of the Jungle to be picked up by, what else, the old WOT 6's when we would be treated to yet another exciting ride back to Base. Here we would sit drinking Char Walla's Tea, and talking late into the night relating the daring feats we had undergone earlier in the day. Every man had landed in a taller tree than anyone else and the point at which his Webbing Strop had fallen short of him reaching the ground was far more than anyone had ever seen before.

The next day followed the same routine, and the next, and the next. It was all very exciting stuff but it did tend to start wearing a bit thin after a week or ten days.

There was a definite art to this tree jumping lark. On leaving the plane and going down to the canopy of dense trees below, it was very noticeable that when you came to just above tree top level there was always a cross wind blowing. This could be quite unnerving at times especially if you were not expecting it. You could be whipped away at a great rate of knots away from the rest of the Troop and thus become isolated and therefore very vulnerable. We quickly learned the art of steering the Parachute by pulling the Lift Webs (part of the Parachute suspension gear) just a few second prior to when you would normally have done and in this way counteract the cross wind effect somewhat.

We all eventually agreed that the safest and by far the most successful way to jump into the Jungle was to aim yourself at the tallest and most substantial of trees and attempt to get the 'chute canopy well and truly hooked up on it. You could then wriggle around a bit to make sure that all was secure and would stay put as you brought the absail equipment into play as you lowered yourself to the Jungle floor below (or as near as you could get to it).

Various methods of lowering were tried out, some being slightly better than others. Without a doubt the most notorious one was an arrangement which looked like a pair of outsize webbing knickers which had a metal ring sewn into the front part. These were worn underneath the Parachute Harness and were donned prior to fitting the actual Harness to your body. Strapped to your leg was yet another webbing bag which carried the coiled up Webbing Strop which you pulled out two or three feet from the bag and passing around your waist and through the metal ring which was sewn into the knickers. The loose end of the Strop was then securely fixed to a sturdy tree branch, one that would support you and all the equipment you carried. You were now ready to make your decent to the ground below, a matter of some 150 to 200 feet. The trees in Malaya were quite an awesome obstacle believe me.

The inventor of this miraculous equipment, whoever he or she was, had obviously never tried it out themselves or they would have binned it from the outset. You were supposed to have full control of yourself by feeding the Strop through your free hand (if you had one) from where it was coiled in the bag, round your waist and on through the Metal ring which was in front of your stomach after the style of a Bosuns Chair. Its greatest fault was not only did the Strop burn your hand as you attempted to control it but also the Metal Ring had a very nasty habit of turning under itself and digging deeply into you stomach. When this occurred, in some cases men suffered great pain and even lost consciousness. This particular equipment was quite rapidly taken out of service and the Boffins came up with an alternative which proved to be only marginally better but at least a little more useable and what we called "Soldier Proof".

It was essential that this lowering technique should be made as sound as possible as the Terrorists were not averse to staying and having a pot shot or two at the soldiers while they were dangling in the trees. However, once there were one or two of us on the ground and in a position to retaliate, they were off into heavy cover like Badgers with their arse on fire.(Similar to the Ford WOT6s).

After we had done some ten or a dozen descents into the trees we were considered to be ready to make airborne assaults on the enemy. We now looked forward to taking on these Terrorists who were supposed to be living it up in their own version of Jungle Forts and it was not to be long before we were called upon to do the business.

Alas, I was destined to miss this great adventure as I was summoned before the Adjutant on a second occasion.

On being ushered into his office, I was faced by two men who wore civilian suits and who I was sure I had never seen them before. They had copper written all over them. The Adjutant made no comment at all and the taller of the two men asked me to identify myself by giving my Army Number, Rank and Name which I did. They then disclosed that they were members of the SIB (Special Investigation Branch) and that they were going to take me to Kuala Lumpur where I was to be interviewed at Police Headquarters. I asked them what this was all about but all they would say was that all would be revealed when I got to Kuala Lumpur.

Now this turn of events was a complete surprise to me to say the least. No matter how I racked my brain I was unable to fathom the reason behind what was happening to me.

Once inside the Police Headquarters Building I was taken to a room where a third person, also dressed in civvies, sat behind a large metal topped desk. On first sight I took him to be of Chinese extraction, however, on closer inspection across the desk it was obvious that the Oriental touches were quite a long way back in his breeding. This third man was introduced as a Chief Superintendent in the Malay Police Force but I failed to catch his name.

He studied me across the desk for what seemed to be a long time, but on reflection I realised that this was only a matter of a couple of minutes. He never took his eyes away from my face and seemingly never blinked an eyelid during this time. This apparently was an essential part of his business for it had the effect of completely unnerving me. I averted my gaze from his stare and found myself becoming agitated in the knowledge that he knew something about me, something that I didn't even know myself. I began to break out into a cold sweat.

"You are Trooper Charles Hebden and you are serving with the 22nd Special Air Service Regiment out at Sungai Besi"? This sounded more like a statement than a question. I answered with a nod of my head. One of the men who had escorted me in from Sungai Besi said "please, for the benefit of the tape recording, would you kindly respond to questions by speaking your answers"? I stared at the man and rather abruptly said "yes I suppose I can, if you insist that I do, for the benefit of the tape of course".

What the hell was this? Tape recordings and guys acting as if they were Kojak about to nail down a suspect who had carried out a dozen murders. The man replied frostily "thank you very much".

The man behind the desk stared at me most intensely. "Do you have a brother serving in Malaya at the present time"? He asked without breaking his gaze on me.

What a question to have thrown at you right out of the blue. I was completely dumbfounded for almost a minute, and it was only later that day that I wondered how the Chief Superintendent had interpreted they delay. Perhaps he was thinking that I was deciding just what sort of a reply to give to the question. There was only one answer that I could possibly give. I looked him squarely in the eye and said "No Sir I do not". "Do you have a brother serving with the British Forces anywhere else apart from Malaya"?

Bugger me I thought, what was he going on about my brothers for? I had only one brother left alive and he was in the UK as far as I knew. It did cross my mind that it must have been all of 15 years or even more since I had any contact with him.

"No Sir, the only brother I still have alive is somewhere in the UK as far as I know, but I have not been in touch with him for some considerable time".

"Did this brother of yours ever serve here in Malaya at any time"?

I was absolutely flabbergasted. My brother had served in Malaya, but that was a very long time ago. As far as I could remember he had been involved with the RTO (Rail Transport Organisation) people at Kuala Lumpur Station. And now I remembered that he had told me some time ago that he had been the Bus Driver at Sandicroft Leave Centre in Penang for a while. I rather haltingly repeated these memories to the man behind the desk who sat in silence for some time pretending to read something from the papers scattered across the desk.

"Do you have any other relatives serving in the Far East Theatre at this time"?

"No Sir I do not".

I had just about had enough of this business. "What is this all about Sir"? I asked. "I have only just arrived back from a Tree Jumping session and here I am being questioned by you on some subject that only you seem to know about. I haven't even had a shower and I feel crummy and dirty as well as being dog tired and bloody hungry as well. If you can tell me what this is all about, I will do my best to answer any questions you care to put to me, but surely, let's not pretend and longer. I have done nothing wrong as far as I know, at least nothing that would warrant this sort of performance anyway".

"I don't suppose it could have anything to do with the couple of beers I had in a Bar up Batu Road and left without paying for them before we went on the last operation, could it"?

I was beginning to get angry with the situation now and they either came out and accused me of whatever it was that was bothering them, or they could provide me with transport back to camp. Whichever, we could then both get about our business".

"How much time have you spent in Penang since you came to Malaya"? The man behind the desk asked.

"I was on the Penang Operation which the Regiment carried out, and I have been there a couple of times since for leave with the rest of my Troop".

"What did you do during those leave periods there. Who did you spend your time with"?

"I don't understand Sir, I went on leave with the lads and did the usual things that soldiers usually do when they are on leave. You know, get pissed, have the odd bunk up and the like".

This semi Oriental behind the desk smiled for the first time since the interview had started. Apparently my answer had not only met with his approval, but must have stirred some long forgotten escapade or other which had been long forgotten until now. "I see", he said, "and did you have any special girl friend with whom you had this bunk up as you put it"?

Alarm bells began to ring in my mind. Could this have anything to do with that Bridie woman? What if they knew that I was responsible for bringing her down from Penang to Kuala Lumpur? What had I done? Was it illegal in some way or other? Anyway I was not the only one who was shagging her at the Hotel where she lived. I could name at least two others that I knew of for sure, and there was probably more if the truth was known. She was a bit of a goer was that Bridie.

"When did you first make the acquaintance of a European woman called Bridie Delaney"? He asked me direct.

I stopped for just a few seconds, "Bridie Delaney"? I asked enquiringly with raised eyebrows. I thought it was the same Bridie that I knew, but it was the first time I had heard the name Delaney. In fact I couldn't remember her ever disclosing her surname to me all the time I had known her.

"If you are talking about the Bridie that used to work as a Nanny for some German bloke in Penang, then yes, I do know her, but she doesn't live in Penang now, she lives here in Kuala Lumpur".

"Would it be correct to say that it was you who was responsible for bringing her here to Kuala Lumpur and establishing her in an Hotel in Batu Road, where you visit her from time to time"?

""Well yes I did bring her from Penang but that was only because her gaffer tried it on with her and she had to take refuge in one of them Convent places. Poor bugger had nowhere else to go and she looked to me to help her out so to speak".

"Could you explain to me why she turned to you, a married man, to help her out, as you put it"? "How was it that in her hour of need she turned to you for help? Perhaps there was no one else with whom she was on such familiar terms, for her to ask for his or her help"? He went on, "When did you first meet her and under what circumstances"?

I told him how I met her at the dance at Sandicroft and how she had invited me to visit her at her place of employment, which of course I had done. I left out the bit about getting pissing wet through on my way there. I thought he might make an issue about me getting my kit off and taking a shower. The Superintendent thought over what I had just told him and then sat fully two minutes without speaking.

"Well Sir, she was quite willing to have sex with me and that is something you don't turn your nose up at, not when the only alternative is the local Taxi Dancers. You don't know what you might bring home from them, if you see what I mean Sir".

"Apart from the sexual side of things, did she treat you in any other way, such as days out, or boat trips, perhaps a Picnic or something"?

My nerves began to jingle as I immediately thought to myself, this bastard knows something about that trip we took to the Beach in Penang. What was I to do? Should I broach the subject to him? Should I wait to see if he made anymore of it? Did he know about the two Chinese blokes who came and shared our Picnic? Did he know that we had spent most of our time there shagging? My mind was now ablaze with a myriad of questions about the whole affair. But there again I had done nothing wrong, and I thought, why shouldn't I admit it myself? It might be better to do that or the interviewer might think I am trying to hide something, particularly if he does know about it, and I was trying to hide the facts.

"Well Sir, we did go on a Picnic once to the beach. That was just after I met her. I hired a car for the day and we went to a beach on the Western side of the island. Lovely place it was too. Not far off the main road and very secluded too. No one else there when we arrived".

"Did you see any other people at all during the time you were there? Did either of you speak to anyone else while you were there at this beach? How many times did you go there, was it just the once, or perhaps it was a few times"?

At last, here we are I thought. This was what it was all about. I speculated with myself that he wanted the griff on those two Chinese blokes who came up and said they wanted to take me for a Chinese meal. They never did anyway.

"If it's those two blokes you want to know about, the two that came up to us on the beach and bummed a feed from us, well there was nothing in it. I thought it was a bloody cheek anyway, but she didn't seem to be at all bothered. As she had supplied the food, well, who was I to say anything? I would have done if she had wanted me to. I would have kicked their arses out of it in no time".

"Did she introduce these two men to you? Did she talk to them in Chinese or any other language that you didn't understand? You don't speak Chinese or Malay, do you"?

"No Sir I don't speak anything but the Kings English, and I didn't hear her say anything foreign either, but I must admit, she did seem a bit too much at ease with them and chatted away about things in general all the time they were there. I did think it a bit funny when the taller of the two suggested that he would meet me in Georgetown when he would treat me to a slap up Chinese meal in one of them posh restaurants. That's another thing which I though to be a bit strange at the time. He said he could contact me through Bridie when he wanted to meet me again. I thought he might be an arse bandit or something and said to myself, you will be bloody unlucky if that's what you are after".

"Would you be able to recognise these men again do you think if you were to see them again"?

"Oh yes Sir. I recognised them right away when they were at the Ferry Terminal the day I brought Bridie down to Kuala Lumpur. They came up and had a chat with us saying how they hoped we would have a nice journey and promising to make contact with me when either of them were next in Kuala Lumpur".

"And have either of them contacted you since then"?

"No Sir they have not".

"How often did you visit Miss Delaney at the Hotel where she was staying? Did she or you ever make any effort to find either a flat or a job for her and if so, who took the initiative in this search, you or her"?

"When I was not on Operations, I would pop round a couple of times each week but not always to stay the night. She didn't seem too keen on me staying the night for some reason or other. As regards the job and flat, well she never mentioned it to me and I never said anything to her either. I must say though, she always seemed to have plenty of money to spend, and it couldn't be cheap living in that place either. I don't know where she got all her money from but I do know that she used to have other visitors, other than me calling on her".

"Do you know the names of these other visitors"?

"Well Sir, I'm not the sort of chap who would drop his mates in it, but I can say that I think that there were other members of the Regiment who occasionally called on her".

"Is it that you refuse to disclose the names of these men, or is it purely and simply that you do not know of anyone for sure, and you are speculating that there may have been others"?

"I have seen blokes in the Bar at the Hotel and used to wonder what they were after. You know it's hardly the Ritz where she was staying, and it would not be the sort of place you would hang about in if you were having a night out on the town. I do know there was a Chinese bloke used to be sitting chatting and drinking beer with her sometimes when I called, but he always scapered when I came in".

"He was not one of those men from Penang was he? You said you would recognise him if you saw him again".

"No Sir, this bloke was a different one. Much shorter and fatter I would say".

"Did you ever see Miss Delaney with anyone other than the chap you have described? I mean the one who sat in the Bar with her.

"No Sir, I did not".

The Superintendent fell silent for what seemed to be for some minutes. He appeared to be weighing the job up before he went on with what came next.

"I want you to listen very carefully to what I am about to say to you Hebden. The reason why you are here right now is because this woman Delaney has reported to the authorities that you and your brother, who incidentally we have been unable to trace, have some sort of scheme going where you supply information to the Terrorist Forces. For these services you are supposed to receive payment, but here again we have been unable to detect any evidence of secret Bank Accounts which would be for your benefit. Now, can you think of any reason whatsoever why she would say such things, if it were not true? She also tells us that

161

you have told her all about it and ever since, you have given her a sum of money each week, which she says was supposed to keep her mouth shut about it. She further tells us that it is you who keeps her supplied with funds for the Hotel rent and you have refused to pay for a flat for her as you are quite content to support her, providing that she continues to grant you certain privileges on a regular basis".

"That's a load of crap" I said, "The truth of the matter is that she is always on the scrounge for cash, whenever I go and see her. I don't know why she was always on the tap because, as I said previously, she seemed quite flush whenever she opened her purse and that wasn't very often I can assure you. The other thing is that I never paid her rent at the Hotel. She never mentioned rent to me and I certainly never broached the subject. Beside, I just couldn't have done it even if she had asked me".

"Then you have no explanation as to why this young woman should make such allegations against you? I will tell you now Hebden, I believe what you have told me. This young lady has been very sparing with the truth I fear. It seems that you have let your basic instincts cloud your thinking, and you gave little thought as to what the outcome could be".

"I can't think why she should tell such lies" I said. "Maybe she got all bitter and twisted because when she asked me to take her to Penang for a long weekend I said I couldn't because I was not allowed. Apart from that, I just couldn't afford it".

The Superintendent seemed to renew his interest as a result of what I had just told him. He asked "Did she say why she wanted to go up to Penang? Do you know if she ever went up on her own, or perhaps someone else went with her"?

"I don't know what she did; she might have gone up with someone else. I just don't know. I haven't seen her for about three weeks. I haven't bothered. I'm a bit cheesed off with the whole thing. I wish I had never clapped eyes on her and I certainly rue the day I let myself be talked into bringing her down to Kuala Lumpur. What would my wife think if she were here now? What a Pratt I have been, and all for the sake of a quick bunk up".

The Superintendent studied me once again and then said "Now Hebden, as far as I am concerned, you have been a prize Pratt as you put it, and all over a bit of skirt, but now I shall send you back to your Regiment and you must forget all about coming here. No one, with the exception of your Commanding Officer, will be told about anything we have discussed and I would ask you not to tell anyone else. You were quite right about other members of your Regiment being involved, but like yourself they don't know about you, anymore than I shall tell you who they are. You will all do well to forget about the whole thing and remember, be very careful who you go jumping into bed with in the future".

I learned not long afterwards that the lady had been forced to take up residence in Pudu Jail after being arrested by the Special Branch. She was apparently suspected of being a Communist sympathiser with the specific aim of forging links between servicemen and local Chinese Communist leaders. She had apparently been under surveillance for some time. It was only when she became confident enough to move to Kuala Lumpur, with the assistance of an idiot, that the authorities decide to take a closer look at her and do a bit of digging into just who her contacts were and where they could be found.

That was the last I heard of Bridie Delaney, which proved to be a great relief to me. Whether she did time in Malaya or was returned to the UK to answer for her misdeeds, I never did know,and I didn't want to know either. I had been taught a lesson which I would remember for the rest of my days.

CHAPTER 14

As time went on, I became more and more disgruntled with the way things were going. I had been seen by the Commanding Officer after my visit to the Special Investigation Branch. He gave me a damned good roasting which I suppose he felt he aught to. He assured me that the matter was now closed as far as he was concerned and further commented that I was not the first soldier to have climbed into bed with the wrong woman. I must admit that I rather had the impression that he was keeping a tight reign on himself throughout the whole incident.

It was later made known to me by someone who was surely in the know, that under normal circumstances he would have booted me out of the Regiment. I learned from the same source that there were four men altogether who had been quizzed by the Special Branch as a result of bedding the Irish Colleen. It would seem that a loss of four men from the Regiment right at that time would hardly have gone down very well with the powers that be at the War Office. Consequently, as a means of self preservation I suppose, the C.O. could ill afford to send us all packing right at that time. As an alternative he decided that it was a case of least said soonest mended. His final words to me were that as the matter was now closed, I should not discuss it with anyone else in the Regiment and the episode would never be mentioned again.

This all seemed very well but I did notice, imaginary or not, that certain members of the Regiment tended to keep me at arms length where previously they had always been pally with me. Even some members of my own Troop seemed to have some reservations and life was far from comfortable although no one referred directly to what had gone on.

Here, yet again I was at a crossroads in my life. I was generally confused about the situation I now found myself in, and it was no one else's fault but my own. As the title of this book reflects, I had sinned once again, against what was considered to be the correct thing to do. Would I never learn?

I was rapidly approaching the end of my contract with the Special Air Service and it was time for me to give some serious thought as to what I would do with myself. I had a number of options open to me and I must apply my mind to the task of selecting just what I considered would be the best route for me to take. I was offered a second tour with the Regiment, which came as something of a surprise to me in view of what had gone on in the past, but there again, I knew that almost everyone had been given that option when the time came. This I felt was entirely due to the fact that they were desperately short of men. It was not that the end of contract men were leaving in droves, but that recruitment of replacements had failed dismally. The Gaffers of the Regiment felt that it was better to keep what they had rather than rely on new members turning up.

I decided that staying with the Regiment was not for me and duly notified them of my decision. I had become Pig Sick with the same old thing. Sure there was a certain excitement jumping into the trees but this was invariably followed by mooching around for an unspecified time looking for Terrorists that you knew damn well was no longer there. Never making any contact with the enemy was the soul destroying part of Jungle Patrols and most of the men began to resent being sent out on such missions. They knew it was just a waste of time. Apart from all that, we were expected to exist on very meagre rations as the 24hour pack left much to be desired. The powers that be, had hardly taxed their brains when deciding what the contents of these would be.

When operating in an area where there was no Jungle Fort, we had to sleep on the ground out in the open. The men were constantly cold and wet, or alternatively hot and wet, but without exception we were always wet right through to the skin. Then there was the nightly ritual of removing Leeches from various parts of your body. This always took the best part of an hour to carry out thoroughly. The creatures would bury their heads under the tenderest parts of your skin and then set about filling themselves with blood. If they were removed by just pulling them off the body, then you were inviting trouble as when they came away they left their heads under the skin. Within a very short time you had a septic place which was prone to rubbing itself even more and you ended up with a situation that was far from satisfactory. The approved method of making the blighters give up their quest for blood was to touch them with a lighted cigarette. They came away immediately, head and all. All these things accumulated and clearly pointed the way that I must make my choice. I decided that there must be far better ways of being a soldier.

It was while I was down in Singapore doing my Parachute training at Changi that I met a chap who had been in the Army Apprentice College in 1947 with me. In fact he had slept in the very next bed to me for the best part of two years. This young man had gone off into the REME (Royal Electrical and Mechanical Engineers) while I had been posted out to the RE Royal Engineers). The young fellow was now sporting a Warrant Officer Class 2 badge on his uniform while I was still just a Trooper. If I had not chosen to seek adventure and all that it offered with the Malayan Scouts in the Jungles of Malaya, well, how far up the promotion ladder would I have been now?

In the days that followed I became increasingly browned off with my lot and my thoughts increasingly turned to the young man I had met in Singapore and all that he had apparently achieved since leaving Boy's Service.

I was now in a position where if I exercised my right under my contract and was to opt for a transfer to the REME. I considered that this would be the right move for me. Accordingly, I consulted the Squadron Office who in turn referred me to the Regimental Orderly Room. I was assured that all that could be done would be done, and when the time came, I was posted to the REME just as I had requested.

CHAPTER 15

I was first sent to the Command Workshops right there in Kuala Lumpur. I had rather been hoping that I might be sent to someplace other than Kuala Lumpur, after all I still had bad memories of the Irish bird and all that went with it. I need not have worried however, for after an initial assessment of my capabilities and a check on how much of my Apprenticeship I remembered, I was posted up Country to an Infantry Workshop which was situated close by the town of Ipoh.

It was here at this workshop that I set about this soldiering business with "mucho gusto". I was determined that I would catch up in the promotional stakes, which I seemed to have missed out on so long ago. I was fully aware that my best chance of success could be achieved by hard work. Coupled with this I made sure that my conduct was exemplary and that my turnout was second to none. This paid off as within three months of my arrival I was once again on the move.

I was promoted to the rank of full Corporal (two stripes) and was selected to head up the REME element attached to the Motor Repair Section of the 1/6th Regiment of the Ghurka Rifles. This outfit was also close to Ipoh so being posted to them meant that I just had to go to work at a different Army Camp every morning.

Again I set out to impress by working hard. I was informed that the post I was filling was meant for a Sergeant and this in itself spurred me on, as if a promotion was in the offing, it was going to be mine. I was always there or thereabouts if any of the unit's motor transport ailed anything, and I got along very well with the Ghurka soldiers who drove the vehicles. At this time the Army still had National Service Conscripts within its ranks and all those under me when I was with the Ghurka's

167

were such people. They were not interested in the Army or promotions in any way shape or form. Their sole interest was in getting back to Blighty and back into Civvy Street.

In spite of all my efforts I remained a full Corporal for the entire year that I remained there. It was after the completion of that year that I was informed that I had now come to the end of what was considered to be a full tour of duty in the Far East . I was now to prepare myself for my return to the U.K. where after a spot of leave, I would be re-allocated to another Unit somewhere in Europe this time.

Oh how I hoped that this time I would be posted to some exciting place, perhaps Germany or the like. I would then be able to have my wife with me and I could settle down to something that was called Family Life.

I was to be disappointed yet again. I was shunted around England going from one Unit to another, where it seemed that the British Army was undergoing difficulties when the National Service started to run down and manpower became scarce. I suffered a couple of postings to holding Units where the daily chore seemed to be nothing else but an excuse for giving me something to do until they could decide just where to send me where I could at least do something constructive. It was bloody soul destroying and made me sort of wish that I had signed for another spell with the SAS Regiment.

Then came the big day. I was to be posted to Germany. No, they couldn't tell me exactly which Unit I was destined for, but all they could tell me was that I would first go to a holding Unit in Hanover. That was it.

I arrived in Hanover and the daily routine was much the same as it had been in the U.K.

It took some six weeks before the order finaly came that I was to be posted to a Workshop which supported a Royal Engineers Bridge Building Unit. Believe me I was absolutely pig sick at the way I had been pushed from pillar to post but at last it seemed that I was to have a purpose in life and I could get on with my soldiering.

I enjoyed my life in Hanover where the Workshops were based and set to once again to make myself noticed by virtue of my hard work and of course, when we were on a Regimental Parade, I made sure that my turnout was second to non. It worked once more apparently, for within six months of my arrival, I received my third stripe and became a member of the Sergeants Mess which had been my primary goal for sometime.

The Captain who was in charge of the Workshops was a fatherly figure, and it was obvious to me that he had a wish that I should get on in life. Within a very short period he sent for me and asked if I would be interested in sitting the entrance examination for a place on the REME's Armament Artificers Course. He felt that I was now ready to do that, and of course success at it would guarantee my way for my promotion through Staff Sergeant and onwards to Quartermaster Sergeant and eventually to the top rank of a Warrant Officer Class 1. He emphasised that if I was able to achieve the WO 1 Rank at an early age, then there was every possibility of me receiving a Queens Commission which of course would mean a great difference to my Pension Rights which would be awarded to me when I had served for a total of Twenty Two Years in the Army.

This I liked to hear and after discussing the whole thing with my wife, I decided that it was the thing for me to fight for and I quickly agreed with the Workshop Commander that I was up for it.

I eventually sat and successfully passed the entrance examination for entry to the Artificer Training Course which was to be held at Bordon in the U.K. It was only a matter of six or seven weeks before I was transferred to Borden to start my course.

On completion of the course I was promoted to Staff Sergeant and then on to a Royal Signal Unit where I was in charge of the Workshop responsible for all the Motor Transport which the Unit used in their day to day exercises. It is strange how some things come about but it was while I was serving in this appointment that a great opportunity presented itself to me and I was both quick to appreciate it and to the opportunity in both hands as it were.

In the first instance the LAD (Light Aid Detachment) Commander reached the end of his service and left the Unit to return to Civilian Life. There was apparently another Warrant Officer Class 1 who had been nominated for the post but he would not become available for some six months or so. This in turn left the Warrant Officer Class2 (Quartermaster Sergeant) in charge, while I was left to cover the duties which were his, in addition to those that were by their nature, my own.

I was a very busy chap, but I didn't mind as when the annual reports came out on how one was behaving as a Senior N.C.O. I came out of it very well and received a grand report.

This state of affairs lasted some six or seven months when suddenly the Acting LAD Commander was suddenly stricken with a terminal Illness which necessitated him being discharged from the Service and returned to Civilian life.

Right at this very point I received a posting from REME Records which to my absolute delight, I was to go to Hong Kong, a place I had always wanted to go to.

The post I was to fill was an accompanied post and accordingly I would be able to take my family with me to the Far East for a three year period. Life had seemed to have turned up trumps at last.

Now there is a saying that "All's well that ends well". I had always been a firm believer in that but alas it was not to be so in this case. Hard on the heels of the initial letter informing me of my posting, there came a second letter which addressed all the trials and tribulations which befell the LAD attached to the Royal Signals Unit right at that time. If I was to proceed to Hong Kong the Unit would have no Senior N.C.O. who would be responsible for the day to day running of the Workshops. No Warrant Officer Class 1. He was now a civilian. No Warrant Officer Class 2. He had become too ill to continue.

Well as we are at present quoting saying, as above, it would appear that the one about "It's an ill wind which blows no one any good". You've guessed it. My posting was to be delayed for three months to allow REME Records to manoeuvre three Senior NCOs to be posted to the LAD. There was an additional benefit for me in this communication, I was promoted to Warrant Officer Class2 and made the temporary Commander of the LAD. It also promised that my posting to Hong Kong would be honoured when all the changes had been brought into effect. Talk about two Birds with one Stone. Things were definitely on the up.

The Military machine did indeed honour their promises. I together with my family, were flown to Hong Kong and settled in a magnificent flat at Kowloon Tsai which is just across a small stretch of water from Hong Kong Island itself. We were all very happy indeed.

The happy state of affairs got even better when I was informed that I would take charge of a detachment workshop looking after a Company of the Brigade of Ghurkha's who went under the name of The Ghurkha Transport Company. All this seemed fine to me at the time but boredom started to set in after a couple of months. You see the place was staffed by local Chinese Fitters who couldn't speak English, at least they said they couldn't, so I was stuck out at the detachment six days per week with no one to talk to except the Chinese Foreman whose English was somewhat limited. He only understood what he wanted to understand and my part in the running of the workshops was somewhat curtailed.

Although life was very pleasant in Hong Kong I began to think that there must be more to life that staring out of an Office window wishing that the time would pass a little more rapidly.

My three years tour of duty passed oh so slowly and it came as something of a relief when the time came for my family and I to return to the United Kingdom.

After a spot of leave, I once again reported to the R.E.M.E. Depot to find that I was now to be posted to Western Germany where true to form, I would take charge of the day to day running of a Vehicle Workshop which was responsible for the maintenance of the vehicles used in transporting Guided Missiles and their Launching Platforms.

This was quite a large set up which was Commanded by a R.E.M.E. Captain who was supposed to be aided by a WO Class 1 Artificer. I didn't like either of them from the start. It wasn't just that I thought little of the pair of them, for neither of them were what you could call efficient. My attitude to the Craftsmen who worked as fitters (Vehicle Mechanics) in the workshops was that I would recognise a good job well done and as a result I would give the chap concerned a few extra hours off work.

Oh dear me. When this became apparent to the Captain and his side-kick the fertiliser hit the fan so to speak. What did I think I was doing? Why did I not consult them before doing it?

The truth of the matter was that they had never been able to gain the respect of the workshop staff, probably because they just had no idea what went on beneath the bonnet or the Mighty Antar Trucks that were being serviced and maintained by the workshops. Alas I in my own way, told them just what I thought of them. This resulted in the Captain ordering the workshop to work overtime not only in the evenings but also at the weekends too. They thought that this would be a good way of showing that as I had given some of the lads an afternoon off occasionally, I was getting behind with the scheduled maintenance of the Workshops. This I am afraid was just not so and I told both of them that it was not. I was quickly informed by the Captain that he didn't like my attitude and it was his intention to report me to the Brigade Headquarters for disciplinary action to be taken against me.

I was bloody fuming at this and told him I would welcome the chance to visit the Brigadier when I would be able to give him a picture of just what was going at 39 Missile Regiment Workshops.

It was on an exercise on Hohne Ranges that one of our Cranes had broken down and the young lads who had been sent out to fix it had run into some sort of difficulties. When I heard of this, I jumped into a Land Rover and made my way to the Map Reference where the casualty was supposed to be. It had been a long day and apart from the snow coming down like sheets of the Daily Mirror and Ice everywhere, I was just about knackered. Still they were my lads that were in trouble and I saw it as my duty to go to them and see what was what.

I duly found them, they were rolling around on the cold wet earth trying their best to fit a new Propeller Shaft and a Lay Rub Coupling. Now these lads were newly out of the Boys School of Army Apprentices. I could see immediately that the job was probably beyond their capabilities them being newly into the Workshops. I asked who was in charge to which they seemed to be at a loss for the answer.

I collard one of them and questioned him further only to learn that the Warrant Officer Class1 had ordered them to accompany him to the breakdown. Upon their arrival he had bid them to get to work but he himself failed to get out of the Land Rover to assess just what the problem was. Within minutes he had fled the scene. I suppose this was to guard himself from being asked for advice by one of the young lads.

I got underneath the Crane and was having a look at the thing when suddenly I felt a tap, tap tapping on the sole of my boots. Who the hell was this I wondered and shuffled my way out from under. I stood up and was confronted by the Brigadier himself. He asked me what I was doing out here on the Ranges at this time of the day. Now I would have thought that it would have been obvious even to a blind man, but apparently not so.

I'm afraid I did go over the top at him, which he clearly did not approve of. In my anger I slated the Warrant Officer Class 1 for leaving these lads to fend for themselves. I slated the quality of these lads who had just come out of Boy Service, saying they had been ill prepared for soldiering in the raw as it was. Then I am afraid I blew him a gut full. He seemed to be not surprised when he asked me my name to which I added that I was waiting to go and see him a Bielefeldt as my Workshop Commander seemed to doubt my motives for the way I ran the Workshops. He promptly jumped into his Land Rover and disappeared across the Ranges.

I am afraid I never did get to see him at Brigade Headquarters. I was posted back to the UK. There are no prizes offered for guessing where I was posted to. You've got it. The Army Apprentices College at Hadrian's Camp in Carlisle.

I had sinned yet again and was now being punished for it. The Apprentice Colleges were not the most popular of posting in the R.E.M.E. I was expected to act as a Nursemaid to the --

Apprentices and the teaching of the way they should go on when they went out into Man Service, well I am afraid this took second place.

CHAPTER 16

Life at the Army Apprentices College as an Instructor turned out to be real trial and I knew immediately I arrived that this was not for me. There was little doubt that I was being punished because of what I had said to the Brigadier about the products coming out from the Apprentice Colleges. They may well have quite a good standard of theory in their given trades but as regards putting their knowledge into practice, well it just didn't happen. I was soon to find out why when I had been at Carlisle for a very short time.

The way that these lads, all potential soldiers when they moved on into man service upon reaching the age of 18, was to my mind anyway, little short of a mamby-pamby existence. They were all but spoon fed and were in no way being prepared for life at the sharp end as it were.

I was a soldier with a not an inconsiderable amount of service both at home and overseas, and some of that spent on active service, but none of the Officers at the College seemed to care two hoots about that. The truth of the matter seemed to hinge on the fact that the complete staff, from the Commandant down to the most junior Lance Corporal, who was a Regimental Policeman, all were in the twilight years of their Military Service. You know, not long to go to my Pension and I must not rock the boat and keep my nose clean at all costs. If I had been aware of these facts when I blew off at the Brigadier perhaps I would not have belittled the Apprentices but instead I would have had a go about the way they were being brought up by old farts. Who knows, perhaps I would never have been posted there, perhaps he might have agreed with me. Ah well, it was not the first time I had let my mouth run away with me, and suffered the consequences at a later date.

I was treated to numerous embarrassments, things like having to spend a complete weekend confined to the College Buildings. There was no going home for me to see my wife and kids. I had to remain on stand by to either summon immediate attention myself or, alternatively summon the appropriate authority to render attention to any unfortunate Apprentice who suffered a mishap of any nature.

At least once each month I was detailed to roam the streets of Carlisle accompanied by two Senior Apprentices. We were supposed to be there to ensure that no one attacked the little darlings from Hadrian's Camp. . The truth of the matter was that almost all of the Apprentices frequented the Public Houses, at that time they were State run and sold a damned good pint, the youths, after say, a couple of halves, looked for trouble with the local lads and we had to break up many a jolly, to save the little darlings from getting a bloody good hiding I might add. Of course if I should decide to take the names of our lads and order them back to camp there and then, I would be treated as if it was I who had caused the bother for I would be summoned to appear the very next morning before the College Adjutant who would carry out an inquest as to why and how I had dared to take such an action.

The Army Apprentice College, Carlisle was not the place for me and I made it quite clear to them when I applied for a posting back to a unit where I would have a real job to do and put being a Nursemaid behind me. I was refused and told straight forward that here I was and here I would stay right up to the end of my Military Service.

"That's what you think mate" I told the Chief Clerk in the Orderly Room. At this point I saw little point in unsettling my family and therefore made enquiries about what the form would be if I applied for discharge from the Army and became a Civilian once more. I of course said nothing to me wife or anyone else for that matter about me considering packing the whole thing in. When the answer came back I felt a bit downhearted about the idea. Apparently I would loose all my rights to a Pension and would however, receive a lump sum the value of which would depend on the actual date that I wanted to leave the Services.

You see although I was credited with 21 years and 180 days service if I were to take my discharge on the 1st March 1969 I would not be en-

176

titled to any Pension, as they said that my time in the Army Apprentice College, where I served from 1947 to 1950 did not count towards an Army Pension. I was shattered at first hearing this news but after really thinking it over seriously I decide that I should put it to my wife, or as we had always done when a serious decision arose, we would have a family conference about it in order that we all had a say in what we should do. I calculated that in order to qualify for the Pension I must serve on for another 2 years and 184 days to bring my total service up to the required 22 years in total. The thought filled me with absolute horror.

The Christmas duties list appeared on Part 1 Orders and I must say "not to my surprise", I had drawn the short straw as I was listed as the Duty Warrant Officer for the coming Christmas Day. Now the number of Apprentices that would be present throughout the Christmas period would be something less that a dozen. These were the Apprentices whose parents were themselves working overseas and the result was that they had nowhere else to go. Tough Titty I thought. What about my wife and kids, they would have to eat Christmas Lunch without their Dad as he would be wiping the noses of ten or a dozen other kids and all because of the fact that their Parents had probably had the foresight to put the little buggers into the Army Boy Service to relieve them of the troubles they may encounter if they were allowed to stay at home with Mummy and Daddy.

Christmas 1968 proved to be a non event for the Hebden family. The frame of mind I was in at that time made me determined that this would never happen again if I had anything to do with it. Now I am fairly sure in my own mind that I used the Christmas thing as a means of satisfying my own wishes. I was having no more of the British Army and was giving serious thought about moving to South Africa, complete with family. The South African Government had made approaches on two occasions asking if I would consider serving in their Special Forces they would apparently welcome me with open arms. Quite how they were aware that I was ex S.A.S. I know not, but the opportunity appeared to be there if I cared to take it up.

Our family conference was held in January 1969 where the main topic for the children seemed to be where we had lived during the past few years. Hong Kong was a definite favourite with them, but my wife and I had the Pension bit uppermost in our minds. The children looked on this subject as "it's only money, what the hell we'll get some more. Let's live a little". (Providing it is in Hong Kong).

At the end of the Christmas break and at the start of 1969 I returned to duty and immediately requested that I be discharged from the Army at my own request. A few days later I confirmed with the powers that be, that I would leave the Service on March 1st 1969. I really had no idea how I was going to earn our daily bread at that time but in true Mr Macawber fashion, something was bound to turn up.

I had been told that I was wasting 18 years of my life by leaving right then, but I cared not one Fig. I had always been a firm believer that as one door closes, another opens. I had done the deed then and I would stand by the decision which in the end had been mine alone.

CHAPTER 17

With what at first seemed to be a newly found freedom, I tried a number of jobs but they all seemed to be very mundane to me. Alas none seemed to suit me. When someone employed me, I invariably found that there was a long established little Hitler in the system somewhere who was determined to get right up my nose. Consequently after a couple of clashes, I decided that my only way forward was to become a self employed person. At least in this way there would be no one to antagonise me with their petty stupid ideas. I would be my own boss, but what field would I enter? What would put bread on the table for my family and yet at the same time provide the challenge that I so desperately sought.

I still had the South African idea niggling away on the back burner of my mind. I must not leave it too long or they may change their mind.

I was to try my hand at being an Insurance Assessor at my first attempt. The work proved to be fine as I could get out and about being a free man. Furthermore I could progress at my own pace without anyone breathing down my neck just to see what I was doing. There was however a down side to things. The biggest snag I found was that the cash seemed very slow in putting in an appearance and having no pension coming in from the Army; well I didn't have a bottomless pocket with which to meet my outgoings. Apart from that it was not a very exciting prospect if I had to go and have a look at some old dear's carpet which she swore that it had become burnt through a coal falling from the fire grate. The fire marks always looked as if they had happened some considerable time ago and I couldn't help but think that the very sad carpet had been the subject of a good number of claims previously. I always signed the claim in approval and the old dear would receive a small sum from the Insurance Company in due course. Oh what a dashing and exciting existence that was proving to be. (I wonder who they gave the job to when a Bridge collapsed into a river which resulted in multi million pound claims from a number of concerns including those who had lost their lives and vehicle in the tragedy.) Never mind, one must learn to crawl before one can walk and one must then learn to walk before one can run. ?????

I next purchased a Newsagents shop. At least this would provide the instant cash flow that I felt I would very soon be in a position where the need for this would have an increasing part to play in my daily life. The children were growing up and the growing bit seemed to be aligned with their growing demands for funds which I was expected to provide to maintain them in the style to which they had become accustomed.

I was not cut out to be a Newsagent. This was apparent on the first day I took over from the man I bought the business from. An Old Girl gave me a right dressing down because the needle threader, promised in the previous week's issue of the "Peoples Friend" magazine, had not been present in the issue which had been delivered to her house that very day. I advised the Lady that if my services were deemed unsatisfactory by her, she was at liberty to get her copy of the said magazine elsewhere. I lost a customer on that day but I was to lose many more in the days that followed.

Believe me, it was no small relief to this Newsagent when a small man with moustache and Bowler Hat presented himself one day saying that he was from the Local Council. He informed me that it was the intention of the Council to knock down my shop in order to make way for a new shopping centre and would I be interested in taking on one of the new units which had been designated as a Newsagent's. I told him that he should offer such a golden opportunity to someone else.

I packed up in two months and received a small sum of money as compensation from the authorities when they completed a Compulsory Purchase Order on the Premises.

Easter holidays came round and the children were their usual irritating selves having nothing much to do except annoy Dad who was now listed as unemployed. Although we were not flush with cash we decided, as a family, it would do us all a power of good if we were to get away on holiday for a few days. We would take a Caravan Holiday in North Wales, which was about as far as our budget would stretch at the time.

We arrived on a Saturday and it was raining. We rose on the Sunday morning only to find that it was still raining and we were faced with yet another day all cooped up together in the Caravan. This prospect did very little for my holiday spirit, which was already at a very low ebb. I asked my wife if she would like to come with me to hunt down some Sunday Papers. The children all clamoured to come with us but were soon pacified when I told them that I would book somewhere nice where we could all go to eat that evening.

After a fairly comprehensive tour of the town Barmouth, we eventually secured the papers and then set about finding a Pub where we could eat that night. After finding a number of prospects it was some half an hour later that it seemed that our world had gone into reverse and I said, not for the first time either, "why did I ever leave the bloody Army"? What had caused this oft-used comment to be trotted out at this time was our discovery that this being Wales, and this being the Sabbath, the Pubs, which were now shut would remain in this mode until opening time the next day. Despite a further search there were no food shops open either. This of course meant yet another sumptuous meal based on baked beans and tinned tomatoes was all that the Hebden family had to look forward to on this the second day of their holiday. It was still raining by the way.

We returned to the Caravan and gave the children the good news knowing full well what the resultant bleating and shimfing would be. We were not to be disappointed. In absolute disgust I turned to the Sunday Telegraph and made my first choice the Situations Vacant pages. Being an unemployed person I always made it my standard practice to view these pages thoroughly before looking what the rest of the world seemed to be up to at the time. I scoured each section line by line, even those that didn't apply to me directly they all came under close scrutiny. Eventually there was only the General Classifieds left. These were in small print and each one took up only three or four lines at the most.

Suddenly I was fully switched on. I even forgot about the prospect of the Baked Bean's Supper. There it was, "WANTED. Ex Serviceman. Must be of Warrant Officer standing and be fully qualified in Mechanical Engineering (Motor Vehicles). To teach in a Technical College in Central Africa (Malawi)". It went on to say that family passages would be paid and a Schooling Allowance was available. Furthermore it promised a Gratuity on completion of tour and the Contract would be renewable.

I read it through two or three times and then breathed a great sigh of relief. At long last here was just such an opportunity that I had been searching for, a job that seemed to be tailor made for me. I re-checked all the requirements the advertisement specified and was more than happy that I fitted the bill exactly. I turned it over to my wife to read the advert and she immediately showed her enthusiasm and appeared to be no less excited than I was at the prospect.

The first thing she asked me was "Where on earth is this place Malawi"? I am afraid we all drew a complete blank as none of us had any clue except that it was in Central Africa. The Advertisement said it was. As for myself, I neither knew nor cared very much where Malawi was. I was too excited thinking about the possibility of getting out abroad again. My total contribution to the general discussion going on was that it was somewhere overseas and that was good enough for me.

The rest of Sunday was awful. The children squabbled about insignificant little things. I was grumpy all day and my wife was at her wits end thinking about what she was going to feed her brood on that evening. And by the way, it continued to rain all the rest of that day.

When we found it was still raining on the Monday morning we held one of our famous family conferences in the Caravan which by now we were all thoroughly fed up with. We discussed the idea of kicking our Welsh Caravan holiday into touch and shooting off home there and then. The vote was unanimous and chuffed me up no end. We packed up in record time and were on our way within thirty minutes. I would now be able to follow up the advert which we had taken such an interest in. I couldn't wait.

It was still raining but somehow that didn't seem to matter any more.

The first thing I did when we arrived home was to dig out a world atlas and search for this place Malawi. The atlas, being rather old, showed nothing resembling Malawi. Determined not to be beaten I made a bee line for the local Library where a very knowledgeable young lady informed me that the country which was now known as Malawi was formerly called Nyasaland and had been part of the Central African Federation together with Northern Rhodesia and Southern Rhodesia. She added that these later countries were now known as Zambia and Zimbabwe respectively. They had all parted company when the Federation had collapsed in disarray and each of the three members was now independent countries in their own right. Each country had a Head of State and Doctor Kamuzu Banda was the President of Malawi.

I wasted no time at all writing to the address given in the Sunday paper and requested an application form for the post advertised. The form arrived just a few days later and I filled it in and returned it the very same day together with my C.V. which incidentally, I had prepared some time ago.

As is always the case with these matters, things never move fast enough for the applicant. Consequently I found myself becoming increasingly agitated about the situation. At that time I had managed to get part time work in a Bookmakers shop in the high street. The job was hardly taxing and after all I needed something to do with my time while I waited for an answer to my application. Every time I rang my wife to see if there had been any response, when her answer was negative she said she could almost feel the disappointment in my voice coming down the telephone. She always tried to placate me by saying that perhaps it would come in the following days post. A week went by and this stretched to a fortnight. I had all but given up hope when at last a letter arrived inviting me to London for an interview. The letter stipulated that the only document I should take with me was my Army Certificate of Service Book (Army Form B.108).

My first thought was that I would take Jean, my wife along with me as it would be a chance to have a day out in London which was something we had not done for quite some time. On second thoughts

I wouldn't take her with me as the interview may take a long time and she would have to wait around for me with nothing much to do. Anyway I would see what she thought about it and we could decide later. In the event we both decided it would be more sensible for me to go alone as in this way I would only have myself to worry about and not have my mind wandering worrying if she was O.K.

The letter I had received stated that I should present myself at Milbank Chambers at 0900hrs and it was just five minutes to 9 o'clock when I entered the reception area there. I told them at the reception desk who I was and why I was there. A rather stunning young lady, giving me a ravishing smile, told me to take a seat in the Foyer and wait. I didn't have to wait long when an equally pretty young thing came asking for me by name.

Milbank Chambers proved to be a real Rabbit Warren for it took some minutes just following the escorting young lady to an office somewhere on the third floor. I recall thinking that I didn't mind the length of time it took after all the scenery was mind boggling, if you know what I mean. The young lady tapped on the door and entered announcing Mr Charles Hebden, 0900hrs. She then requested my Military Certificate of Service saying that it would be returned to me when the Interview was over.

I was shown into a comfortably furnished office where there were three men, two of them were obviously serving Military Officers, or they could have been recently retired. Anyway they bore the unmistakeable mark of Army personnel. The third man however came from a different mould. He was a typically weedy looking bespectacled Civil Servant type. All three sat behind a table which was covered in green baize material. The guy in the centre of the three, the Civil Servant type, greeted me and directed me with a wave of the hand to occupy the single chair which was at the opposite side of the table to the three interviewers.

Each one in turn questioned me on a variety of subjects none of them I thought to be of any significance to the post that had been advertised. As a matter of fact one of the military types did ask me if I knew how to bleed brake shoes and when I explained to him that brake shoes could not be bled but the hydraulic cylinders which operated them must be bled to expel all the air which might have entered the system, well he just looked at me and smiled but said nothing in return. As a matter of fact he said very little after that. The questions which were mainly put by the other two didn't seem to be leading in any particular direction and I quickly came to the conclusion that apart from the Civil Service type, the other two were not in the least interested in what I had to say. I guess they had been appointed onto the interviewing panel just to keep them out of mischief while they waited for their pension fund to mature, if it hadn't already done so. The only line I was able to decipher from the questioning as a whole was just what did I think of Civilian Life now that I had left the British Army after such a considerable length of time? What were my thoughts about Malawi now that it had become an independent state? I told them the truth saying I was not impressed by what I had seen of civilian life so far and that I had indeed had only a little time at my disposal to make any measured view on the situation in Malawi at the present time. All three of them seemed to be nodding their approval so I shut my trap at that stage intending to leave it to them as to what would be the next step. One of the Military chaps then asked me about my experience as a Military Instructor at the various Army Technical Teaching Establishments and wanted to know if I had enjoyed the experience. Alarm bells rang at this point. Had the bastards been a digging in my Army records to see just what I had been up to before I left the Service? Again I thought that honesty was the best policy and I told them that I hardly approved of the methods adopted at the Army Apprentice Colleges. The Apprentices had their heads stuffed with theory but very little was taught hem about the practical side of the life they would encounter when they moved away from the Training College and were then expected to earn their corn an a day to day basis.

My answers appeared to be satisfactory to them at this stage and then we progressed to the Civil Service type going into detail about my family. His first question was what had been their reaction when I had suggested that we may go to live in Malawi? He was assuming that I had discussed the matter with them I suppose. He then asked straight out if it were my intention to take the family to Malawi with me should I be successful in securing the post advertised, the one which I was now applying for. He went on quite a bit and gave the impression that this was the main reason he was there on the selection board. I began to get bored with questions that did not seek to plumb the depths and in fact seemed to be a bit low key as they, in only a cursory way did they explore the extent of my technical skills.

After thirty minutes of this, whether the Military types could see that I was getting a little pissed off with it; they suddenly upped and left the office leaving me alone with the Civil Service type.

I had already figured that this chap was the main man and the other two merely made up the required number of bodies for the purpose of carrying out an interview. The man before me suddenly seemed to relax and in fact offered me a cigarette which I declined. He then offered Tea or Coffee which I also refused. I had come here in search of an Overseas Post and I wished to make the most of things while ever the opportunity lasted. I had dozens of questions that I would have liked to put to this guy but I held my tongue for fear of rushing things and perhaps buggering it all up before I had even got started.

I was questioned closely about the time I had spent with the Special Air Service in Malaya. He seemed to be sympathetic to the reasons I gave for leaving them after my two year contract was up. What was more, he seemed equally sympathetic to the views I held about my subsequent service since leaving the Special Forces. I did express my regrets at leaving the Military without completing the extra bit of time which would have automatically qualified me for a pension. I followed this quite hastily by saying that this was no ones else's fault but my own, it was a mistake I had made but I could live with that.

The interviewer didn't appear to be interested in the least about what I was doing at present. In fact it was never mentioned. He did however; seem pretty keen to hear how the family had reacted to the idea of moving to Africa. When it seemed that I had reassured him that there would be no problems with this he followed on with some general chit chat about Africa and the aid our country was giving to them.

At last we seemed to have arrived at the meat of the matter. There was a vacancy within the Overseas Development Administration for someone to teach young African men the basics of Motor Vehicle Technology together with some basic education in Machine Drawing, Mathematics and of course English. This post was in Malawi where married accommodation would be provided and schooling for dependant children under the age of sixteen would be made available in Malawi. Children above this age would be eligible for boarding school fees here in the U.K. and their air fares to and from Malawi would be provided for three holidays each year. All this sounded great to me and after discussing the type of accommodation provided and the standard of the schools in Malawi we went on to talk about salaries and things related such as end of contract gratuity and the aspects of Income Tax matters. It was disclosed that a normal tour of duty would be for thirty months and this would be subject to renewal after a leave period in the U.K. and of course a satisfactory report in respect of performance while in service. The whole package seemed to me to be very attractive and even more so with me being seemingly trapped in the present U.K. system for what seemed to be such a long time. Finally I was faced with the question of when I could make myself available for a move into post in Malawi, qualified of course with "providing you are successful with your application". My reply was almost instant and was in the form of a very definite statement. I could be ready to travel, with my family in four to six weeks time. That was it. The young lady came to escort me back to the reception area where she returned my Military Certificate of Discharge Book to me. The reception staff paid me a sum of money in reimbursement for the expenses I had incurred in attending the interview and I left with the promise that they would contact me as soon as possible with the result of the interview. I could hardly wait to get home and tell the family just how things had gone.

As always when you are anxious to have word of something important the people who are responsible for corresponding with you seem to take ages to get round to it. Some ten days had now passed since my trip to London for interview and I had heard nothing from them. It was only natural I suppose that I began to think that I had been unsuccessful with my application.

It was on the sixteenth day that Jean rang me at work to tell me that there was a letter from the Overseas Development Administration and was she to open it? It said that they would like to see me again and that I should report to Milbank as it was highly likely the following Monday at 10.00hrs. They also advised that I should take an overnight bag as it was highly likely that I would be required to stay for a second day. This indeed sounded very promising and it was with something of a spring in my step that I caught the early train to Euston and was in Milbank well in advance of the appointed time.

The receptionist seemed to remember me and with a really dashing smile she informed me that a car and escort would be along shortly to take me to yet another office where I was expected. I sat and waited for less than ten minutes when the escort appeared asking for me by name.

We went across London to the Edgware Road and just before the roundabout which connects the end of Old Marylebone Road and Sussex Gardens; we turned into Crawford Place and almost immediately right again into Cato Street. This proved to be a cul-de-sac with the office which we were to visit being right at the very bottom of the street. When I reached the top of the steps leading up to the door, which I suspected might be made from steel, I noticed that there was no door handle or knob and there was no letter box either. Barely visible above each side of the door were what was obviously security cameras which would record the presence of anyone who had mounted the steps. There was no need to knock as the escort was obviously expected with his visitor, consequently the door opened outwards almost immediately. A large Victorian Hallway was immediately inside and there was a very Military looking gentleman sitting at a single table which was situated right in front of the doorway to the hallway. A Visitors Book lay open on the table. How different it all seemed from that which I had seen at Milbank Towers.

My escort reported to the Military looking gentleman telling him who I was and then disappeared through a door which formed part of the wood panelling which covered the whole surrounding area.

"Would you kindly sign the book Sir"? This came from the gentleman who was obviously in charge of the reception area. I gave no verbal response but signed in at the point indicated by him. "Someone will be along in a minute Sir to show you the way". I answered with a curt "thank you" and left it at that.

A smart young man appeared as if by magic from behind the wood panelling, he was dressed in Mufti but there was no mistaking the signs that he was a young Subaltern who was learning the trade. "Mr Hebden? Good morning to you Sir, would you like to follow me please Sir? We shall be going to see Brigadier Parker, Sir, as you know he is expecting you". All this came with the broadest of smiles as if the young man felt he must impress me. After all he didn't know who I was and what was more, he wouldn't have a clue as to why I was visiting the Brigadier. His Tact and Charm was obviously why he had been chosen as an aide and assigned to the post he now held. Up to the top floor they went arriving at yet another large impressive door. This one had a highly polished brass plate screwed to it which informed anyone who didn't know that beyond this door one would find Brigadier Parker. Following the name was a string of initials representing a number of awards and honours that the Brigadier had had bestowed on him.

It was quite noticeable that once inside, the rather stiff Military overtones disappeared and a very well groomed lady showed me to a comfortable chair telling me that the Brigadier would not keep me waiting long.

A buzzer indicated that all was now ready for my interview and I was ushered into the presence of the man himself. He proved to be one of those people who you either take an instant dislike to, or on the other hand you felt at ease with him and are prepared to bare your chest to every query he cares to throw at you. I liked the man instantly. The broad face with a clipped Military moustache bore a large open smile as he greeted me. He invited me to sit in a nice easy chair next to a coffee table as opposed to the more formal upright chair which stood on the opposite side of the Brigadiers desk to where he would normally sit.

After spending of minutes exchanging pleasantries it was down to business. We covered my S.A.S. experiences and then the period immediately following that right up to the time that I resigned from the Services. Why had I resigned? What, if any, were the underlying reasons? Did I now regret leaving the Services? Had I ever considered going back into the Services, either here in the U.K. or perhaps the Armed Forces of some other country overseas? The story was an old one to me. It seemed that the Brigadier must have managed to have some sort of secret access to my thought processes for all his questions seemed to match exactly the questions I had asked myself the very same things scores of times since that fatal moment when I had packed it all in. The replies I gave him were as truthful as I could possibly make them and it seemed that my inquisitor appreciated that.

"What is your present economic situation now that you are a civilian"? This question again could have not been more forthright or to the point, as a result I replied that life had become something of a struggle financially. What with the children growing up and the cost of living etc., I told him that I was extremely keen to secure a position that would give me a decent living wage. I also sought to provide myself with more purpose to life and give me back my old dignity once again.

"Have you any special views on Religion"? This Brigadier asked this question in something approaching a hushed tone. I told him that I had nothing against those who wished to believe in such things but from my own point of view I was not a Church goer and I had no opinion to offer either one way or another. He nodded his head wisely as if he was in approval with my answer but said nothing further on the subject.

"Are you a Royalist Mr Hebden? Or do you simply think that King and Country is one and the same thing"? The old warning bells were ringing again. That was a strange sort of question I thought and was a little surprised at it. Where were we going? Where was he leading me and what was the purpose of it all? There seemed to be a little more to this interview than just an instructors post somewhere in Africa. I was now intrigued even further and found that I was now actually beginning to enjoy the questioning which the Brigadier was now pursuing. Both the interviewer and I seemed to be walking the same path. One knowing where we were going, and the other, although most willing to follow, didn't quite know where we were going.

At this point the Brigadier asked if I would like some tea or coffee and when I said yes, this appeared in no time at all. It was almost as if someone had been listening at the door of the office just waiting for some sort of signal that the time had come for refreshments to be made available.

The tea break seemed to act as a natural break in the more formal part of the proceedings and we chatted about such things as the aid Britain was giving to the third world countries and how important it was that such aid should continue to be made available in spite of the many instances where the system was being abused by certain officials in some countries where funding was being applied to projects other than what it had been intended for. The standard of poverty in many African countries was not only due to the local environment but was, in many cases, due to the mismanagement by some Government Officials the Brigadier said. In some cases they were milking huge sums of money from the aid provided by, not only the United Kingdom, but many other countries as well. I was non committal about any of this. I was far too long in the tooth to fall into the trap of being interviewed when the questions were of the hidden type and smoke screened by by a cup of tea and a biscuit.

With the refreshments cleared away we returned to business but now I detected that we were being a little more serious than before.

"You undoubtedly have all the requirements for the post in question Mr Hebden and I am sure that you would make a jolly good job of it, but there is another matter that I would like to discuss with you. However, before we can deal with that I must ask you to attend for a medical examination. An escort could take you right now to our medical centre which is almost on our doorstep I might add, that is of course if you have no objections to this". I said that I did not mind in the least believing in my mind that this was something of the routine existing in the selection procedure for such an overseas post. At this point the Brigadier said he would see me again after lunch and told me to be back at Cato Street by 14.00hrs.

The keen young subaltern appeared as if by magic once more presumably in response to some form of signal sent by the Brigadier to the outer office. He took me back to the reception area where he passed me on to the same escort who had brought me there earlier that morning. The escort and I walked the short distance to the Medical Centre. On arriving there he asked me if he would be required to accompany me back to Cato Street for my afternoon appointment. I thanked the man and assured him that this would not be necessary.

The medical proved to be a very thorough affair but as I expected I passed with flying colours. The only ricket I made was that when the Doctor asked me to about turn, I turned left about instead of right about. This brought the comment that it was typical of a REME man to turn about in an altogether un-military manner. We both appreciated the joke and parted company the best of friends.

I now had the best part of an hour to kill before returning to Cato Street. I wandered around the streets looking in shop windows without the least bit of interest. My mind was working overtime speculating just what it was that the Brigadier had in mind. I glanced at my watch for the umpteenth time just to make sure that it hadn't stopped. I mustn't be late. Eventually I resigned myself to the fact that whatever it was all about I would hear all about it in a very short time.

The Brigadier informed me that all was well with my medical and that all the qualifications I had claimed had been verified and he was very pleased that all was in order. He then went straight on by saying that there was a very great need for people such as myself to serve the needs of our country and with this in mind, how did I feel, apart from the instructional job, about serving in one of His Majesties Departments? This would entail paying attention to what was taking place around me and submitting reports from time to time to a person who would be on the ground with me in Malawi. This of course would be an additional duty to my teaching at the Technical College which by the way, was located in Lilongwe which was in central Malawi and was at the very moment being built up to becoming the Capitol City of Malawi and was due to replace Blantyre as the main administrative centre and seat of the countries Government.

I had a distinct feeling that the interview had been sort of loosely leading up to something of this nature and it came as no surprise to me that such a thing had eventually suggested. I said that I had nothing against such duties and in fact the whole idea held something which appealed to me.

I felt that it was now time for some sort of clarification and asked the Brigadier to explain just who it was that I would be working for. Would it perhaps be some little known Government set up or even for the Overseas Development Administration, for it had been they that had originally placed the advertisement for a Technical Instructor? Was it possibly the Government of Malawi?

The reply came, "If you were interested and were in fact to be appointed, you would be placed under contract to the British Government, Foreign and Commonwealth Division with subsequent secondment to the Overseas Development Administration and you would, in the event, be responsible directly to me". There must have been something given away by my facial expression, as the Brigadier now appeared to catch himself up and wound down all of a sudden.

"Mr Hebden, I gather that you were asked to bring an overnight bag just in case you were wanted to stay over for any reason. Well, I would like you to stay and come and see me again tomorrow morning when I will introduce you to a member of my staff who is extremely well versed in all matters that will affect you and your family. You know such things as Pay and Allowances, Accommodation, Schooling and Travel as well as Terms of Service etc., I am sure you will have many questions to ask him and I am equally sure that he will do his level best to answer anything you wish to ask him".

The jolly Subaltern put in his appearance seemingly out of thin air. Once again he took me back to the reception area. Bert, that was the name of the Military type man went by, had already retrieved my overnight bag for me, It was funny but everyone in the place seemed to be fully aware of what their colleagues were up to even before they were told it seemed. Hence Bert getting my overnight bag ready even before I put in my appearance at his work station that afternoon.

It was the same escort who had been in attendance on me earlier in the day who took charge of me once again and informing me that it was just a short walk to the "Firms" Hotel which was apparently in Sussex

Gardens. He said he would show me round there as they were expecting me for a one night stay.

The Hotel had been part of the set up for some time apparently. It was for the exclusive use of the members of "The Firm" as it was known. Any member visiting Cato Street who had to stay overnight, for whatever reason, was accommodated at the Firms expense. It was not a palatial affair by any means but the rooms were comfortably furnished and the Dining Room was very well appointed. There was a Bar which I visited but left after one drink only. I weighed up the Barman and the five or six other customers and decided that for a new boy, this was hardly the place to stumble into conversation with anyone and most certainly not to over imbibe as it were. I was a far too experienced man to be caught out in such a way and it crossed my mind, how many people had brought about their own downfall due to the performance they had put up in this place?

I was up at the crack of Sparrows. I couldn't possibly be late for my appointment at Cato Street. I was practically on the doorstep anyway and I was consumed with that burning feeling of wanting to know what the outcome was to be.

I arrived five minutes before the specified time and could see the look of pride on Bert's face at the Military precision being observed by Mr 'Ebdon, as he addressed me. I signed in and was immediately taken to the office of what could best be described as a weedy little man who obviously was a Civil Servant. It's funny but they all have the same look about them.

"My name is Sidney Clements and it is I who will be in charge of all your financial arrangements such as Pay and Allowances, School Fees etc., etc., I have been given to understand that I am to run through the financial part of any proposed appointment which may or may not affect you and also to do my best to satisfy any questions which you might like to raise in this connection. If there is any part that I am unable to answer, which is highly unlikely, then it also my duty to direct you to another person in the Department who will be able to do so".

Pompous little bastard I thought. Typical Civil Servant. Think their

194

shit doesn't stink. No doubt he resented people such as I who were making something of their lives and took some sort of perverse pleasure from giving the impression that he knew it all but he wasn't going to tell me unless I asked him. Still the reason I was here right now seemed to confirm that I had got the job, or at least I was next door to being given it. They would never have discussed money with me if they didn't intend taking me on.

Sydney Clements made a good job of describing the system and never faltered once nor was he ever stuck for an answer in spite of the many questions I had for him. There was one point when he visibly showed disapproval of Mr Charles Hebden. That was when he asked for the Bank Code Number where my account was held. Now 99% of the population would be at a loss to tell anyone that one, without looking it up. Sydney tapped his pen on the table impatiently while I fished out my Cheque Book from my pocket and read the Code Number somewhat triumphantly to my inquisitor. Sydney was now back in full flight explaining about family transportation and schooling arrangements for the children.

He followed this up with the ins and outs of the Gratuity System which would be payable at the end of each overseas tour. I must admit, he was a very efficient little man but that was no excuse why he should be such a miserable little fart.

The whole process took up just over an hour and then I was passed over to the administrative people for them to record, yet again, the most minute details of what made up Mr Charles Hebden and his family.

The time had by now raced around to lunchtime and I was on my way up in the lift to see the Brigadier for a final chat before I left for home. I had a warm feeling of coming home as I was shown into the Brigadiers office and greeted with a broad smile and a warm handshake. "Well Hebden you will have gathered by now that you have joined the staff and I want to congratulate you on that. I am sure that you will be happy with us and will make a fine job of any task you are set in the future. How do you feel about it now that we are all finished with our tiresome questioning"? "I feel fine Sir and I can hardly wait to tell my wife that we are going to Malawi along with our two youngest children.

Of course she will be just as pleased that our two eldest will be coming out to us during school holidays from their Boarding Schools here in England".

"Is there anything else you would like to ask me? I know that you will have many questions in the near future, things like Planes and Trains and Baggage to mention just a few. Feel free to telephone the Staff here for anything you need to know, they will be only too happy to help. If you have nothing further to ask at this time, I will say goodbye and hope it will not be too long before we meet again". The two of us shook hands warmly looking each other straight in the eye.

I was full of the joys of spring as I left Cato Street and almost immediately popped into one of those delightful London Pubs which was, at this hour of the day, packed by the lunchtime trade.

CHAPTER 18

Jean was absolutely delighted at the news I brought, but, as was her way, she started to worry about Boarding Schools and School Uniforms in addition to other things. The business of fixing up Boarding Schools for our two eldest children proved, with a little help from Cato Street, to be very easy indeed. We managed to get them into schools which were situated in the same towns, (Shaftsbury in Dorset). At least they would be able to see each other at weekends and of course when it came to school holidays, they would be able to travel together when they visited us in Malawi. Although the arrangements seemed to be ideal I knew at the bottom of me that Jean was far from being happy at the prospect of us "leaving them behind" as she put it. We got over this as best we could by just not talking about it, however, we were to suffer an even greater blow when we arrived in Blantyre only to find that our two youngest children were expected to go to Boarding School there whilst Jean and I would be expected to take up a post in Lilongwe which was hundred's of miles up country.

There was one matter which was of a rather urgent nature and that was what were we going to do about our house in England? It was on mortgage and we hesitated in selling it as neither of us had any idea really just what we getting ourselves into. We may find that Malawi proved to be not for us or our family and those we would want to come home to England when we had been there only a very short time. If we went ahead and sold our house then we would be closing off that option. One day we were going to sell it, the very next day we would decide it was best to keep it and rent it out perhaps. Of course the next day we would change back again. We found it most difficult to make up our minds. Fate took a hand in the end and we at last able to make up our minds.

An advert appeared in the local Evening Paper. A buyer wanted a semi-detached, three bed roomed family house with a garden and garage and most important, he wanted to move in within a month and he was paying cash.

We sold our house, gave the dog to the next door neighbour, put our eldest two into Boarding School and all our furniture into store and off we went. The clean sweep had taken just short of one month and we were absolutely delighted with the way things had worked out.

CHAPTER 19

The Hebden family arrived at Blantyre Airport in Malawi after having had a very pleasant flight from London Heathrow with stops at Rome and Entebbe in Uganda. Although the flight had been enjoyable, there had been one rather tense moment at Entebbe Airport when our youngest son had pointed to a large photograph of Idi Amin prominently displayed on the wall and enquired rather loudly I'm afraid "Whose that fat black man dad"? The enquiry unfortunately fell on the ears of one of the many soldiers who roamed the Airport armed to the teeth with automatic rifles and festooned with bands of spare ammunition belts crossing their chests.

Ignoring the child the soldier turned on me and threatening menacingly with the gun demanded in broken English that I should apologise to the President for failing to recognise him and also failing to educate my small son what a beautiful man General Idi Amin was. This outburst rather took me aback, but having some knowledge of such "soldiers" I decided that an apology would not be amiss and hopefully, there would be no further trouble. The soldier stood his ground and watched us head for our plane, I think he was at something of a loss as to what further action he should take but let us go on our way at last.

When we arrived in Blantyre it was raining cats and dogs. Surely this was not Africa, it never rained in Africa, it was sunshine all the way and this had been one of the factors that made us take the job. However, this was the observation our two children made at the time just as children are apt to do. I suppose they had a picture in their minds that it would be all sunshine and wild animals just as they had seen on the television back home in England. Let them dream on was the only comment that their mother made. They will either get used to it whatever the weather or they could always return from whence we came and leg it back home.

As we stood gathering our thoughts and searching for our elusive baggage which it seemed the Malawian baggage handlers had their own ideas how to make the task as difficult as they possibly could, a short rather rotund little man, who introduced himself as a representative of the Malawian Ministry of Education, approached us. He lost little time in making it quite clear that he was in charge of all Technical Education and this meant that he was my new boss.

He had an official car waiting for us and he followed in his car as we were transported to The Ryalls Hotel which proved to be the typical Colonial Style Hotel which must have been built a good number of years ago in the days when the country was called Nyasaland. It now, sadly, needed no little attention to it to bring it up to the 1960's standard.

After such a long flight we were all more than grateful to have somewhere to lay our heads.

The man from the Ministry stayed only a short while, in fact it was just long enough to see us installed in our rooms. Before he left he said he would come and see us again on the following day but it would not be much before lunchtime as he thought we would want a good long sleep. Both Jean and I were most grateful about this as we had not seemed to stop to catch our breath for the past month or so.

The man arrived just before mid-day as he said he would. He ordered drinks for all the family and then suggested that he and I went off to somewhere quiet where we could discuss various matters and iron out any potential difficulties which may occur.

This guy liked his iced lager and summoned the waiter some five or six times to replenish his glass while we talked. Each time this happened I made a mental note that he was putting the tab on the Hotel bill and wondered if it was me that would eventually have to pick it up. Subsequently it proved that I had no need to worry at all as the Ministry of Education paid for it all, at least I believe that to be the case as I never was presented with a bill for any part of our stay at Ryalls Hotel.

He was one of those men who apparently knew it all but he wasn't going to tell me if he could avoid it. I had to ask specific questions, and then he would give me an answer. Strange that I thought, could it be that he would turn out to be the chap that Cato Street said would contact me once I was in Malawi? On second thoughts I decided that he was not the expected contact as he was supposed to get in touch when I had settled in and this guy had been waiting for me and my family at the airport.

I was not impressed at all by the man who sat next to me casually telling me that my two youngest children were about to be parted from their parents as they would be educated at a Boarding School here in Blantyre whilst Jean and I were due to head north to a place called Lilongwe where I would take up my post at the local Technical College. This was a blow to me and I hated to think how Jean would take it when I relayed to facts to her. This Head of Technical Education condescendingly granted us the two next days to settle our offspring into the School and then on our third day in the Country we were due to fly up to Lilongwe.

Jean proved to be most unhappy at this prospect of her being parted from our two youngest. I was so serious that there was talk of returning to the U.K. there and then. She just couldn't believe that I had not been told about it previously and persisted with "you must have known that was going to happen before we left England". I was on the verge of packing it all in and legging it back home. That was until the children had seen the Boarding School and to my utter amazement were really taken up by the prospect of staying there and flying up to Lilongwe every couple of months, staying at home for a couple of weeks and then flying back down to Blantyre. They obviously felt that they were suddenly grown up but I was not so sure.

We said our goodbyes to the children a couple of days later and made our way to Blantyre Airport where we were due to join an internal flight up to Lilongwe. Now we were not the happiest of people bound for Lilongwe, but in true Military fashion, we had spent a long time in the Army together, we put our best foot forward determined to give Malawi and the Technical College every chance. After all we had come a long way since I had packed in the Army life and we both now felt that this might still be the opening we had been looking for despite the fact that our children were at one end of the country and we were at the other.

The flight up to Lilongwe is truly worth a mention here. The plane was a World War Two Valletta which had been adapted for internal flights between Blantyre, Lilongwe and Kasungu up in the far north. There were two Pilots, one being an Australian and the other a local Malawian. The Aussie sported a pair of canvass plimsolls, very brief shorts and a loose floppy sweat shirt which was novel indeed for any airline representing their country. The second pilot was a local Malawian who obviously hadn't been at the game very long. He presented himself in grey flannels; a well worn blazer complemented by a snow white shirt but alas no neck-tie.

The interior of the plane had been fitted with a number of bucket type seats with little thought being given to passenger comfort. There was no stowage bins for luggage and the all luggage was dumped in the back few passenger seats. I gathered that with the exception of the children travelling between school and home, there was not a great deal of air traffic demand. In true Malawian style the attitude seemed to be, "It gets you back and forth within a few hours so why spend money on unnecessary items"? As it was used mainly for the school kids it was fondly known as the "Lollipop Special".

Rumour had it that navigational aid was in short supply too. The Pilots were said to take off from the grass track field at Lilongwe "Airfield" and make a circuit in order to get sight of the one main road which ran the whole length, north to south between Kasungu and Lilongwe and so on down to Blantyre. Once they found the road, the only decision they had to make was turn right for Kasungu and left for Blantyre. The rest was easy they only had to follow the road.

The chap who had met us on our arrival from the U.K. when he had set about giving us the good news that we were destined to take up a post at Lilongwe Technical College, had given us the low-down that the President of Malawi, Dr Hastings Banda, had decreed that Lilongwe was to become the new capital of the country and work was already underway building new premises to house the various Ministries and their associate Branches. We were to consider ourselves fortunate indeed that we were to be part of a very vibrant economy where we would be at the heart of things and be able to see the new capitol take shape, as it were.

Now the fellow hadn't struck me to be the type who would feed me such information if he himself didn't believe it to be true but when we saw just how far things had developed in respect of the grand new Capitol, it was then that I considered the man himself had either never been up to Lilongwe, or perhaps he told me this story to cover up the fact that no one else would take the post at the Technical College with the subsequent blow of their children having to be split up from them as there was just no provision for their schooling except in Blantyre. I just didn't know, but what I did know, was that during the first interview I had for the post, I had been assured that education would be provided for the children, in Malawi, until they reached the age of sixteen.

The man from the Ministry, (Head of all Technical Education), had made no forecast as to when the new Capitol would be up and running which was just as well I suppose when we considered just what we had got ourselves into. Still as I said before, time and time alone would tell.

It wasn't raining when we arrived at Lilongwe and we were not too dismayed to find that the Airport consisted of just a grass track runway together with a corrugated iron shack erected in one corner of the field. I was more than a little pleased that it wasn't raining as we had some two hundred yards to trundle our baggage from plane to "terminal" and this without any help whatsoever. Baggage handlers, what were they? Still it was just after mid-day and as it would be the hottest part of the day well I suppose they were all taking a siesta. There was no airline, or any other official for that matter, to see us into the budding Capitol of the country. However, we were eventually greeted by a very tall European chap who introduced himself as being a teacher from the College who had been instructed to meet my wife and I due to the Principal of the College being unable to do so. It was only some considerable time later that I learned the reason why the Principal was not available at that time, he had been summoned before some person who was In authority at the Ministry of Education to give good reason why he should not be "P I'd " (made a Prohibited Immigrant) which was the term given to anyone that the Malawi Government chucked out of a job and sent them back home, wherever that may be. Just what he was accused of I do not know even to this day. It didn't have to be anything serious anyway as I was very soon to learn myself when I was carted off to the local nick to explain why I had defaced a newspaper picture of the President. On that occasion I was explaining the mysteries of spray painting just a portion of a vehicle and needed to protect the window glass by masking it off with newspaper and tape. I never gave it a second thought; I just got on with it. Unfortunately the particular sheet of newspaper I used had a picture of the Kamuzu, President Banda on it and one of my students, thinking he would possibly score a few "Brownie Points" or something, made it his business to report the facts to the local Police Station who promptly picked me up, while I was at home taking my lunch, and carted me off to Jail. My incarceration was not to last long. When the College Principal got wind of what had happened he sprang into action. He visited the local nick and passed over a brace of Malawi ten Kwacha notes to the man in charge and I was released immediately and allowed to return to my post at the College. I never did find out who the culprit was that reported me but it never happened again during the rest of my tour of duty.

But I digress. Let's return to the first day when we arrived at Lilongwe the future Capitol of Malawi.

We learned from the chap who met us that a new bungalow, which had three bedrooms, had been constructed specially for me and my family. He made no mention that it was hardly finished and consideration was being given to my wife and I being sent to the one and only "Hotel" in the town, the Lilongwe Hotel. He even showed us the place as we passed through the town on our way to the Technical College. When I say "passed through", we did notice that there were a few Indian shops on either side of the road that must have numbered about twenty or so. Nearly all had an Indian watchman lounging on a rope strung Charpoy (type of bed) on the dusty veranda outside the shop. The whole thing gave the impression that time didn't seem to matter, tomorrow would do. Such was our first impression of the town and I am afraid it didn't improve much as time passed by.

There was a branch of the South African Kandodo and we were most surprised that nearly everything we wanted in the food line could be obtained here. Sitting on the dusty area outside were a number of enterprising Malawians who offered various kinds of vegetables for sale. These were not offered at so much a pound or even a kilo but by the heap. Five tomatoes or potatoes were carefully made up into a heap and the shopper negotiated a price for so many heaps together. The vendors needed to be watched closely as it was not unknown for them to, by slight of hand, do you out of one or even two of the heaps you had bought and paid for prior to him/her slotting them into you shopping basket.

We arrived at the College after a trip lasting around a quarter of an hour and it was a very pleasant surprise when we had our first sight of it. It was built within a compound with a high boundary fence around it and this was complimented with a well established row of Malina trees which also completely surrounded both the College and the staff bungalows which were very attractive but had the usual African corrugated iron roof. All the buildings appeared to be built from bricks but as with the bungalows they all had corrugated iron roofs. In true British fashion, the guy who designed and built it was obviously an ex-member of the British Army. The main entrance to the College was dominated by a Guard Room which was magnificently bordered by flower beds which boasted a riot of colour and fragrance that would hardly have failed to impress anyone passing into the College. Flower beds and exquisite grassy areas abounded throughout the whole College area. I was very impressed with it all and so was my wife jean.

We were duly deposited in the home of the chap who had met us at Lilongwe Airport and he introduced his family to us. His name was Helmut and he was a German National as was his wife, Girder. They had two lovely children who were seven and nine years old which meant that they were luckier than we were as there was facilities in Lilongwe where they went to school and would do so until they reached the age of eleven. Here we were duly fed and watered for which we were very thankful as the vitals at Ryalls Hotel where we stayed in Blantyre left something to be desired.

Apart from the Principal there were apparently four European Lecturers and five Malawian both Lecturers and Educational Teachers who were all accommodated within the College compound. The Students were all boarders and apart from Education tuition the trades taught were Bricklaying and Building, Wood Machining and Carpentry, Plumbing and Pipe fitting and last of all Motor Vehicle and Mechanical Engineering. I was to take on the latter but it seemed that I would have some six months to wait for my first student as all the equipment necessary to operate the course had not so far materialised. I could hardly wait to see where this was all due to take place but first I must get my house in order ready for our children to visit which I had the impression would be in about six weeks.

I made enquiry on two separate occasions as to which would be our bungalow and when would we be able to go and see it. I felt I was being fobbed of by Henry and when I pressed the matter he came clean and told me that the place was not ready for occupation and it would depend on the Principal's return, if in fact he did return, to show us our new accommodation.

The Principal did return a little later and after welcoming us he explained that, again as was the way in Africa, the builders department had left the painting of the floors till the last minute and they were just not dry enough to allow us to take up residence. I must explain. The standard practice in Central Africa is, or was at that time, to paint the floors either green or red. In the absence of any form of carpeting this was the most sensible thing to do when the floors were made of concrete. Good idea it may well have seemed at that time but the fact was that for some considerable time after we eventually moved in, if you should walk across the room without any sort of footwear on you found that the soles of your feet became either bright green or bright red according to which room you were in at the time. Make no mistake it was just one unholy swine to get rid of once it had taken root.

The school was far from the finished item as was the Staff Bungalows. One of my first duties was to organise the completion of the Mechanical Training Workshop facility. While this was taking place, the opportunity presented itself for me to have a good look round the other workshops and buildings which were all part of the complex. All proved to be constructed along similar lines to that which the Mechanical Workshop was now being brought into existence.

It was during this period of general nosing around that I came across a situation which seemed to be more than a little odd to me. In one of the outhouse store buildings there was some twenty or so tool chests filled with a wonderful array of brand new Carpenters Tools. Now these still had the protective wax wrapping on them and they had obviously never seen the light of day as indeed the chests in which they were housed were in a similar state. Each chest was proudly marked on the lid with the information that these were a present to the people of Malawi from the people of Western Germany. Curiosity itself made me check four or five of them only to find they were all in the same unused condition. I carefully replaced the Tarpaulin which was used to cover them up and after carefully closing the store shed high tailed it back to my temporary office near where my workshop was being built.

Now I know that I am the possessor of a suspicious mind, but something didn't seem to sit right here. There was a Carpentry Course in residence at the School right now but from what I had seen of them they were scratching along with the barest of tools and equipment. I took it upon myself to make enquiries of the Principal, a man of very few words who was conversely, a man of many eyes or so it was to be proven to be at a later date. I asked him why the Carpentry Class suffered from a sad lack of tools and equipment while there in the stores laid the answer to all their problems either real or imagined.

"When you have been here a little while Mr Hebden, you will quickly learn not to ask such questions". This was all he had to say on the matter and switched the conversation with an enquiry as to how the building was progressing on the new workshop. I was amazed at his attitude and certainly not a little curious as to why he had taken such an off hand stance. I was to discover less than three months later, the Tool chests together with their contents had disappeared from the stores and the poor old students in the Carpentry Class were still scratching along in the same old rut.

Was this the kind of thing that Cato Street was expecting me to report to my contact here in Malawi, whoever he might be? Surely it would not be long now before someone made contact with me. I was becoming increasingly impatient with life in general, what with one thing and another. I suppose the cause of this could be blamed on the fact that I found that I had very little to do from day to day and time lay heavily on my hands.

Lilongwe had very little to offer in the line of leisure facilities. There was of course the Hotel but this had, unfortunately, become a drinking den for the locals and fighting was quite common apparently, invariably about women as was the usual way with the indigenous population. There was another bar which had been set up in what was once a shop apparently. This place, known only as "Bushy's" sported a Restaurant which it must be said turned out some pretty good food the most popular of which was the Portuguese Steak served with Asparagus and their own version of chips which came in all manner of shapes and sizes according to how the vegetable cook felt on that particular day. The establishment had apparently been simply named after the chap who owned it. No one, as far as I knew, ever did discover the man's proper name and any enquiry as to the whereabouts of him was met with a plain statement that he was off hunting in the Bush somewhere. All the time I spent in Lilongwe I never clapped eyes on the man. At least I think I never did. What a Strange place the Countries of Central Africa were in those days.

Now hunting was illegal except for persons in possession of a Government Permit. It was quite possible that "Bushy" had never heard of such things. He simply went in search of the most lucrative type of Game. If in fact that is what he did. Many people had their doubts but all seemed to be reluctant to talk about him especially as it was but a few kilometres from Lilongwe to Dedza and the border with Mozambique and the Frelimo Terrorists. "Bushy" being of part Indian extraction was a very discreet man and you could have laid money on it that if there were a few Kwachas (local currency) to be made he would not be far away from the source.

The only other place to go was the local Sport's and Social Club. This boasted a Tennis Section, a Cricket Section and a thriving Golf Section due to there being a well laid out Eighteen Hole Golf Course which sported "Greens" made from Sand which was kept oiled to stop the Sand blowing away. When one was preparing to "Put" you would first use a "Scrapper". This was two pieces of smooth timber; about an inch and a half square each piece. The bottom piece would be about two feet long and the top piece, the piece you pulled along with your hand, was a little longer say about the length of a "Driver" and arranged as a "T" with a small swivel attaching one to the other. First you would "Mark" where your ball had come to rest; next you would draw the "Scrapper", starting at the hole and make a straight line back to where you had marked the position where the ball was to be placed. The business of "Scrapping" was indeed quite a skill. Too much pressure on the handle and you ploughed a furrow. Too little pressure and you left lumps and bumps in the line that you were to "Put" the ball on. Many were the arguments and equally many were the ruses tried out to outwit your opponent when the "Scrapping" techniques were applied.

There was just one other Section in the Club and this was The Boozing Section. This Section was a thriving one indeed and was always well subscribed. The Club Bar never seemed to close. A member, meaning every Expatriate within fifty miles of Lilongwe, could order and receive a drink at anytime of the day or night. It was a very popular place with all Expatriates irrespective of whichever nation they had sprung from.

Jean and I joined as family members with no affiliation to any of the Sections although at a later date I did become a member of the Golf Section. Our family membership provided us with the means of breaking up the monotony of just sitting on the Khonde (Veranda) of our Bungalow and drinking Red Wine. We were able to buy plenty of the wine if we crossed the border between Malawi and Mozambique at the little town of Dedza south of Lilongwe. The trouble with this was that it was only available in five gallon lots and this was sold in large Carboys housed in a thick straw wrapping. This practise was of course quite illegal, but when crossing the border back into Malawi if by some strange reason there was a Border Guard who had somehow managed to stay awake, if you were to allow him to siphon off say about a gallon, presumably for his own consumption, all was well and as you departed down the dusty unmade road he would cheerfully shout, "see you again master" as you gathered speed on your way back to Lilongwe.

Life was pretty slow. In fact it could best be described as painfully slow. There was no Television, the Kamuzu, Doctor Hastings Banda, refused to have it in the Country as he said it served only to corrupt the minds of those who watched it. Radio reception was unfortunately not so hot either. You could occasionally manage to get the BBC's World Service and catch some of The World at one which was broadcast at Thirteen Hundred Hours every day except Sunday. This all proved to be a little irritating but there were other things happening which seemed to be directed exclusively at the Expatriate population, a bunch of men and women who gladly gave of their time in order to improve the lot of the people of Malawi.

The Kamuzu and his Government had formed a movement which were known as The Young Pioneers. They comprised a small army of youths; all dressed in Khaki Drill uniforms and put one in mind of the Hitler Youth Movement. They were meant to be the Government's eyes and ears when it came to the matter of Expatriates. Not only did they strut about but also enforced a rigid form of control. Ladies were not allowed to appear in public with any part of their legs showing, that was apart from their feet of course. Long skirts were the order of the day and it was woe betide anyone who fell foul of the Young Pioneers if they considered that the law was being disregarded. I recall one Saturday morning in Lilongwe; this was the day when most expats did a bit of shopping in town prior to retiring to the Club for a few bevies before returning to their Bungalows for the rest of the weekend. On this particular Saturday people were going about their business as usual when suddenly a couple of truckloads of Young Pioneers arrived. Right before my eyes I saw two well fed young "men" approach an English lady who had a couple of youngsters in tow, One seized her by the shoulders while the second youth attempted to hold her skirt close to her leg in order to determine just how much of her leg remained uncovered. The lady became extremely frightened and the children of course were terrified by this time. The skirt was considered to be too short; it came to about one inch above the ladies ankle. The youth holding the ladies shoulders renewed his grip to make sure that there would be no escape while the one who had made the damning judgement, withdrew a razor blade which he had secreted in the band of his hat and without any hesitation stated slashing at the unfortunate ladies leg. Due to exuberance with which the youth carried out his attack, the ladies skirt was not the only thing that was badly cut to ribbons but her leg also suffered a most frightening wound right down the side of her calf. The wound was appalling and as far as I could see at that time, the depth of it appeared to had exposed to muscle. As the lady fell to the raised sidewalk, children by now hysterical, the two very brave Young Pioneers stood back and surveyed their handiwork and then both laughing fit to kill they jumped up into their transport and we rapidly driven away. They bore no means of identification on their uniforms and they left in the knowledge that the might of their beloved Kamuzu together with the rest of his Government would protect them from any form of criticism

I never saw the lady again but rumour had it that she had been repatriated back to the UK where unfortunately, although she partially recovered, she was wheelchair bound with little chance of any improvement to her mobility.

There was yet another experience in store for all Male Expatriates entering Malawi. It wasn't such a shock if you had passed through Blantyre Airport before because you knew what to expect. If it should be your initial trip to the Country, well that was something quite different. Again the Young Pioneers were in charge of what they referred to as "Air Cut" mainly I think because the majority had undergone very little schooling and they probably had never been taught how to sound their "Haitches".

Apparently the Kamuzu in his wisdom had decided that Expatriates with long hair were unhygienic and constituted a health hazard. He therefore devised a test to ensure that all men who entered the country had their hair shorn to the official length. The method adopted, vigorously I might add, was to place a rubber band around your head with the front part being located just below the nose and the back of the head having the rubber band in a straight line with the front. Should the erstwhile Young Pioneer, that is to say the one who was in charge of the others

211

on that particular day, spot just the most minute amount of hair sticking out below the rubber band he summoned up the services of the one who was in charge of the hair shears, on that particular day. Rectification of the misdemeanour was swiftly carried out. Off came the rubber band and the one in charge of the hair clippers, on that particular day, set about the perpetrator in a manner not unlike the Aussies when they are shearing Sheep.

The best way to describe the result was that they made complete balls of it. But here is the rub; they then charged you one kwacha for the pleasure of having your head mutilated. It almost goes without saying that should a new arrival fail to submit to the test, he was unceremoniously bundled onto the very next International Flight irrespective of who the carrier was or indeed which country it was headed for.

This sounds all very tedious and annoying, but there were also other restrictions which must have taken a great deal of time to think up and even longer to enforce. There was the one about censoring the U.K. newspapers which, if nothing else, gave the majority of us expats a damn good laugh. That was of course when no locals, who were dab hands at trying to curry favour with anyone in authority, were conspicuous by their absence.

One which readily springs to mind is the overseas edition of the Daily Mirror which was occasionally available. This comprised the six daily editions, plus the Sunday Mirror which were all stapled together and sold as a single unit. Although this was eagerly sought as it kept one in touch with home, it was generally six or seven weeks old by the time it became available to us. This publication from the "Decadent West" did not escape the attention of the Government watchdogs. They painstakingly went through each and every page of every single copy and took it upon themselves to stick big black patches over all the pictures showing women who exposed their legs. Not only this however, they also stuck their censors tape over any footballer who they considered to be wearing shorts that were too short.

Apparently the Kamuzu had decreed that these pictures were guilty of lewdness and would be damaging to the good people of Malawi. Quite how the men were to play football and not wear shorts was never quite made clear by the watchdogs. Perhaps the pictures in the Daily Mirror had shown the players without shorts let alone short shorts, and that is why they had been censored. I always said that it was not just a Government ploy to keep the unemployment figures down, oh goodness me no. This army of censors, and there must have been an army of them, were gainfully employed carrying out Government policy. Still the aid they received in the form of cash from the British and other Governments had to be spent somehow I suppose. What a waste it would have been to have purchased such things as Carpenters tools and the like.

There were many such restrictions which seemed to make little or no sense at all. However when you are an Expatriate serving in such a country, the only alternative to toeing the line was, apparently, immediate expulsion from the country and a very large Red "P.I." would be stamped in the most prominent part of your Passport. The "P.I." of course stood for Prohibited Immigrant. Some punishment for failing to get your hair cut.

It was to be a full school term later before I saw my first set of Students and believe me I was quite impressed at their general standard of education. They were, to a man, extremely keen to learn and were to prove that their thirst for knowledge was quite insatiable. I enjoyed teaching them; they seemed to hang on to my every word and appreciated all that I said on matters Mechanical Engineering. Life was beginning to be quite pleasant and despite my excellent relationship with the Students I was to be brought down to earth with quite a bang due to this obsession the Malawians seemed to have to curry favour with anyone they considered to be in position to do them, as an individual, even a little bit of good.

Amongst my first crop of Students was the son of the head of the Malawi Army, General Mateweri. It was through this connection that I obtained two worn out Land rovers which were of no further use to the Military as they apparently had neither the funding nor the expertise to breathe a glimmer of new life into them They became an absolute boon to the Lilongwe Technical School and my Students not to mention how they affected the content I could now put into my lessons. It was directly due to this equipment that I found myself arrested by the Police and taken away to the local jail where I was locked up without any explanation whatsoever.

I was sitting having my lunch with my wife in our Bungalow when suddenly a Police Land rover, containing four armed Policemen, screeched to a halt just a few feet away from our Khonde (Veranda). They leapt from their vehicle and with guns cocked and ready to shoot, I.was ordered to "come out with hands up". Being at a complete loss as to what this was all about I did as I was ordered only to find myself handcuffed and unceremoniously bundled into to back of their vehicle where I was made to lie on the floor with an automatic rifle only inches from my head. I couldn't think clearly but it did fleetingly cross my mind that this perhaps had something to do with Cato Street.

I was placed, no pushed, into a cell at the local nick but no one told me why, or for how long I would be there. There seemed to be no one of any authority present. My hands were still in handcuffs behind my back and I desperately needed to take a leak.

The guys who had brought me in seemed to think I was showing them my party piece with the antics I went through and they rolled around laughing fit to kill when disaster finally struck and I stood bedraggled and, I am sure a very sorry sight. A Police Inspector finally arrived after something like an hour and informed me that I had been arrested because I had defaced a picture of "Our Beloved Kamuzu". He added that I was to be fined Fifty Kwacha upon payment of which I would be free to go, provided that I made a promise that I would never again commit such a felony.

Defaced a picture? Who? When? How? Who said I did and when was I supposed to have done this grave act? Besides how was I to pay the fine if they wouldn't let me out of Jail to go and get the money? He would have none of it. I sat and tried to think with not a great deal of success. Then suddenly after a couple of hours my cell was unlocked and the handcuffs removed and I was told that I was free to leave but not until I swore an oath that I would not do anything bad ever again. I obliged and took a very deep breath as I left the confines of the local nick.

It was a great relief to see a friendly face for there in the car park sat the Principal of the Technical School with a welcoming grin which stretched from ear to ear. As I opened the car door to get in, his only greeting was "You owe me twenty Kwacha; I just paid that to get you out of jail".

Apparently within seconds of my being arrested during the lunch hour, the facts had been brought to the Principals attention by one of the labourers who worked in the school grounds. He had then tried to make contact with the police by telephone to see just what the score was, but they were having none of it. He then came down to the local nick but was not allowed to see me, however, he was very promptly informed that they required a payment of twenty Kwacha before he could even speak to me. Now the Principal had served in a number of countries in Africa and as a consequence he immediately grasped the situation and hightailed it to the local Bank to withdraw the required amount. On returning to the nick and paying up, he was informed of the crime I had committed and I was discharged into his care.

It was a few weeks afterwards that I learned that the informant was one of my own students who had taken exception to my behaviour and reported me to the Police. It had arisen from a lesson I was giving them on the repair and re-spraying of accident damage and I was using one of the Land rovers which we had been given. Without any thought on the subject, I had demonstrated how the unaffected area of the vehicle should be masked off from the damaged area prior to applying a coat of paint using a Spray Gun. To mask it off I used a couple of sheets from an old newspaper showing the Students just how important this part of it was. I then applied a coat of paint and as I did so the paper did its job and protected the unaffected area of the vehicle. One bright spark in the class had noticed that whilst I did this, some of the paint went onto a picture of the Kamuzu which had been a feature in the very newspaper that I had used.

I never did know for sure which one it was but of course I had my suspicions.

CHAPTER 20

I had now been in post some six months and still had no approach by anyone, as far as I was aware, on behalf of Cato Street. However, it was about this time that I became increasingly aware that a certain person seemed to make a beeline for me whenever I paid a visit to the Club. I knew the man as Harry but was not familiar with his surname. He apparently ran a small Mechanical Engineering business on the outskirts of Lilongwe. The firm made such things as Oxcarts which were sold on the local market. It was also known that they would repair and refurbish Agricultural Machinery and Implements. I was not sure if this chap owned the business or if he managed it for another person, a Portuguese man, who wasn't always present and seemed to frequently be off on his travels, in much the same way as "Bushy" seemed to do.

This Harry character was a very pleasant sort and had an easy going attitude to life it would seem. His wife was also of a similar nature and on each occasion we were in their company she seemed to get on rather well with Jean, my wife. They invited us to visit them at their home which proved to be a small holding some five or six miles outside Lilongwe. We went for Sunday Tea which proved to be a very pleasant experience. We hardly had time to politely enquire after their health etc., when Harry took me to one side and lost little time in getting right to the point.

"How did you find them all at Cato Street"? He asked.

I was immediately on my guard. True, I had been expecting someone to contact me for sometime now but when faced with such an approach I felt unsure of myself.

"What do you mean Cato Street? I'm not sure that I understand" while making sure that my facial expression gave nothing away.

"Is old fag ash Lil still dolling out the expenses with the same attitude that she acts as if it were coming out of her own pocket"?

I kept my gaze steady and never switched my facial expression.

"It's perfectly OK Charles; I understand why you seem so reticent to talk about it. I have worked for the Firm for sometime now and I know both the Brigadier and Cato Street very well indeed. He then began searching his pockets to find something and as he did so he said "both myself and the other guy I work with, thought the proverbial had hit the fan when you were dragged off to the nick the other week. Had to make a report about it back to Cato but they informed me that they were in possession of the facts and there was nothing to worry about". "Ah! Here we are" he said as he found what he had been searching for. He presented his official pass which bore his full name and emblazoned in gold lettering across the front were the words "Representative of HM Government of Great Britain".

I broke into a very broad grin and I said "Harry Willis eh! I have often thought it might be you that would have a word with me and now that you have, and I am aware that your second name is Willis, I am very pleased that it is". "I admit that I had half formed the impression that you were in business on your own behalf here in Lilongwe".

"So does everyone else and to some extent it is true that that is what I do. I am only the Manager of Lilongwe Engineering as we call ourselves, but the business is owned by a Portuguese Chap who you will meet later. His name is Manuel. He fell foul of one of the Government Ministers who tried to get this little Small Holding where I live and the Engineering set up, away from him by using threats against him. He is a smart cookie and managed to stay one step ahead of the game. He was eventually forced to do a bunk to Mozambique where he lives just over the border at Dedza. You know where that is I think. You go there to buy your wine don't you"? "I go and visit him every two or three weeks or so and pass on a proportion of the funds that we generate. I have to be very cautious about it all as I know the authorities watch me from time to time in the hope that I will lead them to Manuel, but so far so good".

"You are very well organised Harry, I would never have guessed that you were anything other than what you project yourself to be. Cato Street told me that someone would be in contact with me once I had settled in and the only reason why I marked your card as being the most likely one was because you always bought me a beer whenever you saw me.

"I must learn to curb that habit" he said, "You can buy them in the future".

We talked on for some minutes and agreed the basics of our relationship. I would not visit him at his workshops and he would have no contact with me through the Technical School.

"Well there we are then" he said, "Life is full of surprises you know. However there is one matter which seems to be rather urgent. Cato Street is a little concerned about some toolkits or other. I don't know how the matter arose but then you may have mentioned something to them in one of your reports. I would like you to look a little closer into this if you would. You are of course aware of the items I refer to"?

"I do indeed", I said, "There were twenty or so Tool chests fully equipped with brand new Carpenters tools. They were there when I first arrived and I was more than a little surprised that the woodworking students were scratching along with inferior, and in some cases, the wrong kind of tools, while there in the store shed was all these perfectly new items which could be made available to them. In fact I was so concerned about it that I raised the matter with the Principal. He fobbed me of with a short retort that when I had been here a little while longer, I would learn not to ask such questions. "I didn't quite know whether it was the kind of thing I was to look out for, so I bunged it in one of my reports which was sent in the usual way".

"Are they still there? Harry said, "Or have they been taken into use by the Students, or what? Have a bit of a scout round and see if you can throw any more light on the matter. Don't go making it obvious by showing too much interest. We don't want to put the wind up anyone now do we? Besides, it is my bet that they away into South Africa by now but I would like to know who was responsible for outing them and if possible roughly when they went, if in fact that is what has happened to them".

"You can rely on my discretion" I said, "I will have a little dig around without anyone knowing I am there".

"Good said Harry. There is however another thing that has connections with the Technical School. Cato Street has already been asking questions about it. It concerns a Bradbury Car Lift that was supposed to have arrived at the School for use on the very course that you are teaching. I know for a fact that it was delivered but it seems to have been mislaid or something as I have been assured that it isn't there now. Find out who ordered it? Where did it come from, and if at all possible, was it ever brought onto the Equipment Register by the School? You know the sort of thing, anything that might give us a clue about just what went on. I am afraid someone may have been a little too ambitious this time".

"Funny man that Principal" I said. "Seems to be a bit of a loner and so does his wife. We have never been introduced to her and they seem to want to be left to their own devices. In fact I have a feeling about the pair of them. Oh well worth watching I think. By the way Harry, there is something you may be able to set my mind at ease about. When we first arrived he was apparently on the carpet for something or other and it was only late in the day that he was back at the School to see just what the O.D.A. (Overseas Development Agency) had sent him. Now I was never able to find out just where he was supposed to have been at that time or in fact what it was all about. I feel sure that he would have been there to welcome us onto his staff if it had been at all possible".

"Your feelings are not wrong. He is a strange kettle of fish and seems altogether far too wrapped up with the American Evangelists who have a place not too far from the School. They churn out leaflets by the thousand but they are all thinly disguised by being shrouded in Religious Jargon. I have had my doubts for some time now but did nothing about it once Head Office told me that you would be arriving to work at the School. As regards the other matter you asked me about. Well, the facts are anything but clear. It would seem that it was something to do with a man who is now a member of the Government in Zomba. It appears that it is not too long ago that he was a Store man at the Technical School here in Lilongwe and had apparently been there right from the time that the place was first built. He had been very friendly with the man who was the first Principal there and he apparently continued this type of relationship with the man who is currently the Principal there. There was some talk locally that there was some kind of mismanagement of School Funds and in particular, That portion which was provided to run the boarding facilities. Apparently one of the Students, who happened to be very well connected, complained that there was never enough food and the bedding issued to them was of a very poor standard. Anyway, an enquiry was held and this Store man chap and the Principal were called to account for the whole thing. True to form the Store man had been sent to Zomba on promotion and was now holding a position which had a bit of clout about it. He apparently knew someone higher up the ladder who managed to sweep the whole thing under the carpet. I expect the Principal was under the impression that he would have to carry the can and that he would be PI'd over the matter. It was all kept very quiet in the end anyway and as result your Principal is still here in residence is he not?"

After this introductory meeting we met on a fairly regular basis. We would usually meet at the Club and have a general chat about one thing and another. Alternatively we would take turns to met at each others home for a spot of supper. This seemed to be the best way as it was the usual thing for friends to meet socially now and again.

We never discussed business when the ladies were present but on the whole we all got along extremely well together. The outcome of our liaison was that between us we invariably came up with a pretty accurate answer to the questions asked of us by Cato Street. I was never quite sure how Harry maintained contact with them and he never told me. I didn't ask.

I did find out however, during a conversation with one of my colleagues at the Technical School, that a truck of Portuguese origin, it had a Mozambique registration number and the driver spoke very little English, had collected the Tool Chests late one afternoon just before nightfall. They had been spirited away under cover of darkness, presumably to someplace in Blantyre from where they would be sent on to South Africa by road. There they would be disposed of for a cash sum but quite who benefited most from such a transaction was not at all clear. What was clear however was that a member of staff suddenly had a new engine fitted to his car to replace the tired old thing that had broken down at fairly regular intervals?

The building of the School went on but it was proving to be a very slow process. One of the main reasons why progress was proving to be so slow was the fact that Cement seemed to be constantly in short supply. That which did come into the country from South Africa was quickly seized by members of the Government who were having large palatial bungalows built on land they had somehow secured where the Capitol City was destined to be situated. It was one of the O.D.A. personnel who came up with a very bright idea. Most of the local Shop's, Housing, Police Station etc., were constructed in the past using what was referred to locally as "Dambo Sand" instead of Cement. Some of these buildings had stood for a good number of years and still showed little sign of any major faults. It seemed quite a logical solution that the School buildings should be constructed using "Dambo Sand" as a substitute for Concrete. The sand is dug from the bed of a river and piled up and allowed to dry out thoroughly. During this process large lumps are formed and these must then be crushed into a fine powder like consistency before it could be taken into use.

I know not how it came about but a very ancient Pug Mill was unearthed at the rear of some premises in Lilongwe and this was transported to the School where the Staff and Students set about bringing the thing back to life. It comprised a large granite wheel which was some three feet six inches in diameter. This wheel was housed in a shallow steel circular type construction in which the wheel would revolve round and round thus pulverising any of the contents shovelled into it. The whole contraption was supposed to be driven by an engine but alas the engine had long since gone and would now be providing the motive power for someone's Maize Mill or the like.

We were now presented with a problem. It was suggested by someone that if we could "Borrow" an Oxen this could be tethered to a pole lo-

221

cated through the hub of the granite wheel. When the beast was encouraged to walk round and round the Pug Mill, the wheel would turn and hey presto, we would be in business refining our Dambo Sand prior to it being used as a Concrete substitute. After a long conference in the Club and the quaffing of a number of bottles of San Miguel beer it was finally decided that the idea of using Oxen power was all together impractical. Someone would have to be employed to encourage the beast to continue round and round all day. The animal, assuming that we could acquire one in the first place, would have to be fed and housed which could prove to be a considerable drain on the Schools operating funds. Another round of San Miguel was called for and the out come was settled. It fell to me, being the Mechanical Engineering Instructor, to investigate the possibilities of a proper engine being acquired which would drive the Pug Mill just as it had always been intended even as far back as the days when Malawi was known as Nyasaland.

The acquisition of a suitable engine proved to be quite an easy matter in the event. "I had a quiet word with a chap I knew who ran an Engineering works in Lilongwe". He was most helpful and almost immediately produced a well seasoned Wolseley 1Horsepower Single Cylinder Water Cooled Engine together with a suitable Drive Coupling and Propeller Shaft. A couple of weeks went by and after a couple of false starts and the application of the tried and tested Heath Robinson affairs; we were in business with our Pug Mill running somewhat like a Rolls Royce. Well almost anyway.

Our entry into the Building Supplies Business put fresh life into the School building programme and work went on Apace. By the time I was due to receive my first set of Students I had a workshop built and up and running. I also had some stout wooden benches made by the Carpentry class, despite their sad lack of suitable tools. On these benches I would introduce the Students to some basic skills which, I hoped, would serve them well in the future.

At one of my casual meetings with Harry Willis, the subject was raised in respect of cash payments claimed by the Ministry of Education (Technical Division) for equipment purchased for the use of Students. He asked me to find out why the Lilongwe Technical School had paid, and claimed back, 1000 Kwacha (local currency) for a Pug Mill and an additional sum of 500 Kwacha for a Wolseley Engine to drive it. There was no need for me to pursue this matter any further as I myself had been responsible for scrounging both these items, the engine itself from none other than Lilongwe Engineering. The truth of the matter was that it had not cost the Technical School a single penny to acquire these working items. It was also during our conversation that Harry mentioned the fact that it was now common knowledge locally that a Cement substitute could be obtained from the School which could even be delivered for a very reasonable price. (Half the cost of Cement).

I once again took on my Sherlock Holmes role and came up with some quite amazing facts. A very lucrative business was being operated right there under our very noses. The Dambo Sand, which cost nothing, was dug out of the local river by the schools labourers and transported back to the School using the Schools Transport. The Lime which was added tò it as it was processed was purchased from School funds and booked off as cleanser for the many Monsoon Drains around the School Compound. The Petrol used to fire up the old Wolseley was booked off as being used on the School's Grass Cutting Machinery and therefore all receipts from sales was indeed pure profit. What is more, none of this ever appeared in any books of account whatsoever.

There were many such instances where funds either went missing without trace or were diverted into questionable disbursements, such as claims for expenditure, which to put it mildly, were a little questionable. Those which came to my attention was indeed quite small beer in comparison to what was happening in higher places. I suppose there were other people who worked for "The Firm" who were altogether much closer to the apex of Government Affairs but their brief would be much the same as mine.

It seemed that the longer I served with the O.D.A., the more detail of dodgy dealings came to my notice. A quite striking incident of this was as follows. When I had been in post for about eighteen months the Principal announced that he thought the Students should have their own Football Pitch within the School Grounds. Now there was a sad lack of other teams that could be invited to play there but he insisted that it was a facility which would greatly enhance the School. An area of ground was measured out and work started in earnest to clear it of stones, old scrub bush and rubbish in readiness for the planting of a grass called Kapinga. This grass, when planted in individual bits, would spread in all directions and eventually cover the whole ground and would be thick enough for it to be cut by a grass cutting machine.

The Principal showed a great deal of enthusiasm for the project and cajoled both Students and Staff to give of their time freely in order that the pitch would be completed in record time. Alas the interest was proving to be of "not of the highest standard" and consequently progress was very slow indeed. The expatriate staff made it known to the Principal that they were there to teach while the Malawian Students made little secret of their attitude that they were there to learn and not labour in the fields.

If nothing else, the Principal was not a man to give up so easily. He approached the Governor of Lilongwe Prison (an Expatriate himself) and offered him the facility to provide a number of his inmates with some remedial occupational therapy. They could clear the ground and what was more; he would allow them to plant the Kapinga as an additional incentive to them. The Governor was delighted and some two hundred men were transported daily from the Prison to the Technical School were they laboured ceasesly in the broiling sun. Their enthusiasm seemed to know no bounds and this was perhaps because they now had something to do to pass the time as opposed to just sitting around in a dusty compound where time must have hung heavily on them.

It was sometime later that Harry asked me how much the Prison Service had charged the School for the work they had carried out? My immediate response was that there was never any mention of payment for the Prisoners labour as the Prison Staff, including the Governor, welcomed work for their charges. Harry told me that the Malawi Government had submitted an Invoice to the O.D.A., which claimed a large amount of money for the construction of Student Facilities at the School. i.e. One Football Field.

During this time I had become quite friendly with the Prison Governor who invited me to tour the Prison just to see what facilities were available to those who broke the countries laws. Now, I am pleased to say that I had never seen the inside of a Prison before but there must be little doubt that perhaps I had luck on my side as I can think of a few occasions when the gods seemed to be smiling on me.

I was most surprised to find that the inmates of Lilongwe Prison were not all Malawians by a long chalk. There were Indians, Chinese and a host of additional nationalities including Europeans, mostly English, German and Greek's. They were incarcerated for a variety of reasons but the main reason seemed to be the misappropriation of funds or outright theft according to what the Governor had to say. They were all treated, apparently, in the same way as the local inmates. By far and away the most common crime amongst the locals was that of murder. When I was shown round, I asked my escort what the twenty five foot brick tower was for. This appeared to be the only brick construction in the whole of the Prison complex. My escort smiled at my question and then quite proudly it seemed told me that that was where the hangings were carried out. He went on hurriedly to relate that down at Zomba Prison they had a much grander affair which sported a Trap Door and everything. Unfortunately it seemed that here in Lilongwe; the accepted method of despatching the unfortunates was to simply push them off the board on which they stood while the Noose was put in place. This board was of course at the top inside the Tower and was reached by a wooden ladder also inside the Tower. I was truly amazed at what my escort had just explained to me and considered that such barbarity would be frowned on in most civilised communities. I resolved to enquire of the Governor just what the facts were.

The Governor gave me a full run down in respect of the hanging procedures carried out at Lilongwe. On a good week he said they would despatch six or seven murderers. His Warders, all local men, would compete for a place on the hanging detail as a bonus was paid to them after they had taken part in a hanging. Similarly, it was Government policy to pay a fixed sum to the next of kin of anyone who was hanged.

This amount was indeed a pitiful sum for the loss of ones Husband or Father.

He also told me that the next of kin would queue up outside the Prison Offices in the Boma (Local Government Office Complex) on a daily basis to enquire on which day of that week their loved one was due for the chop. Each in turn would make a plea to the Prison Governor, not for the man's life, but to see if he could give them an advance on the cash sum they would be due once the deed had been done. Life was, and I am afraid still is very cheep in Africa.

The gap between the have's and the have not's was wide indeed. Quite rightly, I felt that the aid being made available by a number of countries was intended to ease the pain being suffered by the majority of the indigenous people. Unfortunately there were many feeding from the honey pot and sad to say, they were not all local people either, although many were. Others held positions of authority and had been sent by their own mother country to give aid in the form of guidance to the local population. It had become something of a real problem which organisations like "The Firm" strived to redress the balance a little through people like myself.

At the end of a two and a half year tour of duty in Malawi, I was recalled to London and after a spot of leave I was up for re-assignment. This time we were sent to Zambia where I was not as close to the Government department as I was employed in the role of Training Officer in an Industrial Complex. Although I found the job to be quite a challenge, I am afraid I just did not like Zambia. The people I had to work with were of a different breed to me altogether. None of them had seen Military Service and it showed. My wife and I did make some new friends but in view of the fact that food was in extremely short supply, we were more than happy when Head Office in Cato Street recalled us to London after barely a two year stay.

The next station we were assigned to was a brand new Technical College in the town of Kwe Kwe in central Zimbabwe. This posting meant that we had covered the full set of countries which had previously made up The Central African Federation. Malawi was of course formerly known as Nyasaland before it became independent. Zambia was the former Northern Rhodesia while Zimbabwe was known as Southern Rhodesia prior to independence. Life was far from being comfortable at the new Technical College which had been built and presented to the Zimbabwe Government by the American Company, Union Carbide. They had made a first class job of the College which comprised modern workshop and classroom facilities. They had also not skimped on the equipment they installed and it could be rated as the equal of any Technical College I had the pleasure of seeing in the United Kingdom.

The war (between Smith's Southern Rhodesia and Mugabe's Independence Party) had been over but a few months and the Student's who turned up for the initial classes were indeed an arrogant lot. They had scant respect for their instructors who were all of European origin and white. The Instructors, who had by necessity, been dredged from various European countries, as the new Government had been unable to recruit anyone suitable locally, came mainly from the United Kingdom and Sweden and were considered by the Students to be completely unsuitable. The black Students were of the opinion that the posts should have gone to their own countrymen who had fought in the Bush for the independence of Zimbabwe. They gave no thought to the fact that those very men were ill equipped to teach technical subjects. The white Students on the other hand, looked on us as traitors to the white race who only when all the fighting was over had come from Europe to live off the backs of the former Southern Rhodesians.

During the time I served there I became absolutely appalled at the antics of Students and Staff alike. The Zimbabwe Government was always late in paying us our salaries and this did make life very difficult for the Expatriates. Quite naturally the local tradesmen and shop keepers, who were to a man, Asian (Indian) origin, were reluctant to advance any form of credit as they had been sold short a number of times due to maladministration throughout the system.

Things went from bad to worse and when fighting broke out once more, although it was only sporadic skirmishes, I decided that I had had enough. I requested that I be withdrawn from Zimbabwe and re-assigned to a different theatre where life would be all little more stable for my wife and me.

After what proved to be a most unhappy and frustrating period we eventually managed to get on a flight from Harare (formerly Salisbury) back to the U.K. After my de-briefing in London I was granted indefinite leave. I suppose this was to give the Brigadier time to consider what he was going to do with me next. This leave caper seemed to go down very well indeed but after a few weeks I started to get a little restless. As a result I became an increasingly frequent visitor to Cato Street in an effort to seek out a new post overseas.

At last an opportunity did arise. A post became available in South Africa. The nature of the work was entirely different to that which I had been engaged in previously. No longer would I be expected to root out the misuse of Aid Funds and the incompetence of Expatriate Staff who were in the employ of the British Government. Instead I was to enter the murky world of Apartheid and make any contribution I could after observing the attitudes of both Blacks and Whites towards each other. Additionally, I held one further brief. I was invited to comment and give an opinion on cases that became public knowledge through the South African National Media. My prime task would nevertheless remain the reporting of those misdemeanours that failed to meet the public eye.

Arrangements were put in place for me to take up a post in a Publishing House in the Northern Transvaal. Here I would dispense my technical knowledge as a Technical Author, a calling which was in very short supply or so I was led to believe. I was situated not far from the hub of things being half way between Johannesburg and Pretoria. My wife of course accompanied me and to all intents and purposes we were a new family of Immigrants who had come to South Africa in search of our fortune.

Life suddenly became very sweet again for the Hebden family.

CHAPTER 21

I was about to have breakfast with my wife Jean when the telephone sprung into life. As usual with its persistent ring, ring, ring, it was not to be ignored and we both glanced at each other briefly and then quickly looked away. Neither of us spoke, neither of us seemed to want to leap into action and answer it. A silent question was passing between us as to who would go. The phone continued with it's insistence until eventually it began to grate on the nerves. One of us had to give in and attend to it but it was not going to be me.

"I'll get it dear" she said, "You get on with your breakfast". She jumped up from the table fully expecting that the jangling bell summoned her and not her husband. The caller was more than likely to be their daughter confirming that she would meet her mother at Preston Rail Station later that day. This had all been discussed and arranged the day previously without the knowledge of me her husband. It was their intention to do what women seem to do best when unencumbered by men. Go shopping together not for anything in particular, but just shopping as women do when they are released either in pairs or in packs.

I was by now well engrossed in the "Daily Telegraph", partly as a guise for not answering the phone and partly because I was becoming obsessed with what the Media were reporting, on a daily basis, stories about what was happening in South Africa. From my own experience I knew they were talking a load of rubbish. I considered that my knowledge of South Africa was pretty well up to speed right now. After all, my wife and I had lived there for getting on for five years now and the job that I was doing made it essential that I was fully aware of just what was going on around us. Frequently, I totally failed to agree with just about everything I read in the Newspapers about the country that we now considered was our home. Well, currently our home anyway.

I strained my hearing in an effort to catch what Jean was saying and perhaps get some sort of a clue as to whom she was speaking. She had pulled the door shut behind her as she had gone out into the hallway where the telephone was situated. This was a sure sign that she knew who would be ringing and what she and the caller had to say to each other had an element of secrecy about it. It was also a sign that she didn't want me to know anything about it. She would tell me eventually. She always did.

Although I continued to stare at my Newspaper, letting my breakfast get cold in the process, my mind started to wander as it often did when I was contented with life as I was right now. My mind drifted to the day when I had been offered the post in the Transvaal when my old boss had broken the news that I was to go to South Africa.

"You will enjoy it there Hebden. The only trouble you are likely to encounter is that between Black and Black and White and White. The Blacks prefer to stick to themselves and if you have any bloody sense at all, you will do the same".

My wife and I had been very happy in South Africa and it was not only there that we had found contentment with our way of life. Malawi in particular held some very fond memories for us. The predominant Tribe in Malawi was the Ngoni who were basically a very gentle race of people. Their men folk were true gentlemen and they acted with deep dignity and respect, not only to the expatriate community, who they seemed to appreciate their being in their country, but also to each other. Above all, they were completely trustworthy. Of course there was the odd exception, as there is in any community, but generally speaking they were happy and somewhat content with their lot. A picture sprung into my mind of our esteemed Garden Boy and how he would stand for the best part of the day, holding the garden hosepipe but only moving occasionally to a new spot. This process, while giving him some form of Job satisfaction, ran up an enormous water bill which came in at the end of every month without fail. I recall trying to explain to him that this was not good for his Master and Missy but as they say, some fell on stony ground, and I refer not to the water. Oh yes, I thought, the differences between the various people who make up the populations of the various countries which collectively make up the African Continent, were many and varied indeed.

There was a story which I would relate whenever the opportunity presented itself. This was invariably when we were either holding our own Dinner Party when, in spite of our guests having heard it before, some of them a number of times, it never failed to be appreciated.

My wife and I decided that when the School broke up for a holiday it was perhaps a good time for us to take a months break back in England. When we left, what with the exciting prospect of seeing England again and the general hustle and bustle of last minute rush to Lilongwe "Airport", we completely forgot to lock the front door of out Bungalow. When we returned from holiday, we realised the mistake we had made and of course expected to find chaos within. To our utter amazement everything was exactly as we had left it. Nothing had been touched during our absence. The listeners to this tale were suitably impressed and invariably would voice the opinion that it was extremely foolhardy of us to go away and leave the Bungalow open to all manner of things. On hearing this, I would continue with my story.

We were not worried because we had taken precautions in another direction I would tell them. When the Bungalow was first built apparently, everyone had said it was very close to the native village as well as being exposed to the animals of the Bush, hence the erection of a six foot high perimeter fence. All the long standing local experts expressed their opinion; each one in turn saying that the six foot fence would prove to be no deterrent and the day would come when they would be proven right in their assessment. My wife and I paid scant attention to the things that were said at the time.

It was really at the urging of our Garden Boy, who lived in the village close by. He said that for a very small fee he could arrange for the local "Gully Gully" man to visit our Bungalow and perform a ceremony. This ceremony would not only protect us from the evil spirits, but would also ensure that the beasts of the wild would be deterred from making entry into our garden compound. What was more, with a little extra skilful negotiation by him, the Garden Boy, he may be able to persuade the "Gully Gully" man to work some extra special magic which he assured us would cover all eventualities. I suppose it was something like a Fully Comprehensive Household Insurance Policy really.

Now our Garden Boy was a pretty sharp guy it would seem, especially when he smelt the possibility of netting a few extra Kwachas for himself. He seemed to have made up his mind that we were hooked and putting on a suitably resigned look, he broached the subject of money once more and informed us that the additional work that the "Gully Gully" man would have to perform would necessitate an additional charge being made. When I pressed him as to how much this extra charge would be, he quickly averted his eyes and said that it was impossible for him to say right now but, with our permission, he would negotiate a favourable price on our behalf.

He looked very wise for some minutes and when he considered the time was ripe and his estimate of the extras stood a fair chance of being accepted, he made a suggestion. It appeared that due entirely to his own negotiating skills, a sum in the region of say ten shillings or so, he hadn't quite got the hang of the Kwacha yet, would be necessary to persuade the "Gully Gully" man to cast a spell which would protect us from the entry of any bad men into our Bungalow.

A verbal contract was agreed there and then and money changed hands that very same day.

The Garden Boy failed to report for work on the following two days. Neither hide nor hair was seen of him and on his second day of absence, that normally being his pay day, enquiries were made of our Houseboy regarding the whereabouts of the absent Garden Boy. After a little cajoling it was revealed that he could possibly be drunk in the village. He and the "Gully Gully" man had been inseparable since the arrival of the Garden Boy who not only had the contract for the services to be provided, but was also the stakeholder in the whole affair.

The big day eventually arrived, which on reflection, would have coincided with the running out of funds on the part of both of them. Garden Boy, with the "Magician" in tow, set about the duties for which they had been contracted to perform. They applied their efforts with much gusto, singing, dancing and casting a bag of doubtful looking bones against the perimeter fence at varying intervals. This procedure took the pair of them all of ten minutes to complete and just as they were about to pack up, prior to making good their withdrawal from the property, I enquired of my employees when and how the protection of the Bungalow itself would take place?

A conference was held right there and then between the two men. It seemed that this part of the contract had not been discussed previously when the initial bargain had been struck between the two. After much waiving of arms and gesturing of hands, with both men shouting at each other, at the same time, as loud as they possibly could, agreement seemed to have been reached. The two men shook hands and money passed from one to the other and all appeared to be well.

The "Magician" produced a FW Woolworth's carrier bag from the confines of his none too clean robes and carrying this aloft, he made a full circuit of the Bungalow. He then set about dusting the bottom of the house walls with a white powder. I was convinced that this was nothing more than Self Raising Flower but in the event it did seem to do the trick.

We lived in that Bungalow for some three years and were never robbed, nor bothered by anything or anyone. Needless to say, the vegetables and flowers flourished year after year all due to the efforts of the "Gully Gully" man with perhaps just a little help from the Garden Boy. There was most certainly a large slice of help from the Municipal Gardens Department in Lilongwe Town who strangely, always seemed to grow exactly the same flowers and vegetables that grew in abundance in our garden patch.

This type of scenario would not have been evident in either Zambia or Zimbabwe, which were both ideal places for Expatriates to live and work not so very long ago. Today your house is burgled on a regular basis and you employed an armed guard to protect your property during the hours of darkness. Bars would be installed on all windows and doors and everything that was moveable would by necessity be locked down. It was not unknown for the robbers to telephone you, either at your place of work or your home and tell you that you should not be present in your house on such and such a date as they were going to ransack it. It would have been folly to ignore such blatant warnings.

We were now on our annual leave break in the U.K. and our daughter Shirley had secured us a rented holiday cottage close to the Lake District. It was here that we would make our base while going off fro time to time to spring a surprise visit on our many friends who now lived in England. We had been home barely a week now and were just about ready to spread our wings.

Jean had been on the phone a good ten minutes now when I heard her laugh loudly and then she went into the "Bye" routine which all women seem to do. You know, "Bye then", "See you soon", "Cheerio love", etc., etc., "Look forward to it, Bye". I heard her hang up the phone and she came back into the room and smiling broadly, she plonked herself down at the dinning table.

"That was Shirley. She wants me to go shopping with her in Preston tomorrow. You know nothing special but she wants to choose some new curtain material for her Lounge. She thought I may be able to help. Anyway if it's OK with you I said I would like to go. You can come along if you would like to, but I did say that I didn't think you would".

The phone started clamouring again for attention. Not a word passed between us and I buried my head in the paper.

"It's alright, Ill go" she said pulling herself to her feet and disappearing into the hallway once more pulling the door shut behind her. Almost immediately she re-appeared. "Its for you dear, Head Office I think".

I hoisted myself to my feet muttering as I did so. "What the hell do they want now? I'm supposed to be on bloody leave. They can't leave you alone not for two chuffing minutes".

I wandered through to the hall and picked up the Phone. "Hello, Charles Hebden speaking" I said making no attempt to disguise my displeasure at being disturbed while I was on leave.

It was Head Office. I knew that hoarse gravel-laden voice which had a permanent wheeze in it coupled with the occasional chesty cough. It belonged to Miss Whinstanley; known widely as "Fag Ash Lil". This was due to the fact that her first name was Lillian, or so common gossip would have it, and she was rarely seen without a cigarette hanging from her mouth being a habitual chain smoker. She was of course addressed as Miss Whinstanley at all times. Not even the top hierarchy would dream of addressing her as Lillian. Certainly anyone of us lesser minions would ever dare address her as "Fag Ash Lil" to her face. She ruled the roost with a veritable rod of iron at Cato Street and everyone knew it.

"Mr Hebden, you are expected by the Brigadier at 11 hundred hours tomorrow. Please be prompt. We don't want any repeat of that previous unfortunate incident now do we"?

She was referring to an occasion when I had been summoned to the presence and had been fifteen minutes late arriving. This had been due entirely to the inefficiency of British Rail who had failed to convey me from Preston to London in the time prescribed in their timetable. But this had happened some two or three years previously. What a memory. She must think of nothing else but the misdemeanours perpetrated by Members of Staff and the way that such behaviour buggered up her well planned and critically executed campaign for the Office on that particular day.

"I'll be there Miss Whinstanley" I said into the phone. "Was it something urgent"? I asked, knowing full well that Lil would not enlighten me in any way.

"Eleven hundred hours tomorrow. Goodbye". The phone went dead.

"Bastard" I exclaimed rather loudly. "Typical bloody Head Office. A dictatorial attitude that's what it is, dictatorial".

I stood for a good few seconds absorbing what I had just heard. Turning sharply I stamped back to the breakfast table. I said nothing to Jean at this stage as my mind was fully occupied with moans about Head Office. I was supposed to be on leave wasn't I? What did they think they were playing at? I'd been home barely a week and already they were pissing me about. Was I supposed to sit on my arse at home by the phone for the next month or so in case old "Rekrap" decided he wanted a minute or two chat to one of the Field Agents who just happened to be in England?

The name Rekrap had been bestowed on Brigadier Parker by almost everyone in the firm. This was due to the fact that it was inevitable that he would eventually get everything arse about face when taking it upon himself to explain anything in particular. (Rekrap = Parker backwards).

"Is there something wrong dear"? Jean knew the signs very well indeed.

I sat staring at the Newspaper but she knew from her many years experience that I was not reading it. I was brooding myself into a rage.

"Something wrong is putting it bloody mildly" I said. "I only have to go and see old Rekrap tomorrow, that's what's bloody wrong. The old bastard probably wants to ask me if I'm enjoying my leave or some such thing. You know what he is".

Jean knew that when I was ordered to do something without being given the reason why, my blood pressure would raise a number of points. The best thing was to leave me to sort it out in my own mind without any comments from anyone else come to that. She had finished her breakfast, while I, through being stubborn, let mine go cold on the plate. I pushed it away into the middle of the table as an indication that I would no longer enjoy it even if it were my favourite.

"I'm just popping down to the Newsagents dear. I shouldn't be very long. Put the kettle on there's a love and I will make us a nice fresh pot of tea when I get back. Anything you want while I'm down there"?

"Bring a large bottle of Panadol" I replied. Probably need them when I get back tomorrow night after wasting a full day of my leave just to fill in a few minutes of the old devils day". Jean withdrew diplomatically. She was far too wise to take the bait. If she entered into a discussion about it, I would not let it drop and would keep on all day niggling about it.

I thought about my trip the next day and fumed inwardly about it. After some minute's logic returned to my thought process and suddenly I was in gear again. I would go down to London on the late train this evening and not wait until tomorrow. In the back of my mind I suppose I subconsciously feared that I would invite the wrath of Fag Ash Lil should

I be even a Tad late. Didn't want to cross swords with her, she was the one who signed you r expenses sheet when you visited Head Office. Apart from that, I might as well see them off for a nights Accommodation and a Dinner and Breakfast. Serves them right, they should bloody well pay for the interruption to my leave. I must ring the Firms Hotel in Sussex Gardens and book myself in for the one night stay.

The Hotel had been set up specially to cater for members of the Firm who had to make an overnight stay when visiting Head Office. It was free to me anyway and I never was one to spend my own hard earned brass, especially when it was not necessary. I waited for Jean to come back before I rang the Hotel and I told her what I had decided to do. She appeared to approve of the plan and if anything was quite relieved that I would be off as it meant that she could have a grand day with our daughter the next day.

I rang the Hotel and confirmed that I would be arriving that same evening.

Apart from my journey being thoroughly boring there was nothing of noteworthy significance about it. I duly arrived at Euston Station at something past seven thirty and after fleetingly considering the Station Bar, I decided against it and took a taxi to the Hotel instead.

The booking in procedure took less than a minute to complete and I was then shown to a comfortable room with all the necessary facilities needed to make the visitors stay as pleasant as possible. After a quick wash and brush up I went down to the Dining Room where I dined alone enjoying the usual excellent fare that was always on offer. When I had finished my meal, I withdrew to the very attractive Lounge Bar. This was next to the Dining Room. There were perhaps a couple of dozen people in the Bar but after a quick look round, I failed to spot anyone I knew and swiftly disposed of a couple large scotches chased by a Carlsberg Special Brew convincing myself that they would guarantee me a good night's sleep to ready me for the meeting on the morrow. Apart from that, I knew of the dangers of sitting alone at the Bar and getting a skin full. The waiters and barmen probably had additional responsibilities

237

apart from dispensing drinks and one could not be too careful in such places.

After a good nights sleep I was up with the birds nice and bright and early. I had the usual jolly good breakfast and then killed a little time scanning the daily newspapers. This I did with no great enthusiasm as my mind kept wandering. I was preoccupied with the reason for the call to see the Brigadier. It was probably nothing much at all. There again, in spite of my criticism of Head Office, they were not prone to dragging the staff in when they were enjoying a well earned spot of leave. It must be something fairly important I eventually settled for and I would soon be relieved of my doubts for I was due to see the old boy at 1100hrs sharp. I really did hope that he was not going to spring a new posting on me, not now we were settled and very comfortable in South Africa.

I checked the Rolex on my wrist and registered the time as almost ten hundred hours. I decided that as Cato Street was but a cockstride away and the weather being such a beautiful October day, I was sure that the walk along Sussex Gardens to the Edgware Road would do me a power of good. Walking along I started to whistle softly to myself and felt at ease with the world. Turning sharp right into the Edgware Road, my route called for me to cross over and take a left almost immediately into Crawford Place. This was a most elegant street which was lined with the most impressive doors you could wish to see anywhere. Some had large brass numbers on them while others seemed to be content with just a tiny brass plate which no doubt gave any visitors an idea of who, or perhaps what they would find behind the door.

I did not have far to walk now, the second street on my right was Cato Street which was a cul-de-sac. It was from this street where Head Office was located, that all my doings over the past fifteen years had been directed and controlled. The objects of my present visit lie in the last building in the street on the right hand side. A range of steps fronted it and these led up to a very impressive front door. The shiny brass plate screwed to the wall adjacent to the door informed anyone who was interested enough that this was the NEXOS IMPORT & EXPORT COMPANY and it had Offices in Nairobi, Durban, Singapore and Hong Kong.

I checked the Rolex once more as I mounted the steps to the oversize door and quite unavoidably a hint of a smile crossed my face. It had always been a source of amusement to me that the huge door boasted neither letter box nor doorknob. There was no identifying number to be seen either. I glanced upwards to both left and right and there, unobtrusively above the door were two security cameras. These were no doubt giving someone within the bowels of the building both a full frontal and a profile view of the visitor who was right now thumbing the brass surrounded button which bade all users to "Ring and Wait".

The redoubtable Bert Dillon opened the door, as indeed he had done on every other occasion that I had visited Head Office. Bert, six feet two inches in his stocking feet (according to him anyway) was a most impressive figure of a man and every inch of him screamed ex-Army. Clipped military moustache, regulation short back and side's haircut and highly polished shoes the toecaps of which would dazzle even a partially sighted man. The creases in his trousers looked to be capable of sharpening a pencil should the need ever arise. Indeed he was every inch the soldier and to prove it, if proof should ever be needed, he sported a chest full of ribbons which included both the Military Medal and the British Empire Medal.

"Good morning to you Mr Hebden, Sir. Eleven Hundred hours, Brigadier Parker, is it?" He questioned me in his usual brusque manner which, although business like, was not unfriendly. Without waiting for a reply he opened the door further and bade me to step inside.

"Could I ask you to complete the formalities in the Visitors Book, Sir? You will find it on the table inside the Hall".

Thanking him, I entered, wiping my feet (quite unnecessarily, but one felt it to be obligatory under the circumstances) on the coconut matting set into the orange and black Quarry Tiling which extended all the way from the front door right to the inner entrance door at the opposite end of the Reception Hall. This inner door bore a sign which simply said "Entrance" just in case anyone should entertain any notion to the contrary.

I made my way to the very highly polished Refectory Table which, just as Bert had predicted it would, provided a resting place for the red leather bound volume which bore on its cover in gold printed letters, "Visitors Book". Adjacent to it, one to the right side for right handed persons and the other to the left side, presumably for those of a different persuasion, was a pair of regulation issue Biro Pens. Each one of these was stamped O.H.M.S. and each had been arranged with the Arrow Sign (War Department Property) and the inscription both on the upper flat side of each pen. Such meticulous preparation ensured that the user would have no choice but to replace the pen in exactly the same position as it was prior to its use. This was of course down to Bert who would have no slip shod ways in his Reception Area. No Sir, discipline must be maintained at all times.

Signing the book I noticed that another appointment was pencilled in for the Brigadier which was due to take place at 11.10hrs. It seemed that I was only to be allowed ten minutes for my appointment which indicated that there was not to be anything of great length to be discussed whatever the subject might be.

All the Office staff and members of the Hierarchy were in the inner sanctum which lay beyond the door marked "Entrance". I glanced at the Rolex once more and made a mental note that I was here and booked in with all of five minutes to spare. I smirked at the thought of "Fag Ash Lil" being a little disappointed being a little disappointed at being denied the opportunity to administer a bollocking to me.

The inter departmental phone situated on Bert's highly polished desk broke the silence with a most refined burp. "Yes Miss he is. Yes Miss I will attend to that". Bert looked across at me and said "Someone is on the way down for you Sir".

Almost immediately the door marked "Entrance" smoothly opened and in came one of those secretaries who make you think instantly, wonder why she is wasting her time here? She surely should be a Model or something. The lady was stunning with bumps where bumps should be and all the rest matched as well. I thought it had been worthwhile making the trip to London even if it was only to have a ride in the lift up to the third floor with this lovely creature.

"Mr Hebden" she questioned looking directly at me. "Yes, thank you my dear" I said with a somewhat dry mouth. I rose and made my way to the door marked "Entrance" which she held open for me. That sign had always amused me whenever I had visited the building in the past. Now it would be etched on my mind forever. My escort smelled lightly of violets. Delightful.

"Fag Ash Lil" greeted me frostily and sneaked a swift glance at the clock on the wall just to make sure I supposed, that she was not to be denied a quick rebuke if it was at all possible. She wore a watch more suitable for a man on her right wrist, which again, she didn't offer me a chair; consequently I stood feeling a little awkward at it all. I would never have presumed to have sat in the empty chair which stood in her office although it was obviously provided for the purpose of accommodating visitors who were subject to a slight delay. Such was Lil's silent power over all that passed through her office. Guys bigger than me and some of them much more senior were secretly afraid of her and all the power she wielded. She glanced at her watch and then up at the clock before fingering the Intercom Button which put her in touch instantly with the Brigadier.

"Eleven hundred hours, Mr Hebden is present Brigadier".

"Send him in please".

The Intercom went dead and Lil pointed with her finger at the interconnecting door which led to the Brigadiers Office. She didn't speak; she didn't have to as I was gone in a flash only too pleased to get away from her penetrating stare which went right to the marrow of my bones every time she looked at me.

The Brigadier sat behind a large desk which was covered in green leather. The indications were, at first glance, that it had been in service for some considerable time. It fleetingly occurred to me that whatever action that piece of furniture had seen, had hardly been carried out by its present Pilot. The desk was devoid of all except a pen stand which also incorporated an ink well. The ink well appeared to be empty. The person sitting behind the desk was of the same ilk. No, not green in appearance but equally weather beaten with thinning pure white hair and a clipped Military Moustache to match. Guessing his age would have been difficult due to the Military bearing he still carried, he was nevertheless, marching on in years as was the desk.

"Morning Hebden" He did not wear his customary fixed smile that I remembered so well. I though this to be a little strange and when he didn't offer me his hand in welcome the alarm bells began to ring and I gathered that that which was about to come was not going to be pleasant. My natural inner defences came into play immediately, there was something wrong for sure and that something was about to be made known to me. The chair on my side of the desk was empty and looked most inviting but in the absence of any invitation from the Brigadier to sit, I decided that discretion demanded that I remain standing.

"Now Hebden" the Brigadier began, "there seems to be some sort of a problem as regards you remaining in Post at your present location. In fact, I have here", and at that point he produced a single A4 sheet of paper from a draw in his desk, "a request from the Host Country Government, that you be relieved of your post and removed from their country with immediate effect". I could see that he was studying my face intently for any sign of a reaction that may be apparent. I for my part just stood with my mouth agape and showed that I was absolutely gob smacked at what had just been said. "Is there anything you would like to tell me" the old boy said quietly, "anything that could possibly be the reason why they have made this request"?

I had imagined many different reasons as to why I had been summoned before the Boss, but I was now at a complete loss at what had just transpired. What was it he had said, problem with staying in Post? The South African Government had requested that I be withdrawn immediately? What on earth could that mean? I had done nothing wrong as far as I could recall off hand. Sure I had crossed swords with a couple of people lately but nothing that would warrant me being removed from my Post.

"I am afraid I am at something of a loss to find something that I could say to you Sir. I just have no idea what you are referring to. Surely there must be some mistake"?

The Brigadier sat and said nothing for perhaps some fifteen or twenty seconds or so. All this time, which seemed to be much longer than what it actually was, he stared at his desk top as if he was reluctant to meet my gaze. Eventually he looked up and caught me straight in the eyes. Then without a flicker of emotion he said "I have here a basic outline of the allegations that have been levelled against you by the Government of South Africa and I am duty bound to take due note and carry out their wishes with immediate effect. These allegations, if true and correct, are very serious indeed. So much so that, until further light can be thrown on them, they warrant the action I am about to take".

My mind was in top gear now going over the events of the past few weeks and months. I was searching for anything or anyone who I had trodden on their toes. The Brigadier looked up at me with something of a pained expression and he was obviously working himself up to say to me just what the verdict was to be as a result of the allegations made.

"I am afraid you will be suspended from duty with immediate effect and of course according to the undertaking you made when we first recruited you, you will receive only half of your salary while under suspension. Should it ultimately be proven that there is no blame to be attributed to you in respect of the allegations made, you will of course be fully reinstated with the reimbursement of your salary, which will in these circumstances be back dated to today's date".

I couldn't believe what I had just heard, I was flabbergasted. I took a very deep breath and said "Just what is it that I am supposed to have done Sir? Surely I am entitled to know who accuses me and what I am accused of"?

"I am afraid there is no obligation on my part to say anything further at this stage" said the Brigadier. "You will of course receive confirmation of your suspension in writing in the next day or so and I notify you herewith that you must hold yourself in readiness to attend any investigation into the matter. You will be fully reimbursed for any costs you incur in attending at these offices for such meetings. You will also be appraised of the full allegations against you in due course. I am truly sorry about this Mr Hebden but as you are aware, rules are rules and we must all strive to abide by them. I do hope that we can get this sorted out quickly and have you reinstated as soon as possible.

I thought I would give it just one more try. "Is it not possible Sir, for you to give me some sort of indication as to what the allegations are against me? This is most distressing and in view of my suspension, I would have thought that the least I would be entitled to would be some sort of indication of just what it is that I am accused of".

The Brigadier looked at me very seriously indeed and then said "Well Hebden, it has been reported to your Station Supervisor that you have been visiting the Local Township of Sasolburg, on more than one occasion. As you are no doubt aware, this is something that the South African Government can ignore. It is strictly forbidden under the current Apartheid Laws and although we might not like it, we must nevertheless respect those Laws while we are guests in that country. This is a very serious matter indeed and it could have far reaching repercussions. We have here a full list indicating dates and specific times, duration of stay and even the registration number of the vehicle you travelled in. All this will be thoroughly checked I can assure you and then you will have the opportunity to have your say in the matter. That is all I am prepared to say at this time and would bid you Good Morning".

I moved into the outer office where "Fag Ash Lil" sat at her desk. She didn't even look up at me but instead picked up the telephone and said to the person at the other end "Would you collect Mr Hebden now please"? That was all; she replaced the phone and still did not look up at me.

My escort was a different one to the lovely lass who had brought me up in the first instance. At least I thought it was, however, things other than lovely ladies occupied my mind right at that time.

I was taken down to the second floor where my Government ID Card was withdrawn. I was also relieved of the document which was my special means of identification. I was from that moment on, so to speak unemployed with half of my livelihood disappearing down the tubes.

What was it old Rekrap had called the allegations against me? Conduct prejudicial to the interests of the Service. It sounded even worse when put like that. I must have a very serious think about it all before doing anything like doing my nut or anything else like that. It had been sort of "Kiss my arse and bugger off". The whole process from the time I entered the Brigadiers office, to the time I found myself back in Reception and on my way out, had something like 12 to 15 minutes.

I was not a happy person right then and I fumed inwardly as I headed for Sussex Gardens to pick up my belongings before going in search of the nearest Bar that was open. It was there in such a place that I would be able to pause and try to absorb what had just happened. What a bloody mess I thought as the bare facts began to sink in. I began racking my brain trying to remember when I had been in the Local Township of Sasolburg. I recalled having been on a couple of binges with some of my pals and we had wound up at one of those Shabeen's but I could not recall with any certainty where it had been. It may have been in Sasolburg, I just didn't know.

I found a likely Bar and as the intake of Carlsberg Special Brew increased, I was less able to recall many of the facts which were now, apparently, very important. My mind was more and more becoming fixed on who the scab was that had seen fit to put the bubble in, in the first place. I would like to be face to face with the bastard right now whoever he was.

I suddenly thought about Jean. What on earth was she going to say, what would I say to her? How could I tell her that it looked likely that I was going to get the push eventually? I knew that she was strong enough to take such a blow in her stride but then she would surely expect some sort of explanation from me as to why this sort of thing had happened. She would show no outward signs but I knew that she would worry inwardly. I would of course give her all the facts as far as I knew them, I always did. I certainly didn't relish the task ahead of me but there again, what other option was there?

I checked the Rolex. Christ, 1400hrs. I had been in this Bar for the best part of three hours and I was no further forward than when I came in.

"Get a grip Hebden, get a bloody grip" I muttered to myself.

I desperately tried to unscramble my thought processes and decide what the next thing should be that I should do. I didn't want to face Jean right now and that much I was sure of, but the Carlsberg was having a drastic effect on my thinking. I was supposed to be able to think quickly while on my feet and come to some form of logical conclusion. That was why the Firm had taken me on some ten, or was it fifteen years ago. Here I was with my arse on a bar stool, glass in hand and in a very unsteady state when I did try to stand up. Even so I was still capable of some sort of thought process albeit a little woolly. It was indeed so woolly that I found myself at a complete loss as to what I was going to do next.

I felt grim as I stretched and slowly surfaced from the extended period of oblivion which had been self inflicted by a prolonged session in the tap-room of The Rifleman's Arms the previous day. I had consumed a large quantity of cheap Brandy mixed with strong Cider knowing full well what the consequences would be. I cared little about the consequences at the time, in fact I seemed to care little about anything after the first couple of slugs had hit the pit of my empty rumbling stomach.

I fumbled blindly in the half light that the meagre curtains permitted to enter the room. My fingers scrambled around on the bedside locker in an effort to locate the Rothmans packet which I instinctively knew should be there. With a feeling of some relief I located the packet and with eyes tightly closed against the daylight, I tried to extract that much needed first weed of the day. "Shit" I exclaimed when I found the packet to be empty. I was absolutely certain that it was only a newly opened pack when I fell into my Brandy sodden coma the evening previously, or whenever it was. The shock as I discovered that I was bereft of weeds brought me rapidly into the land of the living and I sat up in bed. I then set about giving myself a good scratch starting at the head and pro-gressing luxuriously downwards to my private parts via my now ample stomach. Things had not always been this way, not by a long chalk. For one thing my stomach had never been other than lean and knotted with muscle, as indeed had the rest of my body. My mouth rarely tasted as it did right now, it was sort of blanket like and sour. What had been the term used by one of his colleagues in the good old days of not too long ago? "Yes" that was it, "a mouth that tasted like the inside of a Lorry Drivers glove". Having never had the dubious pleasure of sampling such a delicacy, I knew nothing of what that might be but I most certainly could taste something similar right now.

Staring up at the roof of the Caravan in which I had now resided for the best part of two weeks, I saw the screws holding the Hardboard panels in place were in rows of nine. Each one sat in a little metal cup which was in fact rusting away. I had made a mental note of this fact on a previous occasion and given it considerable thought in a forlorn effort to occupy my tortured brain with some sort of function other than how long it was to opening time at The Rifleman's. The conclusion I had come to had varied little. The rusting was most certainly due to condensation formed as a result of the prolonged use of the Calor Gas Heater which now stood unlit and forlorn in the corner of the room. Rest assured, I thought, there would be no further pollution by condensation while I am in residence. The fire had not been pressed into service since the remnants of the Gas left by the previous incumbent of the Caravan, had expired. This was not only due to the fact that a re-fill bottle would cost in the region of ten quid, but also I saw little need for it. In fact I spent most of my waking hours in the Rifleman's Arms which was just across the main road which ran between Wokingham and Reading. Just what had steered me to this neck of the woods, well I just didn't know. If I hadn't been too preoccupied with other things and given it a little thought, I would probably come up with the right answer. My wife Jean was born in Wokingham and it was there that I first met her. I had also spent the early days of my Military Service in the area. All this coupled with the fact that I had a Son who now lived in Wokingham must have steered me subconsciously to the Caravan Park I now found myself in.

It had very quickly become my routine to be up and away from my present accommodation long before the inevitable arrival of the slimy leach who called himself the Park Manager. He visited on a daily basis with his sole mission being to extract additional amounts of cash, for the minimum amount of services that were performed for the "Residents" as he so patronisingly liked to refer to them. I lay in bed this day and after becoming bored with counting the ceiling screws, again, my thoughts finally turned to the immediate future and just what prospects I thought it offered.

I must vacate the Caravan by ten hundred hours the next day, as the current weekly rent ran out at that time. I would then find myself pressed for further payments if the Manager managed to collar me before the clock struck ten and I had not beaten a hasty retreat. Unfortunately I now found myself in something of a dilemma. The cash which I had intended to pay for an extra weeks rent of the Caravan had somehow fallen into the possession of the Landlord down at the Rifleman's. Considering all the facts, I doubted that there was little chance that any rebate could be secured although the Landlord was a very nice chap, well most of the time anyway.

I must make contact with my wife. I had not been in touch with her except for one hurried telephone call to tell her that I would be away for a couple of weeks or so. As was her way, she had not queried why this was or where I would be, she just accepted it as part of my job. It had happened on the odd occasion previously when I had been summoned away at very short notice. I hoped I had sounded convincing when I spoke to her, after all I was under a certain amount of stress, not to mention the other influence I found myself under at the time.

Throwing back the blanket, I made my way naked to the miniscule shower unit. The water was in its natural state as when supplied by the Local Water Authority due to the fact that there was no water heating arrangements supplied with this accommodation. I took a good ten minutes indulging myself in the icy arrows as they struck my body. This action revived life to an acceptable standard, which in turn allowed me to confirm in my mind that there were definite possibilities on the horizon. The shower had been most invigorating and fleetingly brought memories of Bacon, Eggs sunny side up with soft runny yokes, Mushrooms, fried Tomatoes on the inevitable fried slice and freshly ground Coffee, black, no sugar, which when things had been normal, would have been my starter for ten as the saying goes. I sighed because I was a realist if nothing else.

Giving my highly polished Brogues a quick rub with one of my socks, I dressed quickly. I put on a Check Shirt, Regimental Tie, Cavalry Twill Trousers and a Blazer which sported the Winged Dagger Badge of the Special Air Service which was fashioned in Gold and Silver wire and neatly stitched to the breast pocket. This was topped off with a Paisley Silk Scarf and a Military style Beige three quarter length Double Breasted Overcoat with Leather Buttons.

I glanced at myself in the mirror that was built into the wardrobe door and saw a Military Gentleman dressed in Mufti, ready for anything that the world cared to throw at him

Picking up my Pigskin travel bag which contained the residue of my immediately available assets, I swept the Caravan with my eyes just to make sure that I had left nothing of importance behind. I made my way out through the narrow entrance door and slammed it behind me quite deliberately leaving the keys on the so called Kitchen Table in full view through the window. They were tantalisingly inaccessible to anyone wishing to enter the Caravan at least by conventional methods anyway. I dearly hoped that the Management did not have a duplicate set and would therefore have to break the door lock to gain entry. This should give that slimy bugger of a Manager something to think about when he realised that the occupant had now become the former occupant.

Mr Charles Hebden had gone and was never to return.

CHAPTER 22

I arrived at Waterloo Station along with all the Office Workers who were hurrying to their place of work. The train had been packed with the regular commuters from Reading and Wokingham areas and I had to stand for the whole of the journey. This didn't bother me as I had some serious thinking to do and I may as well be standing as sitting while doing this. Should I make a bee line for Cato Street and lay my cards on the table as to why I had not been available for the past couple of weeks or so. I was fairly sure that they would have been trying to contact me at the leave address during the time I had spent in the Rifleman's Arms. I was also reasonably sure that they would have spoken to Jean about where I was. She would have told them that I was not at home and that she hadn't a clue where I was.

Heading for the Station Buffet, I took on some hot coffee which I hoped would help unscramble my thoughts and make me just that bit more capable to decide what the best plan would be. Funds were the obvious key to what course of action I would take and to this end I carried out a very quick audit of the contents of my wallet. How my spirits soared when I unearthed my Barclay Card which had been lurking at the bottom of one of the compartments. I instantly checked the expiry date and confirmed that it was still valid. What a good job I had not discovered it previously as if that had been the case it would have been touch and go if there would be any funds available at this stage. It now became uppermost in my mind that I must now find a Cash Machine and put the validity of the card to the test.

I quickly found a "Hole in the Wall" and inserting my card I pumped in my requirements with all speed. Much to my relief it paused momentarily and then spewed out ten, twenty pound notes and then asked me if there was anything further that it could do for me. I felt an awful lot better right away with the comfortable wedge sitting in my arse pocket once again.

I momentarily considered telephoning Head Office but on reflection I dismissed the thought. Anyway, what could I say to them? Who would I ask to speak to? No, it was much more sensible to ring Jean at home I decided. She must have been worrying her guts out with me just disappearing as I had. After a short search I found a Telephone Kiosk which actually worked and dialled my home number. The Phone rang and rang but there was no reply. Glancing at the Rolex, I noted that it was just on a quarter to eleven. Perhaps she had gone to the shops. I gave up and determined to ring again when I got to Euston Station from where I would catch a train north and homeward.

Life was flowing back into me with every passing moment and I flagged down a Cab to take me to Euston. I booked a ticket to Lancaster and after contemplating a swift half of Bitter, I settled for another cup of British Rail's coffee. I did try to contact Jean again but still had no luck and I had little time left before I had to board the Train.

Arriving on my home doorstep I automatically felt in my pockets for the house key but it was not to be found. I stood wondering where I might have lost it when the door suddenly opened and there stood my wife, Jean. She just stood, mouth open in complete surprise at seeing me there. After just a few moments, she started to shed tears and took me into her arms.

"Where on earth have you been you great chump" she said through her tears which by now were real tears of joy at seeing me standing there.

Drying the tears from her eyes with the kitchen towel she had in her hand, I looked into them and said, "I have been having a few days on my own to think something out. Those Bastards at Head Office suspended me but wouldn't tell me why. I suppose you know all about that now don't you"?

251

She fixed me with one of those knowing looks that she was so good at and said, "Know about it? I have had a call from them almost on a daily basis ever since you went down there for that interview. I have been at my wits end as all that they would say was that you should report to Cato Street as soon as possible. I did say that you were away on duty but they made no comment whatsoever about that. With you not being in touch with me I couldn't help but wonder what was going on. Where on earth have you been"?

"I'll tell you all about that later. I suppose I ought to try and get someone at the office right now and see if they still want me to go down there"? I dialled the number and was immediately in touch with the Duty Officer. As usual with the Staff at Head Office the man was non-committal and simply asked me for a telephone number where I could be contacted. He finished by saying that someone would be in touch the next morning when the Day Staff arrived.

My wife and I talked long into the night and covered the whole aspect of what had befallen us during the time we had been on leave in the U.K. We also went over the ground of our past few months in South Africa. No amount of soul searching and racking of brains came up with anything remotely like a solution to the mystery of why I should be suspended by Head Office at the behest of the South African Government.

We had intended having a much needed lie in the following morning but shortly after 9 am the Telephone began to clamour for attention. I got up and answered it.

The familiar gravel voice came through the instrument in a very matter of fact way. "Mr Hebden? The Brigadier expects you at 14 hundred hours tomorrow. No overnight bag will be needed. Could you please confirm right now that this will be in order"?

I replied that I would be there and on hearing this, she hung up.

Taking the early train from Lancaster I was in plenty of time for my appointment. There was no way I was interested in window shopping, I just wanted to get this thing over no matter what the outcome might be. In fact, I was expecting the Brigadier to terminate my employment with the

Firm as I was still at a complete as to why such a report had been filed against me which, as far as I was concerned, was the sole reason why I had been suspended. After killing time just wandering, I headed for Cato Street and checking the trusty Rolex for the umpteenth time I made up my mind to report in although the time had just turned 13-30hrs.

Mounting the steps, there was the customary delay of a few seconds for security to eyeball who it was that had the effrontery to approach the Main Door. I was apparently expected as the door swung inwards and allowed me access to the building. Bert was as usual, in his hallowed Reception Area and there on the table was the Visitors Book open at the appropriate page with the pens lined up, one to the left and the other to the right.

"Good afternoon Mr Hebden Sir. Would you like to sign in Sir"? he said indicating the book with a waive of the hand. "Brigadier 14-00hrs I believe Sir"? This was more of a statement than a question. I looked him squarely in the eye for some indication of what was to come. Bert would know, he always did, but true to form he swung his eyes away from my stare and in his customary way he said "thank you Sir". He retrieved the pens and restored them to their allotted places on the table and then after crossing back to his desk, he picked up the internal Telephone no doubt to report that Mr Hebden was in Reception for his 14-00hrs appointment with the Brigadier.

It seemed that there was to be no shortcut to my appointment as I was made to sit until on the stroke of two o clock the wood panelling showed signs of life as a portion of it opened and a young Subaltern appeared and approached me.

"Mr Hebden Sir"? He enquired. "If you would follow me Sir I will escort you to the Brigadiers Office".

I was quite familiar with the routine and eventually I found myself in the presence of the dreaded "Fag Ash Lil". She nodded to me but said not one word as she indicated a chair on what it seemed I was required to sit. This she did with a cursory waive of her hand, but still not a word was spoken. The Phone on her desk made what sounded to be a rude noise. Picking it up she said "right away Brigadier" and replaced the phone in its cradle. Her eyes settled on me and she spoke to me for the first time.

"This way Mr Hebden" she said rising from her seat at her desk and tapping politely on the door she opened it and with an inclination of her head indicated that I should enter the office of the Brigadier.

"Good Afternoon Hebden, nice to see you at last. You are something of a hard chap to track down when you put your mind to it, what? I have wanted to see you for more than a week now but you seemed to have gone to ground somewhere or other. Your wife was unable to throw any light as to your whereabouts either so we were left with no option but to think that you did not want to be found. Never mind, you are here now".

"We have had further contact with the authorities in South Africa as a result of our enquiries about this business of you being suspended from your post in their country. I will not bore you with all the detail of what they have said but the main thrust of it is that you visited the Local Township of Sasolburg on more than one occasion. Several occasions it says here, and you have been observed with a Black Female in your private car that was alone with you on each of these occasions".

I just couldn't help myself as my face broke into a broad grin at hearing this and I tried to interrupt the Brigadier with what was, in my opinion anyway, the answer to what was obviously a storm in a teacup.

The Brigadier held up his hand to silence me. He then went on, "Further to this, they accuse you of visiting a Shabeen (Local Village Drinking Place) and they are quite specific with the date you are supposed to have been to this place. What have you to say about these allegations"?

I considered it for just a few seconds and then said "It is true Sir that I did visit a Shabeen. I don't remember the exact date but I am sure that the Authorities will have that one right. It was as a result of a stag party that a number of us held for one of our colleagues who was about to be married. I am afraid we were all a little the worse for wear and when someone in the party suggested that we should go to one of these Shabeen's, it seemed to be a good idea, at the time. We stayed about and hour and then decided that we had had enough and we made our way back to the Golf Club. Here our high spirited antics was not fully appreciated and we were asked to leave. It was purely an error of judgement Sir, one which we all regretted the following day. However, the damage had been done by then. I must say Sir, I am fully aware that we broke the laws of the country and would be more that willing to give either a verbal or written apology to the Government of South Africa in order to make amends for our indiscretion".

The Brigadier said nothing in reply to this but sat and stared at the folder that lay open on the desk before him.

He then said "What of this other matter"? He fixed me once again with his stare. "It seems that this is by far the most serious of the allegations laid against you".

Again a slight delay before I went into the explanation. I said, "Well Sir it is all very simple really. I did drive to Sasolburg on a number of occasions and there is a very simple reason why I did this. I was just trying to be a kind and considerate employer and treat the lady who worked for us in our house with some respect and consideration. As I am sure you know Sir, in Central Africa men usually take up the Household jobs offered by Expatriates and these people are known as Houseboys. In South Africa the opposite is the way they do it. It is Females who do this type of work and they are known as Domestics. Such was the case in our house and the lady who worked for us was extremely conscientious about her many duties. She washed and cleaned and cooked without a word of complaint. When it came to holiday time such as a long weekend or Birthday or Christmas and the like, she quite naturally wished to go back to her Township and visit her children and the rest of her family. My wife and I had been given to understand that such a journey would entail a change of buses on no less than three occasions. Should the bus be filled to its capacity, then she would have a considerable time to wait for the next one to leave in the direction she wished to travel. Well Sir, having a large car sitting in my garage and little else to do with my time, I did offer to drive her home purely out of respect for her and hopefully, some form of recompense for what she did for my wife and myself. I did not realise that this was against the law of the land and certainly no one ever told as much. I am most surprised that Government, or their representative, whoever that may have been, should have considered that such an act of kindness had any such reason other than what it was".

Brigadier Parker studied his folder once more then finally said, "Mr Hebden, I have no doubt whatsoever that your explanation of the events is completely truthful and I thank you for being so forthright. I shall by all means appraise the South Africans of your response to their allegations but I am afraid I must tell you that I have scant hope that they will change their mind on these matters. Past experience with them on similar allegations, leaves me at something of a loss as to say anything which would give you even a glimmer of hope. They do seem to be rather dogmatic once the accusations have been made but I will assure you, I will do what I can to have the allegations against you withdrawn. We should be able to contact you with a few days and let you know the outcome of things. I am afraid however, that I have no option but for you to remain under suspension pending the reply from the South African Government".

I left the building and spoke to no one. I then headed for Euston Station and home to Jean.

She was just as disgusted as I was that such an act of kindness could be misinterpreted in this way. The letter arrived from Head Office some ten days later. All that it said was that with regret, as the South Africans had declared Mr Charles Hebden to be a Prohibited Immigrant, they had no option but to dispense with my services effective the date of the letter. It went on to say that my household goods, which were still in South Africa, must be removed from the Bungalow accommodation as supplied by HM Government. Although I didn't read on, it was Jean who noted that we had just three weeks to comply with this and that we would be responsible for the freight charges incurred in transporting our goods and chattels back to the U.K.

Yet once more Mr Charles Hebden, Ex Soldier, Former Member of the 22nd Special Air Service and Loyal Servant to Her Majesties Government, was left without any form of gainful employment.

I was getting no younger and here I was without a clue about what I was going to do next.

ISBN 1412092620

9 781412 092623